Political Leadership and Charisma

Michael Brecher

Political Leadership and Charisma

Nehru, Ben-Gurion, and Other 20th Century Political Leaders: Intellectual Odyssey I

Michael Brecher
McGill University
Montreal, Québec, Canada

ISBN 978-3-319-32626-9   ISBN 978-3-319-32627-6 (eBook)
DOI 10.1007/978-3-319-32627-6

Library of Congress Control Number: 2016951850

© The Editor(s) (if applicable) and The Author(s) 2016
This work is subject to copyright. All rights are solely and exclusively licensed by the Publisher, whether the whole or part of the material is concerned, specifically the rights of translation, reprinting, reuse of illustrations, recitation, broadcasting, reproduction on microfilms or in any other physical way, and transmission or information storage and retrieval, electronic adaptation, computer software, or by similar or dissimilar methodology now known or hereafter developed.
The use of general descriptive names, registered names, trademarks, service marks, etc. in this publication does not imply, even in the absence of a specific statement, that such names are exempt from the relevant protective laws and regulations and therefore free for general use.
The publisher, the authors and the editors are safe to assume that the advice and information in this book are believed to be true and accurate at the date of publication. Neither the publisher nor the authors or the editors give a warranty, express or implied, with respect to the material contained herein or for any errors or omissions that may have been made.

Cover illustration: © Vincenzo Dragani / Alamy Stock Photo

Printed on acid-free paper

This Palgrave Macmillan imprint is published by Springer Nature
The registered company is Springer International Publishing AG Switzerland

*In memory of my parents, Nathan and Gisela Brecher
and of my brothers, Joseph and Irving Brecher*

Acknowledgments

This book is the product of many years of research and reflection on political leadership and leaders, some of whom were towering figures endowed with the rare quality of charisma, in the formative years of their newly independent states—Nehru and Ben-Gurion—along with brief assessments of other twentieth-century leaders. This lengthy phase can be traced to the late 1940s and early 1950s, when I had the good fortune of witnessing the transition of India and Israel from colonial status to independent statehood: at India's embassy in Washington on Independence Day, 15 August 1947, and in India, 1951–52 and 1955–56, and at Israel's UN delegation in 1948 and in Israel, 1949–51 and 1955–56, when these charismatic leaders were at the peak of their almost two decades of political leadership of their states, Nehru, 1947–64 and Ben-Gurion, 1948–63.

Many persons contributed to the reconstruction of this early phase of an ongoing intellectual odyssey. My wife, Eva Danon, who shared and enriched these educational journeys in Israel and India, wisely emphasized the importance of communicating my findings to readers beyond, as well as in the world of academe. Our children, Leora, Diana, and Seegla, contributed, as only sensitive and imaginative young people can, to our experience and understanding of two civilizations that are very different from their lengthy early-life experience in Canada. Two friends and colleagues, Jonathan Wilkenfeld and Patrick James, provided greatly appreciated comments on an earlier version of this project, as did Diana Brecher, Eric Robbins, and Steven Finestone. And two recent talented students at McGill, Sean Cohen and Cody Levine, provided valuable research assistance. Five persons at Palgrave Macmillan were highly supportive of this book project, Anca Pusca and Anne Schult, current Editor and Assistant Editor for International Relations, and earlier editors Sarah Doskow, Chris Robinson, and Alison Howson. Quality supervision of the production of this book was provided by Jayashree Ramamoorthy.

The following publishers kindly granted permission to use material from earlier books and articles authored by me:

pp. 423–443, from my article, "Succession in India 1967: The Routinization of Political Change", in *Asian Survey*, Vol. 7, No. 7, July 1967, © 1967 by the Regents of the University of California. Published by the University of California Press.

pp. 300–332 from my book, *India and World Politics: Krishna Menon's View of the World*, 1968, "By permission of Oxford University Press".

pp. 251–276, 306–308, 330–349, from my book, *The Foreign Policy System of Israel*, Yale University Press, 1972.

pp. 119–135, from my article, "Turning Points: Reflections on Many Paths to Knowledge", in the book, *Journeys through World Politics*, Lexington Books, 1989.

pp. 23–52, from my article, "Nehru's Place in History", in the book, *Nehru and the Twentieth Century*, Centre for South Asian Studies, University of Toronto, 1991.

I am grateful to all of these persons and institutions for their contribution to this book.

BOOKS BY MICHAEL BRECHER

The Struggle for Kashmir (1953)
Nehru: A Political Biography (1959)
The New States of Asia (1963)
Succession in India: A Study in Decision-Making (1966)
India and World Politics: Krishna Menon's View of the World (1968)
Political Leadership in India: An Analysis of Elite Attitudes (1969)
The Foreign Policy System of Israel: Setting, Images, Process (1972)
Israel, the Korean War and China (1974, 77)
Decisions in Israel's Foreign Policy (1974, 75)
Studies in Crisis Behavior (Ed.) (1979)
Decisions in Crisis: Israel (1967) and (1973 1980)
Crisis and Change in World Politics (with Patrick James) (1986)
Crises in the Twentieth Century: Vol. I, Handbook of International Crises (with Jonathan Wilkenfeld) (1988)
Crises in the Twentieth Century: Vol. II, Handbook of Foreign Policy Crises (with Jonathan Wilkenfeld) (1988)
Crisis, Conflict and Instability (Vol. III of Crises in the Twentieth Century) (with Jonathan Wilkenfeld) (1989)
Crises in World Politics (1993)
A Study of Crisis (with Jonathan Wilkenfeld) (1997)
A Study of Crisis [paperback and CD Rom edition] (with Jonathan Wilkenfeld) (2000)
Millennial Reflections on International Studies (ed. with Frank P. Harvey) (2002)
Realism and Institutionalism in International Studies (ed. with Frank P. Harvey) (2002)
Conflict, Security, Foreign Policy, and International Political Economy (ed. with Frank P. Harvey) (2002)

Evaluating Methodology in International Studies (ed. with Frank P. Harvey) (2002)
Critical Perspectives in International Studies (ed. with Frank P. Harvey) (2002)
International Political Earthquakes (2008)
The World of Protracted Conflicts (2016)
Political Leadership and Charisma—Nehru, Ben-Gurion, and Other 20th Century Political Leaders: Intellectual Odyssey I (2016)
Dynamics of the Arab/Israel Conflict: Intellectual Odyssey II (forthcoming, 2017)
Interstate Crises and Conflicts: Intellectual Odyssey III (forthcoming, 2018)

Contents

1	Introduction: Many Paths to Knowledge	1
2	Prelude to an Intellectual Odyssey	17

    Years of Awakening (1936–46)   17
        Spanish Civil War *(1936–39)*   17
        Munich Agreement *(1938)*   20
        High School *(1938–42)*   22
        Student Years at McGill *(1942–46)*   22
        The Holocaust *(1945)*   23
    Yale Graduate Studies (1946–49)   25
        Pioneers in International Relations   25
        Library of Congress *(1947)*; The UN *(1948)*   29
    Israel: Formative Years (1949–51)   30
    Phases of an Intellectual Odyssey   32
    Encounters with Pierre Elliott Trudeau   34
    Beginnings of the South Asia Phase (1951–53)   40
        Bombay *(May–June 1951)*   40
        Delhi *(June–July 1951, October 1951–February 1952)*   42
        Vale of Kashmir *(July–September 1951)*   43
        Meaning of Kashmir   45
        The Struggle for Kashmir *(1953): Contents*   47

3 Political Leaders: India (1951–91) — 49

In Quest of Jawaharlal Nehru (1955–1989) — 49
  Preparing the Way — 49
  London Phase (May–November 1955) — 49
  Interviews with Lord Mountbatten (November 1955) — 50
  Entrée to Nehru (December 1955) — 56
  Discovery of the Indian Village (January–February 1956) — 57
  Rationale of Nehru Project — 60

Encounters with Nehru (1956–63) — 63
  Tour with Nehru (March 1956) — 63
  Interviews (June 1956) — 67
  Portrait of the Man — 77
  Nehru as an Intellectual — 80
  Interview with Nehru (January 1958) — 83
  Interim Assessment in Nehru: A Political Biography (1959) — 88
  Last Interview with Nehru (December 1963) — 91
  Further Interim Assessment (November 1964) — 97

Nehru and Shastri: Nehru's Mantle: The Politics of Succession in India *(1964, 1966)* — 98
  Political Succession: Universal Problem — 99
  Preparing the Ground — 102
  Key Actors — 103
  Findings on Succession to Nehru (1964) — 106
  Succession to Shastri (1966) — 111
  Two Succession Games: A Comparison; Nehru's Mantle: The Politics of Succession in India *(1966)* — 112
  Nehru as a Political Leader: Final Assessment (November 1989) — 117

Encounters with Krishna Menon (1964–67) — 126
  Rationale for the Menon Project — 126
  Background and Personality — 128
  Content of the Interviews — 129
  Analysis of Menon's View of the World — 135

Intellectual Legacy of the South Asia Phase (1951–1989) — 149
  Other Research-Related Activities in the South Asia Phase — 151

4	**First-Generation Israeli Leaders (1948–77)**	161
	David BEN-GURION and Moshe SHARETT	161
	Contrasting Personalities: 'Courage *versus* Caution'	162
	Contrasting Worldviews	165
	Two Views of the Road to Statehood	166
	Ben-Gurion's View of World Politics	170
	Sharett's View of World Politics	180
	Levi ESHKOL	184
	Road to Aliya *and Early Years*	184
	Jordan Waters Negotiations (1953–55)	187
	Comparison with Ben-Gurion and Sharett	189
	Views on the USA, the USSR, World Jewry, and Germany	191
	1967 Crisis-War: Nadir and Turning-Point Role	193
	Golda MEIR	196
	Early Years and Road to Aliya	196
	Résumé of Government Offices	197
	Personality, Character, Intuitive Approach to Decision-Making	197
	Views of the World, the UN, and Diaspora Jewry	200
5	**Second-Generation Israeli Leaders (1960–77)**	203
	Overview	203
	Generals and Politicians: Yigal ALLON and Moshe DAYAN	205
	Sabra *(Israeli-Born) Roots*	205
	Military Leaders	206
	Assets and Qualities	208
	Differences	209
	Diplomat: Abba EBAN	210
	Zionist Roots and Road to Aliya	210
	Status, Eloquence, Influence	211
	Assessment	213
	Technocrat: Shimon Peres	214
	'Wunderkind'	214
	Zionist Background and Youth	214
	National Security Roles	215
	Role in Labor Zionist Merger and the 1967 Crisis	215
	Insight into Peres, Late 1940s-Late 1980s: Prototype of a 'Bitzuist' *(Activist)*	216

The Four Younger Leaders: A Comparison	217
General	217
Views of World Politics: The USA, the UN, and	
World Jewry	219
Eight Israeli Leaders: A Comparison of Views	224
6 Charismatic Leadership: Concepts and Comparisons:	
Nehru and Ben-Gurion; Other Leaders	227
Sources of Nehru's Power	229
Other Political Leaders	233
Pierre Elliott Trudeau	233
Third World Leaders of Asia and Africa	234
Churchill, Roosevelt, Lenin, Mao	237
Works Consulted	245
Introduction and Prelude to an Academic Odyssey	245
Political Leaders: Pierre Elliot Trudeau	251
Political Leaders: India	252
Political Leaders: Israel	259
Concepts of Charismatic Leadership and Political Leaders	264
Index	267

CHAPTER 1

Introduction: Many Paths to Knowledge

Academe is perceived by many as an ivory tower, a place to which scholars retreat from the real world of stress and strife. To some members of the fraternity, however, it provides a crucial setting in which intellectual resources can be mobilized to attack the great ills that beset the planet—poverty; disease; injustice; and conflict, crisis, and war. To a young Canadian student in the mid to late 1930s and early 1940s, world politics seemed distant yet compelling. The first awareness from afar was the Spanish Civil War and Munich, symbols of Western self-delusion and surrender, events that were puzzling and troubling then and long after. The years of death and destruction on a cataclysmic scale that followed, World War II (WWII), as evil forces swept through Europe and Asia challenging the foundations of a civilization which, in word if not always in deed, placed a high value on human and national rights, strengthened an emerging conviction that systematic knowledge of world politics could contribute, however modestly, to the restoration and enhancement of these values.

An initial encounter with International Relations (IR) as an academic discipline was the stimulating environment of Yale University in the mid to late 1940s, where the Realism of *Nicholas Spykman* (1942, 1944) and *Arnold Wolfers* (1940) held sway at the Institute of International Studies; where *William T.R. Fox* (1944), and *Bernard Brodie* (1946) and their colleagues, were expounding the novel concepts, *The Superpowers* and *The Absolute Weapon*; where *Klaus Knorr* was developing his ideas on international political economy and power (later published in 1956 and 1975); and where *Hajo Holborn* (1951) illuminated the diplomatic history of the inter-world war period. But even prior to that exposure at Yale, then the only university in North America offering a PhD program in IR, I had been influenced by several pioneering works in the field: *Quincy Wright*'s magisterial *A Study of War* (1942); two seminal Realist critiques of Utopianism, E.H. Carr's *The Twenty Years' Crisis* (1939) and *Hans Morgenthau*'s *Scientific Man Versus Power Politics* (1946); and the first power-oriented treatise on world politics, written by a younger member of the 'Chicago School', *Frederick L. Schuman*'s fascinating *International Politics: The Western State System and the World Community* (1933), then in its third (1941) edition. This initial attraction to world politics overlapped with the other early strand in a student's intellectual development.

It was at McGill University during the early 1940s that an undergraduate first became aware of the human condition in the colonial world, primarily through a book that cast a searchlight brilliantly on the crown jewel of the British Empire, *Rajni Palme-Dutt*'s *India Today* (1940). That work, superimposed on an emerging feeling about the innate injustice of the centuries-old domination of non-white peoples by Western imperialist powers, drew one irresistibly to what later became known as the Third World. The analytical perspective of Palme-Dutt's Marxism pervaded the following years at Yale, 1946–49. Its influence continued through a first direct contact with the Indian subcontinent in 1951–52 but waned as the ideologically inspired policies advocated by India's competing Marxist, Leninist, and Maoist parties seemed increasingly irrelevant to the immense tasks confronting India and other Third World peoples in transition from tradition to modernity. Moreover, the doctrinaire mind-set that underpinned their Moscow- or Beijing-oriented postures violated the high value that I have always placed on independence of thought.

A lengthy fascination with South Asian domestic politics, IR, and history, for more than two decades, began with doctoral research on the struggle over the Indian princely State, Jammu and Kashmir, between India and Pakistan, the successors to the near-two-century British Empire of India, 1757–1947. From the perspective of more than six decades, the dissertation phase was a valuable formative experience. The original topic was very ambitious, namely, a comparative analysis of British rule in India and Palestine, with special reference to the triangular relationship among the paramount power and the two community-nations-in-the-making, Hindus and Muslims, in the subcontinent, Arabs and Jews in the Holy Land. However, ambition was excessive: the IR legacy of the 'end of empire' in South Asia, that is, the India/Pakistan conflict over Kashmir, became the focus of the entire dissertation and my first book on that unresolved conflict. To unravel the mysteries of that conflict required *area specialization* and *field research*. This seemed to me then, and over the decades, an important *path to knowledge* about world politics. Thus, I became immersed in the politics, economics, and international relations of South Asia throughout the 1950s, 1960s, and early 1970s.

The counterpart phase of this first intellectual odyssey unfolded in teaching at McGill University and half-a-dozen books from 1953 to 1969, including a political biography of Nehru (1959) and its sequel (1966). I was drawn to the technique of biography partly by an affinity with his ideas and admiration for his roles. This work was also, as cited in the Preface to my *Nehru: A Political Biography*, 'an attempt to view the then-still-unfinished Asian Revolution in its Indian setting. Many persons played a notable role. But only one, Jawaharlal Nehru, links the years of promise and fulfillment, of nationalist agitation and national reconstruction. Indeed, the life of Nehru is admirably suited to serve as the binding thread in a study of recent Indian history and politics. Hence, I have employed the technique of biography to shed light on political events, ideas, and movements' (vii). The Preface to that political biography noted *four objectives* of *this quest for knowledge*: 'If this book provides some clues to the tortuous course of recent Indian history and politics it will have served one major purpose. If it succeeds, at least in small measure, in making Nehru more intelligible to his admirers and critics alike, it will have served another. If it provides some insight into the role of the outstanding individual in history, it will have accomplished a third goal. Finally, I hope that it may contribute to the understanding of the State of mind "among the uncommitted billion".... My concern is with the living, with the actions of statesmen when and as they take place, and with their implications' (viii).

Immersion in South Asia—three intense periods of field research (1951–52, 1955–56, 1964–65) and a dozen shorter visits, from 1951 to 1974—had several other spin-offs for the continuing study of world politics. Perhaps the most memorable experience was a six-week journey in a third-class train compartment, sleeping bag in hand, to the furthest reaches of India, permitting daily contact with the Indian village, still the heart of its civilization. The South Asia experience also provided a stimulus for an initial foray into what became an enduring intellectual interest—*international systems*. Close observation of that region's international politics during the 1950s triggered a conceptualization of a *subordinate system*, primarily geographic in scope, with two or more actors engaged in intense interaction, conflictual and/or cooperative, and deeply penetrated by major powers from the dominant system of global politics (Brecher 1963b). A decade after its initial formulation, by which time my area interest had extended to the Middle East, the concept of system became the organizing device for an analysis of Israel's foreign policy as a *system of action* (Brecher 1972). And 25 years later, after redefining an international system, it served as one of the two 'levels of analysis' in a continuing quest for knowledge about crises in the 20th century and beyond (*Brecher and Wilkenfeld* 1997). This lengthy path was influenced by the seminal books of *Karl Deutsch* (1963) and *Morton Kaplan* (1957).

Another intellectual legacy of the South Asia phase was the concept of *interstate protracted conflict*, initially triggered by the reality of Indo/Pakistani relations, from the carnage that attended the partition of the subcontinent in 1947, through three wars (1947–48, 1965, and 1971), frequent crises, and disputes that penetrated economic, social, political, and religious domains in their early decades of independence. Yet it was not until a no-less deep encounter with the Arab/Israeli conflict in the 1960s, 1970s, and 1980s that the significance of *interstate protracted conflict* as a profound contextual influence on world politics became a major focus of later research (1984, 1997 [the latter with *Jonathan Wilkenfeld*], and 2016).

Another benefit of *field research* in South Asia was an early recognition that world politics is not synonymous with relations among the major powers, which has meant for most Western scholars the bipolar conflict between East and West from the end of WWII to the demise of the Soviet Union in 1991. The centrality of the two superpowers, the USA and the USSR, I became convinced very early, is a necessary starting point for the analysis of world politics since 1945. However, in the hands of the 'globalists', from *Morgenthau* (1948, 1951) to *Stanley Hoffmann* (1965, 1978, 1986), *Henry Kissinger* (1979, 1982), and *Kenneth Waltz* (1964, 1979), it became the exclusive focus of attention, as expressed, for example, in a simplistic dichotomy of international systems—multi-polarity (many centers of world politics, before WWII) and bipolarity (two centers, since the end of WWII).

Those who ventured forth from the ivory tower could not but be struck by the existence of another domain of interstate conflict and cooperation which, although on the periphery of the *dominant system* of international politics in terms of geography, military power, and economic development, is an essential component of a comprehensive paradigm of world politics. Just as the *Third World* became an integral part of the analytical restructuring of international political economy, so too, *Polycentrism* and the dispersion of decisional centers from the early 1960s onward merits recognition in a restructuring of a world politics paradigm. The failure to do so adequately led to grave distortions and lacunae in the dissection of global politics in the late 20th and early 21st centuries (*Brecher and Patrick James* 1988; *Brecher, James and Wilkenfeld* (1990), *Brecher* 2008).

In terms of a long association with Indian Studies, an especially gratifying contribution was my role as founder of the Shastri Indo-Canadian Institute in 1965 (formally launched in 1968) (*Brecher* 1990). The institute began with four members—McGill, the University of Toronto, and of British Columbia, along with the National Library of Canada. Today, there are programs on Indian Civilization at more than 30 institutions of higher learning across the breadth of Canada and a comparable presence among India's universities.

It has been a great good fortune to live in intimate contact with diverse peoples and cultures in several lands. This began in *anglophone-francophone-allophone* Montreal, with its mosaic of ethnic groups. This was followed by three years at Yale in the aftermath of WWII, among older, stimulating students and a talented faculty, noted above, among them Harold Lasswell, whose earlier innovative books on the psychology of politics, such as *World Politics and Personal Insecurity* (1935) and *Politics: Who Gets What, When, How* (1936) opened up new vistas and allowed us 'to drift and dream' in his unique seminar, and Gabriel Almond, then engaged in an original study of periodic mood shifts in American foreign policy (1950) and later, the initiator and major contributor to a multi-volume series on Comparative Politics. Three years in India in the 1950s and 1960s provided an opportunity to witness an ambitious political experiment under a towering leader, Nehru, namely, moving a traditional society in the direction of modernity and economic development, with a firm commitment to democracy and human rights. I also lived for many years in Israel, the political and territorial expression of national liberation for an ancient people after two millennia of dispersion and oppression.

The first direct contact with Israel's foreign policy system and the Arab/Israel conflict was on the diplomatic periphery. In the summer of 1948, toward the end of graduate studies at Yale, I served as a research assistant to *Abba Eban*, then beginning an illustrious career as the 'Voice of Israel' at the United Nations (UN) and, later, everywhere. A one-year sojourn in Israel's Foreign Ministry (1950–51) provided insight into the making of foreign policy and the intensity of the conflict, with its multiple spillovers to world politics. Twenty-five years later, on the political periphery, I helped to draft the first manifesto of the *Israel Council for an Israeli–Palestinian Peace*, along with then leaders of the Israeli peace movement; we were among the first to advocate a two-State solution to the protracted conflict. Few listened at the time, and a resolution of this conflict remains elusive.

Systematic and systemic research into Israel's foreign policy did not begin until the mid-1960s: the research began after the guiding construct of a *foreign policy system* had been developed. In that quest, the major influences were *David Easton's* input–output model (1957); *Snyder, Bruck and Sapin's* foreign policy decision-making framework (1962); and the Stanford perception–action model (Holsti, North and Brody 1968). Moreover, *Harold and Margaret Sprout's* distinction between the operational and psychological environment (1965), along with *Kenneth Boulding's* (1956b) and *Ole Holsti's* work on images (1965), seemed to me a necessary corrective to the exclusive focus on objective reality that pervaded the comparative foreign policy literature at the time. My study of Krishna Menon's worldview (1968), as well as that of Israel's political decision-makers (1972, 1974–75), was an attempt to shed light on the perceptual dimension of foreign policy analysis.

As often in the generation of an idea, concept, theory, or model, students contributed, in a vibrant McGill graduate seminar on comparative foreign policy from 1960 onward. The original intention was to apply this research design to two States in two autonomous subordinate international systems, Israel/Middle East and India/South Asia. But after a decade of concentration on the former, another, closely related aspect of world politics asserted itself. Living in the Middle East for most of each year from 1969 to 2013 made one acutely sensitive to the pervasiveness of *crisis, conflict, and war*. Apart from the earlier Arab/Israel upheavals in 1948–49 and 1956–57, a brief span of six years, 1967–73, witnessed three additional outbursts of major violence: the June Six-Day War in 1967, which transformed the power constellation of the Middle East subordinate system, with Israel at its apex; the War of Attrition in 1969–70; and the October War or Yom Kippur War in 1973–74, with its near-superpower direct confrontation, including the implied threat of resort to nuclear weapons. Ironically, it was that Egypt/Israel War that created the auspicious condition of accommodation that culminated in the Egypt-Israel peace agreement in 1979.

This protracted conflict, in a volatile subordinate system, now posed an even greater danger to global stability than in the past. Yet, ironically, both the 1967 and 1973 wars facilitated important developments in the quest for peace: the first catalyzed a major UN effort to resolve the conflict, Security Council Resolution 242, which envisioned a trade of 'land for peace'—Israel's withdrawal from the occupied West Bank in exchange for the Palestinians conceding formal peace between Israel and Palestine—as the optimal path to peace in the Arab/Israel domain; and the 1973 war set in motion a process that culminated in two Arab/Israel peace agreements—between Egypt and Israel in 1979, which terminated the most crucial dimension of this multi-State protracted conflict, and more than a decade later, between Israel and Jordan in 1994.

Nonetheless, threats to international stability were widespread, with potential far-reaching consequences. In South Asia, the India/Pakistan crisis of 1971, culminating in full-scale war over East Bengal (East Pakistan), later Bangladesh, had significantly changed the structure of that subordinate system to one of India's predominance, until 1998, when both adversaries succeeded in joining the still-small nuclear weapons club. And in Africa, disruptive interaction among the myriad of new States was ubiquitous.

These and related developments highlighted a growing instability in the international system. Many IR scholars recognized that international stability was a 'two-edged sword'. They acknowledged that global or regional stability could, as often in domestic political systems and in history, mask domination of the weak by the strong or of the poor by the rich, or continued control over colonial lands and peoples (the periphery of the global system) by the former imperial powers, the metropole or the core of that system. At the same time, they knew that the escalation of crises to war in a nuclear age and the persistence of protracted conflicts among less powerful States in Third World 'grey zones' of competition between the USA and the Soviet Union made international stability a very high value in the truncated international system during the last quarter of the 20th century and well beyond. This awareness contributed to the launch of the *International Crisis Behavior* (*ICB*) project in 1975: although it seemed unlikely, perhaps impossible, that interstate crises could be prevented or all protracted conflicts resolved, their effective management to prevent often destructive war was a viable and worthy goal.

The first step on the long road to effective crisis management and conflict resolution, and one to which systematic research on world politics could contribute, was the accumulation of reliable knowledge about the phenomena to be managed and resolved in order to prevent runaway turmoil. Viewed from the perspective of the early 1970s, *war* had been the object of systematic investigation for half a century, from *Wright's* ambitious enterprise at the University of Chicago beginning in the mid-1920s, noted above, through *Sorokin* (1937) and *Richardson* (1960a, b) to *Singer's* Correlates of War Project since 1964 (1979, 1980). However, the study of *international conflict* remained in an embryonic State, despite the pioneering work of the Stanford School (*North* 1969, and others). Similarly, work had begun on international crisis: conceptually, on crisis management, and on two celebrated cases since World War I (WWI), the Berlin Blockade, 1948–49, and Cuban Missile Crisis, 1962 (*Robinson* 1962; *Hermann* 1963 and 1969; *Allison* 1971; Holsti 1972). Yet, as these pioneers would agree, much remained to be done. The creative work by *Snyder and Diesing* (1971) came later; and *Lebow's* was not yet on the horizon (1981). It was an awareness of the danger of interstate crises to global stability and the lacunae in our knowledge of this major source of turmoil that led to the *ICB project* in 1975 (*Brecher* 1977, 1979b and others).

How to proceed? There was, and is, no simple and straightforward answer, for contending scholars and schools praise their own, and decry other methods and approaches to the generation of knowledge about this or any aspect of world politics. Endless debates have occurred between advocates of *a priori theorizing* versus *empirical data-gathering*; *quantitative* versus *qualitative* methods; *aggregate data analysis* versus *comparative case studies*. As a convinced pluralist in the matter of research strategy, there is much wisdom in the Hindu dictum that there are many paths to truth and that no single faith (school) has a monopoly over truth. Indeed, the debates over method seemed to be sterile, from the *Bull–Kaplan* exchange (1966) to the more mutually tolerant discussion by *Bueno de Mesquita, Krasner*, and *Jervis* (1985b).

As in other academic disciplines, the 'closed mind' is not unknown among scholars of world politics. An especially disquieting episode occurred in 1963, during a discussion with the then pre-eminent figure in the field, *Hans Morgenthau*: a younger scholar, who had long admired his work, drew his attention to the then emerging body of criticism of his writings, despite the recognition of its significance in the IR literature, and suggested that he owed it to the profession to write a considered response to the critics. He rejected all dissent from 'the truth', as conveyed in his treatise on world politics (1948), then in its widely used third edition: 'There is nothing I have read among the criticisms which is worth replying to!' And he never defended the methods, theory, or substance of his work. In this respect, he was certainly not a role model.

Another peril of academe, especially in the USA, because of its size, self-assurance, physical distance from other continents, and a tradition of isolation, is ethnocentrism. Certainly in the late 1940s, when America stood—and perceived itself—as a giant in the aftermath of global victory, it did not seem necessary to learn other languages or be inquisitive about other cultures, thereby depriving the community of IR scholars access to multiple paths to knowledge in languages other than English. This fallacy was expressed by a respected Yale professor, proudly, to a group of graduate students: 'I have learned only two languages in my life– American English and academic English!' Fortunately for America and the profession, this insularity about paths to knowledge changed in the decades that followed.

Returning to the enduring controversial issue of paths to knowledge in political science and IR: theory clearly occupies a central place, whether deductively or inductively derived. Although the former is accorded higher status in the science enterprise, the evidence thus far in the study of world politics is mixed; and, in any event, the choice depends upon a researcher's disposition. Stated differently, the issue of whether formal theory must precede—and take precedence over—empirical investigation (e.g., espoused by *Bueno de Mesquita, Young, Zinnes*, and all game theorists) or the reverse (e.g., *Russett, Singer*, and all Correlates of War Project researchers) remains unresolved. Others, I among them, advocate a *dual path to knowledge*, framing a priori models and hypotheses and a framework/taxonomy to guide empirical inquiry, leading to the testing of model-derived hypotheses and their refinement or abandonment as the evidence dictates, further testing, and so on.

The stimulus is often, if not always, a puzzle. In this case, the ICB project asked: What is a crisis? How does it differ from conflict, war, and dispute? What are the most likely conditions of an international (macro-level) crisis and of a foreign policy (micro-level) crisis? What is the logical relationship between them? How does one explain its core dimensions—

crisis onset, actor behavior, major power activity, the involvement of international organizations, crisis outcomes, and their severity (intensity) and impact (consequences)?

This, in turn, led to a related puzzle: what path(s) to knowledge should be followed and which method(s) should be employed in order to answer questions such as those posed above and thereby explain the multiple components of crisis? The ICB choice, from the outset, was a two-track strategy, flowing from a conviction about the inherent merit of pluralism. One path is in-depth case studies of perceptions and decisions by a single State, using a micro-level model of crisis that was designed to guide research on foreign policy crises in the military-security issue area and to facilitate rigorous comparative analysis of findings about State behavior (*Brecher* 1977, 1979). The method, 'structured empiricism', was developed in earlier research on Israel's foreign policy system (*Brecher* 1972, 1974–75), and is very similar to *Alexander George's* later 'structured focused comparison' (George 1979): both gather and organize data on diverse cases around a set of common questions, permitting systematic comparison. A series of ICB volumes adopting this research design and method appeared in the 1980s and 1990s, and later (*Brecher with Geist* 1980; *A.I. Dawisha* 1980; *Shlaim* 1983; *Dowty* 1984; *K. Dawisha* 1984; *Jukes* 1985; *Hoffman* 1990; *Anglin* 1994; and *Brecher* 2008).

Comparative case study alone, however, and even more so the 'crucial case' approach advocated by *Eckstein* (1975), cannot uncover the full range of findings about any phenomenon in world politics. For this purpose, a second path to knowledge was necessary, namely, studies in breadth of aggregate data on crises over an extended block of time and space. The result was the selection of a large-scale empirical domain—the sources, processes, and outcomes of all military-security crises of all States in most of the 20th and early 21st centuries, initially from 1929 to 1979, now from late 1918 to 2013, and across all continents, cultures, and political and economic systems in the contemporary era (*Brecher* and *Wilkenfeld* 1988, 1989, 1997, 2000; *Wilkenfeld* and *Brecher* 1988; *Brecher* and *James* 1986).

This 'mapping' exercise was conceived as a three-to-five-year task, an empirical prelude to an analysis of the lessons of crises in the 20th century. It required 12 years of concentrated labor (1975–87), not only by senior staff members but also by a large number of graduate students, leading to the publication of the three-volume work on *Crises in the Twentieth Century* (*Brecher* and *Wilkenfeld* 1988–89), noted above. The first phase of the *aggregate data path to knowledge* was followed by another decade of mapping and analyzing a much larger body of cases over a more extended period of research, from the initial 1929–79 period to the late 1918–end 1994 period, leading to Brecher and Wilkenfeld 1997, 2000. This *aggregate data path to knowledge* continues after four decades with a new generation of senior scholars and many new graduate research assistants, extending the dataset and findings about the world of international crises from late 1918 to the end of 2013, and the beginning of findings on two dimensions of conflict that received much less attention during the first four decades—the role of *mediation* in crisis management and conflict resolution, and the phenomenon of *interstate protracted conflicts*, focused on the causes of their *onset, persistence,* and *resolution.*

The *dual strategy* and the *findings* from this inquiry into a major, continuing source of international turmoil have been elaborated elsewhere (Brecher and Wilkenfeld 1988; Wilkenfeld and Brecher 1988; Brecher and Wilkenfeld 1997, 2000). Suffice it to note here the objectives of the ICB project as a path to knowledge. In terms of IR as a discipline, the primary goal of its case studies is to test the utility of a crisis model and the validity of core hypotheses that have emerged from the theoretical and empirical literature. The aggregate data analysis is designed to generate knowledge about clusters of independent, intervening, and dependent variables related to crisis. This includes an attempt to measure the intensity (severity) and consequences (impact) of crises as international political earthquakes and to discover patterns of crisis management.

More generally, the aim of the ICB project has been—and continues to be—to shed light on a pervasive phenomenon of 20th and 21st century world politics through the accumulation and dissemination of knowledge about all international and foreign policy crises for this time frame; the delineation of the effects of crisis-induced stress on coping and choice by decision-makers; and the discovery of patterns that may exist regarding the key dimensions of crisis, from onset to outcome (Brecher 1993, 2008). In terms of policy relevance to the future of world politics, the aim is to use the findings from this knowledge to enhance the quality and effectiveness of crisis management, that is, at the micro-level, to enable decision-makers to cope more effectively with crises, and, at the macro-level, to reduce the likelihood of escalation of crises to full-scale war, with potentially grave consequences in a world saturated with nuclear and other weapons of mass destruction. In the largest sense, the objective is to apply the lessons of history to the advancement of international peace and world order.

Have these goals been achieved? Certainly not yet. Can they be attained? Unlikely, because of the enormous divide between the academic world and the foreign policy–national security decision-making élite. The latter, with few exceptions, regard academic research on world politics as irrelevant ('ivory tower'), inaccurate ('scholars don't see the cables'), and unrealistic (systematic, where decision-making is chaotic and personal). Academic research allegedly suffers from all of these shortcomings combined. I have personally encountered this ill-founded view in three States, namely, Canada, India, and Israel, the last two profoundly affected by the stress of a protracted conflict.

I have been chided for reconstructing decision processes more systematically than they occurred in reality. 'Your facts are correct', I would (sometimes) be told by professionals from the Foreign Ministry and the Prime Minister's Office, 'but the way the decisions you write about were reached is much sloppier, more haphazard and disorganized than you make out.' To my reply that one task of the research scholar is 'to make order out of disorder', the rejoinder is invariably, 'Michael, you don't understand.' Parenthetically, I have always placed a high value on *interviews* with decision-makers (preferably when they are no longer in office) as a vital path to knowledge about the decision-making process and about specific decisions. Treated with care, checked against other primary sources, when available, for consistency, plausibility, and reliability, they are indispensable for decision-making analysis.

Interviews can illuminate in several respects. First, they add a crucial human dimension to an outsider's understanding of the decision process. One illustration will suffice. During extended interviews with *David Ben-Gurion* in 1966, three years after he resigned for the last time as Israel's prime minister and defense minister, I asked why he had made a provocative speech in the *Knesset* (Israel's parliament) on 7 November 1956, soon after Israel's triumphant Sinai Campaign. In that address, the prime minister figuratively tore up the 1949 Armistice Agreement with Egypt— it is 'dead and buried', he said. He challenged Egypt's sovereignty over the Sinai Peninsula. He implied that Israel would not withdraw its forces from Sinai. And he rejected in advance the stationing of any foreign or international military force in the area. In so doing, he alienated Israel's friends around the world, including the USA, which threatened to terminate all aid to Israel, governmental and private, and to support UN sanctions against Israel. When asked why he spoke so harshly and bluntly that day, he paused for a moment and replied, slowly: 'You see, Mr. Brecher, the victory was too quick; I was drunk with victory!' Within a day, he was to pay heavily for his 'victory' speech: massive pressures from abroad compelled him to agree, earlier than planned, to Israel's withdrawal from Sinai and Gaza.

More generally, interviews with decision-makers help to clarify and elaborate facts and themes, often important pieces in a puzzle, which may be barely mentioned in documents or other written sources. They thereby shed fresh light on the complex process through which politicians and officials cope with a problem for decision. Of course, the danger of distortion, either consciously, to strengthen one's 'place in history', or as a result of a lapse in memory, should lead to caution in the use of interview materials. Yet, even to those disposed to formal theory alone, I would note that this dimension of research would not undermine the quality of their theorizing or the validity of their theories.

In the context of divergent perspectives by scholars and national security officials on the value of interviews as a *path to knowledge* about perceptions and behavior by foreign policy decision-makers, sometimes with serious consequences, an incident relating to Arab–Israeli peace merits attention. In the summer of 1975, I participated in a study mission of North American academics to Egypt, Jordan, Syria, and Israel. While in Cairo, I interviewed members of the Egyptian political, bureaucratic, military, and intellectual élite and was struck by a common theme communicated to a foreign scholar, about to leave for Israel and to meet with political figures, academics and journalists there: 'Egypt wants peace; Egypt needs peace because of its economic, social, and political problems; Egypt can no longer bear the enormous burden of the Palestinian cause; Egypt is prepared to make meaningful concessions for peace.' Among my interlocutors were *Osama el-Baz*, then (and later) the principal national security adviser to President Sadat (and, later, President Mubarak), and *Professor Boutros-Ghali*, about to become Egypt's minister of State for foreign affairs.

In Israel, I presented my findings in public—an article in *Ha'aretz*, a prominent daily newspaper (14 November 1975) and in private, a lecture at the Foreign Ministry. I pleaded for an understanding of a fundamental change in the attitude of Israel's most powerful adversary. 'Michael, what a pity, you have been brain-washed,' was the disbelieving response. *Two years later, President Sadat offered peace to Israel from the podium of the Knesset in Jerusalem.* The rest is history. As one scholar, *Russell Leng*, asked, in an insightful paper on crises, 'When Will They Ever Learn?' (1983). Moreover, *Neustadt and May* (1986), along with *Janis* (1972,

1989), *Janis and Mann* (1977), and *Vertzberger* (1990), recounted episodes demonstrating that decision-makers do not always learn.

What can scholars contribute to the foreign policy process? In rare cases, they can become members of the decision-making élite and, as such, can apply the findings from earlier research to current problems of national and international security, often with profound influence, for example, *Kissinger* (1979, 1982) and *Brzezinski* (1967) on US decisions. More often, they leave the academy intermittently to serve as adviser to a head of government, foreign or defense minister, or lesser officials. For most academicians, the quest for policy relevance is rarely satisfying. The basic reason is the structural gap between a scholar's approach and methods, including his/her paths to knowledge, on the one hand, and a practitioner's concerns, on the other: their paths to knowledge are not reliable, and attempts to influence day-to-day decisions and actions in the domain of foreign and security policy are almost certain to fail. The lack of access to information flowing into the bureaucracy is one obstacle. The natural tendency of officials to protect their turf from outsiders is another. And the scholar's disposition to analyze larger issues than an immediate problem for decision is a third. As for the attempt to influence decisions through punditry, op-ed columns in prominent newspapers satisfy one's ego more than they affect State behavior.

The most valuable contribution of scholars to the foreign policy–national security process is, rather, a two-fold educational role. One is a fundamental, enduring penetration of the mind-set of political and bureaucratic decision-makers on how to perceive the world in which choices must be made, often in conditions of severe stress, for example, *Morgenthau* (1948) in the 1940s and beyond, and *Waltz* (1959, 1979) on the centrality of power in interstate relations, the *Sprouts* on the autonomy of the operational and psychological environments (1965), *Schelling* on the strategy of conflict (1960), and *Keohane and Nye* on the interdependence of global politics and economics (1977). The other path, open to many academicians, is through an impact on students who later enter the public service and who bring to the task of decision-making an approach to analysis and choice learned in the academy. This is far from a direct or immediate influence on policy; but it is not insignificant; and it is more enduring than possible, transient influence on a specific decision.

Scholars have an obligation to make their *paths to knowledge and findings* on any aspect of world politics intelligible for persons authorized to make decisions relating to foreign policy and national security. Decision-makers must disavow their long-assumed monopoly of knowledge and wisdom about world politics. The intellectual gulf remains. Should the efforts be abandoned? No, because too much is at stake—ultimately, human survival—and because the need for improved communication and more soundly based decision-making on foreign policy and national security remains great. In the last analysis, this is the *raison d'être* of scholarship on world politics: to persist, however difficult the task and however little the likelihood of success, to make persons with power and authority to open their minds to the findings from systematic scholarship. If successful, the effort would contribute to a more secure and stable world. If it fails, the cost may be intolerable.

All of the themes discussed in this Introduction will be elaborated in the chapters to follow.

CHAPTER 2

Prelude to an Intellectual Odyssey

YEARS OF AWAKENING (1936–46)

My earliest memories of a world in turmoil are of three high-profile developments in then distant lands in the mid to late 1930s. I awakened to a cruel and violent world at the time of the Spanish Civil War. I first became aware of great power politics during the Munich Crisis and the debate over appeasement. And I was 14 when much of the world descended once more into the abyss of war.

Spanish Civil War (1936–39)

Eighty years after a devastating civil war erupted in Spain in July 1936, I have a vivid memory of what later came to be viewed as a turning point on the road to Armageddon for the second time in the 20th century, WWII. In my then unsophisticated mind-set, this was a crystal clear struggle between Good and Evil: between the forces of Democracy, Secularism, and Socialism, as embodied in the Spanish Republic, despite its mélange of competing parties and ideologies, and a reactionary army officer clique, of which the two most notable rebellious generals were Francisco Franco and Emilio Mola. They were supported by an entrenched Roman Catholic Church, the remnant of a monarchical strand in Spain's politics and society—the last of the Bourbon kings, Alfonso XIII, had abandoned the

Spanish throne in 1931—and the two centers of fascism in Europe, Nazi Germany and Italy.

I was an assiduous listener of radio news reports—TV was still a decade into the future—and I followed with bouts of relief and concern the mix of Republican (Loyalist) victory and defeat on the battlefield: the failure of the initial rebel (Nationalist) siege of Madrid from early November 1936 to February 1937; the Republican victory in the Battle of Guadalajara, 8–18 March 1937; the obliteration of the town of Guernica in the Basque region of northern Spain by German dive bombers on 26 April 1937, a war crime that was captured for eternity by Picasso's magisterial canvas, and a precedent for the mass bombing of Coventry, Rotterdam, Dresden, and other cities during WWII; the Battle of the Ebro, from late July to 18 November 1938, initially a Republican victory, but in the end a total defeat for the Loyalist forces, with enormous casualties on both sides, 70,000 on the Republican side, including 30,000 killed, and 33,000 casualties among the Franco-led Nationalists; the fall of Barcelona, the great prize and symbol of the Republic, on 26 January 1939; and finally, the occupation of Madrid by four columns of Nationalist forces, aided by a 'fifth column' within the capital, on 31 March 1939. (Hugh Thomas, *The Spanish Civil War*, 1961; Paul Preston, *Franco: A Biography*, 1993, Chaps. V–XII)

Apart from the periodic drama generated by the outcome of these major battles, three aspects of the Spanish Civil War left an indelible mark on a young Canadian observer of what was viewed later, correctly, as the beginning of a world unraveling. One theme, close to home, was an admiration for young Canadians—francophone, anglophone, Jews, and many other allophones—who risked their lives in a just war in a far-off land (Michael Petrou, *Renegades: Canadians in the Spanish Civil War*, 2008). The Mackenzie-Papineau International Brigade was one of many groups of volunteers that fought alongside the Spanish Loyalists until late 1938, a total of 40,000 from more than a dozen countries in Europe, along with the USA and Canada, though no more than 18,000 at any one time, along with 20,000 foreigners serving in medical and auxiliary units. Theirs was not the only foreign intervention in the Spanish Civil War: 50,000 Italian troops were actively engaged in support of the Nationalists, along with German and Italian air and naval units, while the Soviet Union provided arms and equipment to the Republican government early in the war and played a key role in organizing the dispatch of the International Brigades starting in October 1936. Many of the volunteers in support of the Republic were pro-Soviet communists; others were socialists, anarchists, and mavericks on the Left; most were motivated by idealism.

Although I was unaware of it at the time, I was not alone in my emotional involvement in this heroic and savage civil war. Many years later, I discovered two stunning comments. One was by the distinguished American literary critic, Lionel Trilling: 'Everyone knows that the Spanish war was one of the decisive events of our epoch, everyone said so at the time it was being fought, and everyone was right' (Introduction to George Orwell, *Homage to Catalonia*, 1952 [1980]). The other was by one of the leading Marxist historians of the past century, Eric. J. Hobsbawm: 'The Spanish revolution was unable to exploit the historical moment when most successful revolutions establish their hegemony.... And so we remember it, especially those of us to whose lives it belongs, as a marvelous dream of what might have been, an epic of heroism, the Iliad of those who were young in the 1930s' (*Revolutionaries*, 1966 [1973], p. 81.)

The second enduring aspect for me was the reality of appeasement in world politics, though I did not fully understand the concept at the time, or even when the term first became known to me, during the Munich Crisis in September 1938. The two exemplars of democracy in Western Europe, Britain and France, created a façade of neutrality at the outset of the Spanish Civil War; and their Non-Intervention Committee, which began to meet in London in September 1936, betrayed the Republic by closing their eyes to Germany's and Italy's blatant large-scale aid to the Franco-led Nationalist rebels throughout the Civil War, a prelude to the Anglo-French betrayal of Czechoslovakia in 1938.

The third lesson of the Spanish Civil War, which remains embedded in my memory eight decades later, was the failure of the international organization, the League of Nations, to mobilize support for the besieged legitimate government of the Spanish Republic at a time of grave threat. It was, I discovered later, a replay of the betrayal of Ethiopia by the League of Nations and the same two major Western powers, passively abetted by the USA. For some inexplicable reason, perhaps because there were no brave young idealists from the West who rallied to the Ethiopian cause as it faced naked Italian aggression in 1935–36—no International Brigades—the Italian/Ethiopian War was not yet on my intellectual or emotional radar screens, certainly not when Emperor Haile Selassie delivered a memorable speech to the League of Nations Council on 30 June 1936:

> *If a strong government finds that it can, with impunity, destroy a weak people, then the hour has struck for that weak people to appeal to the League of Nations to give its judgment* in all freedom. *God and history will remember your judgment....*
>
> I ask the Great Powers, who have promised the guarantee of collective security to small States – those small States over whom hangs the threat that they may one day suffer the fate of Ethiopia: *What measures do they intend to take?*
>
> Representatives of the world, I have come to Geneva to discharge in your midst the most painful of the duties of the head of a state. *What answer am I to take back to my people?* [Emphasis added.]

The (silent) answer was the betrayal of Ethiopia (Abyssinia) and the League's fundamental principles, a glaring precedent for the abandonment of Czechoslovakia two years later.

Parenthetically, for a weak, African state confronted with a dire threat to its existence, abandoned by the major powers and the global organization, Ethiopia coped as well as conditions permitted. It was able to highlight the failure of the League of Nations and did not allow anyone to doubt that Italy was acting in direct contradiction to the League Covenant. However, because of Ethiopia's weakness it was doomed to failure, in light of the messianic aggressiveness of Mussolini's Italy, the perfidious behavior of Britain and France—and the USA, which imposed an arms embargo on both Ethiopia and Italy, in effect, on the former, which was totally dependent on external sources for military equipment— and the inherent weakness of the League of Nations in the face of betrayal of its principles by the Western great powers. (How Ethiopia's emperor and his advisers coped with the threat to its existence is analyzed in my *International Political Earthquakes* [2008, Chapter 8].)

Munich Agreement (1938)

My next encounter with world politics, also from afar, but even more profound, was the Munich Crisis of September 1938. Like many, older and wiser, I was disquieted by Hitler's unopposed annexation of Austria— unopposed by Austrians and the Western Powers alike. Hitler and German forces entered Vienna on 14 March 1938, my 13th birthday; I remember it well, though it was not a welcome birthday gift. However, it was Munich that reinforced my incipient mistrust of the motives and behavior of major powers, which meant, at the time, Britain, 'perfidious Albion', as it was known by friend and foe as long as it remained a great power, and France, as well, of course, as Germany and Italy, Stalinist Russia, and imperial Japan, then engaged in a war of conquest and large-scale atrocities in China; the USA remained immersed in a longstanding posture of Isolationism. Whatever served the euphemism, 'the national interest', in this case the sacrifice of the most democratic small state in inter-world war Central and Eastern Europe, dictated policy: on this occasion it took the form of yielding to Hitler's demand for the immediate cession of the German-speaking districts of Czechoslovakia—Sudetenland—to the short-lived Third Reich (1933–45).

I recall the radio and cinema news reports of the three summit meetings between British Prime Minister Chamberlain, the leading Western apostle of appeasement, and Hitler in September 1938, at Berchtesgaden, the latter's mountain retreat, Godesberg, and then Munich, all located in Germany. In an infamous agreement that has reverberated in the chancelleries of the world ever since, Britain and France yielded to Germany's demands, supported by Italy, setting in motion the dismemberment of Czechoslovakia, initially the imposed transfer of its predominantly German-speaking region, Sudetenland, to Germany, followed by Anglo/French acquiescence in the annexation of the rest of Czechoslovakia in March 1939. The precedent for this behavior by the Western democracies had been created in 1935–36 with their abandonment of Ethiopia to the aggrandizement of Italy—though I do not have a vivid recollection of that act of betrayal at the time it occurred.

To a young Canadian growing up in the mid to late 1930s, world politics seemed distant yet compelling. Spain and Munich became symbols of self-delusion, appeasement and betrayal, and the beginnings of a deep-rooted mistrust of behavior by the great powers of that era. Munich, in particular, was a puzzling and troubling event then and long after. The years of death and destruction that followed strengthened a growing conviction that knowledge of world politics could contribute, modestly, to the preservation and enhancement of the values of human and national rights to which the UN coalition during WWII (China, the UK, the USA, and the Soviet Union) against the Axis coalition (Germany, Italy, and Japan) seemed committed, in word, if not always in deed.

High School (1938–42)

When WWII began, on 1 September 1939, I was 14, entering Grade 9 at Strathcona Academy, which was noted for its high academic standards. Its student body was a mixture of Protestant, Catholic, and Jewish students, almost all English-speaking, without ethnic or religious tension. My favorite teacher at Strathcona was a legend in the school for decades, a history teacher *par excellence*. *Julia Bradshaw* was a tiny wisp of a woman who mesmerized some of her students and petrified others; none was indifferent to her presence. For me and many others, European history since the French Revolution came alive in my final high school year, 1941–42: it was a splendid preparation for an identical university course at McGill four years later, with the newly arrived and, later, Dean of Arts and Vice Principal, *H. Noel Fieldhouse*. I remember her, too, with respect, for telling her students 'the way it was' about a matter that was, potentially, of grave consequence for many of her students. I recall vividly her speaking openly about an unspeakable truth regarding university education in Montreal in those years and beyond.

I had heard from my older brothers, Joe and Irving, who also graduated from Strathcona, about an unwritten and unspoken, but rigid *numerus clausus* (a restricted number of Jews admitted to schools) at Montreal's, and one of Canada's, later one of the world's leading universities, McGill. But it was Miss Bradshaw who alerted us to this rank discrimination one spring day in 1942, on the eve of our 10 High School Leaving exams, each counting for 100 marks. In obvious embarrassment, she related to a predominantly Jewish classroom: 'I feel it necessary to tell you that those who apply for admission to McGill will not be treated equally; Christian students will be admitted with an overall mark of 600, that is, 60 percent; Jewish students will need 750, that is, 75 percent.' In those years, very few graduated high school above 800! There was a stunned silence, though some of us, I among them, had been forewarned. All three Brechers, Joe in 1937, Irving in 1939, and I in 1942, passed the bar; but many, some of whom later became distinguished Canadians in several walks of life, did not.

Student Years at McGill (1942–46)

During my first year at McGill, age 17–18, I recall being awed by the brilliant lectures of McGill's Principal-economist, *F. Cyril James*, on world economic history from the ancient Sumerian civilization to the 20th century: every lecture, delivered in impeccable academic British English, seemed a model of how to inspire students in the classroom: it was a model that I tried to emulate during my 65 years of lectures at McGill and elsewhere beginning a decade later (1952).

Throughout my undergraduate years at McGill, I was fortunate in having a group of stimulating professors. *Burton Keirstead*, author of an undervalued book on microeconomics, *Theory of the Firm*, was an inspiring teacher of both economic and political theory. *Benjamin Higgins*, a pioneer in development economics who was actively engaged in academe until the early 1990s, published an important textbook on *Economic Development* in 1958. Among the historians, *H. Noel Fieldhouse*, who arrived at McGill from the University of Manitoba in 1945, at the beginning of my senior year, was a fascinating lecturer on modern European history, 1789–1939; but his lectures on the 1930s were marred by his unqualified espousal of appeasement, a concept which by then I fully understood, as the correct path for Anglo-French relations with Germany in the 1930s. *E.R. Adair* was a no less talented interpreter of American history. And *C.C. (Charles) Bayley*, who continued to teach at McGill into the 1990s, was a low-key master of the Italian city-states in early modern European history, as well as the history of war and society in medieval Europe.

Yet it was a course on British colonial history that had the most profound effect on my early intellectual development and on the first phase of academic research (South Asia). It was in 1944 that I became aware of the human condition in the colonial world, primarily through a book noted earlier, *India Today*, by R. Palme-Dutt, that produced a devastating '*J'accuse*'-type critique of British rule in India. That book drew me irresistibly to what later became known as the Third World, the first, long phase of academic research, South Asia, lasting from 1951 to 1974, to be elaborated below.

The Holocaust (1945)

Of all the cataclysmic events during my years of awakening, 1936–46, preparing for academe, none had a more profound impact on my early view of the world and world politics than the Holocaust. When the first photographs from Auschwitz and other death camps began to reach the mass public in North America in 1945, I found myself in a state of shock and disbelief: how was it possible for any regime, even an unbridled racist regime like Nazi Germany, to behave with such bestiality, on a scale of horror that defied imagination? Six million Jews and millions of Poles, Russians, Roma, and others were slaughtered in a systematic, organized crime against humanity that defied all rational explanation.

Beyond this portrait of brutality, which was unparalleled in human history, I experienced an unshakeable gnawing sense of a mythical God that failed. Over and over again, I kept asking an unanswered question: how could a Supreme Being, if one existed, observe with equanimity such an unmitigated human catastrophe, initiated and implemented by humans against millions of defenseless civilians, without intervening at any stage of such barbarism. For me, since those days, 70 years ago, this seemed incontrovertible evidence that either God did not exist or, because of a lingering uncertainty, if it did exist, God was unworthy of human recognition, let alone worship.

Many years—six decades—later, compelling words of disbelief were uttered by an unexpected source of authority, Pope Benedict XVI, during his visit to Auschwitz-Birkenau in May 2006: 'Words fail. In the end, there can only be a dread silence – a silence which itself is a heartfelt cry to God'. He then uttered the most poignant words of all: 'Why, Lord, did you remain silent? How could you tolerate this?' (*International Herald Tribune*, Paris, 29 May 2006, p. 3) A similar, more powerful expression of dissent was conveyed by another authoritative public figure, Israel Supreme Court Justice, Haim Cohen: 'I came to an internal realization [in the aftermath of the Holocaust] that I am being merciful to a God I do not believe in. If I did believe in God, I would hate him'. (*Ha'aretz*, Tel Aviv, 25 April 2006, p. 5) These questions remain unanswered 70 years after the end of the Holocaust—by people of all religions, for they cannot be answered. Yet most believers of all faiths did not draw the logical, though difficult to contemplate, inference—either God does not exist, or if it does exist, God is unworthy of human recognition, let alone worship.

The Holocaust led to another fundamental change in my still less fully crystallized view of the world in the mid to late 1940s and, consequently, in the beginning of my intellectual odyssey. Although I was then neither pro-Zionist nor anti-Zionist, but non-Zionist in my ideological disposition, the Holocaust was a crucial catalyst to change. The major effect was to make me well disposed to the Zionist enterprise in 1945–48, though not on ideological grounds. Rather, there developed in my mind a growing conviction that, in light of the tragedy experienced by European Jewry, it was imperative to create a state that would provide a haven for all Jews who felt vulnerable and needed a homeland that was capable of providing them with security against anti-Semitic threats from all possible sources; and this, I became convinced, could only be achieved by creating a state in the historic homeland of the Jewish People and attracting enough Jews to make this state militarily and economically viable.

As I observed the emerging civil war between Arabs and Jews in Palestine, gathering in intensity from 1945 to 1948, this compulsion led me to offer my assistance in an area for which, by 1948, I felt sufficiently trained, namely, diplomacy and foreign policy. Thus, while still a graduate student, I spent the summer of 1948 as a research assistant to *Abba Eban*, the young (33), enormously talented and extravagantly self-confident head of the delegation of the Jewish Agency for Palestine to the UN, who became the State of Israel's representative to the UN upon Israel's admission to the world organization in May 1949 and ambassador to the USA the following year, serving in those two crucial diplomatic posts with great distinction for a decade. (Interviews with Eban over the decades, as part of this research project on political leaders, will be cited later.)

Yale Graduate Studies (1946–49)

I arrived at Yale in September 1946: it was the only social science graduate program in IR in North America at the time: I was the only Canadian and the youngest graduate student (21) in the Department of IR and among the youngest in all the social science departments. It was my first, and most stimulating, encounter with IR as an academic discipline, for IR had not yet arrived at McGill—until 1952, when I introduced it to undergraduates in the then Department of Economics and Political Science.

Pioneers in International Relations

There were very few other centers of IR in North American universities at the time, notably the Fletcher School of Law and Diplomacy at Tufts University. However, there were distinguished and innovative IR scholars elsewhere, whose works influenced me greatly before and during my three years at Yale. Three were at the University of Chicago: *Quincy Wright*, long well-known for major publications in the field of international law, who had recently completed his *magnum opus*, the monumental two-volume *A Study of War* (1942), to which several talented younger scholars who were among my teachers at Yale a few years later had contributed—

Bernard Brodie and *William T.R. Fox*; *Hans J. Morgenthau*, whose thought-provoking *Scientific Man vs. Power Politics* and his magisterial treatise, *Politics Among Nations*, appeared in 1946 and 1948, respectively, while I was at Yale; and *Harold D. Lasswell*, a pioneer in the field of politics and psychology, the author of several classics, notably *World Politics and Personal Insecurity* (1935), and *Politics: Who Gets What, When and How* (1936). I had the privilege of studying with Lasswell, who moved to the Yale Law School from the University of Chicago in 1945, and of getting to know both Wright and Morgenthau, when I was a Visiting Professor of Political Science at Chicago in 1963.

There were several other noted IR scholars of that era whom, regrettably, I never met. *Harold and Margaret Sprout*, at Princeton, framed the fundamental distinction between the 'operational environment', that is, reality, and the 'psychological environment', that is, perceptions of reality, and were the authors-editors of the first and enduring collection of readings in IR, *Foundations of National Power* (1945). *Frederick L. Schuman*, one of many talented younger members of the University of Chicago 'power school' founded by *Charles Merriam* in the 1920s, spent most of his career at Williams College; among his many books was the first power-oriented treatise in the field, *International Politics* (1933), which was revised over 40 years in seven editions.

In Britain, most of the early scholarly work on International Studies focused on international law and organization, and diplomatic history. A notable exception was *E. H. Carr*, a former leader writer for *The Times* (London) and a member of the Foreign Office, before moving to the University College of Wales: his classic *The Twenty Years' Crisis* (1939, 1946) was among the earliest seminal Realist critiques of Utopianism; and his successor volume, *Conditions of Peace* (1942) set down daring Realist guidelines for the inevitable task of creating a viable peace after WWII.

Unlike these individual luminaries, the Yale Department of IR was an institutional expression of outstanding academics that had formed a 'school', the Yale Institute of International Studies, 'organized in 1935 for the purpose of promoting research and post-graduate training in the field of international relations'. During my near-three years at Yale, the Department comprised a high-profile group of IR scholars, many of whom were regarded as pioneers of a new discipline.

Arnold Wolfers was the most senior member of the Yale 'school' when I arrived. A gaunt, severe, analytically brilliant and articulate Swiss expatriate, he was the author of an early IR classic, *Britain and France between*

Two Wars: Conflicting Strategies of Peace Since Versailles (1940), and later, a collection of insightful 'Essays on International Politics', notably two celebrated papers, 'Statesmanship and Moral Choice', and 'The Pole of Power and the Pole of Indifference', in his *Discord and Collaboration* (1962).

William T.R. (Bill) Fox, a young (34) and even more youthful-looking graduate of the University of Chicago 'power school', was the first to introduce the concept—and the term—that characterized the structure of world politics from 1945 to 1989, even before the end of WWII, in his *The Super-Powers* (1944). He later became the founder and long-time Director of the Institute of War and Peace Studies at Columbia University. From Wolfers and Fox, I learned how to think conceptually about world politics.

Bernard Brodie, another product of the Merriam 'power school', was a pioneer of strategic studies in the USA, especially the role of naval power. He acquired high visibility as co-author and editor of the first serious attempt to analyze the likely impact of nuclear weapons on future world politics, *The Absolute Weapon: Atomic Power and World Order* (1946), which appeared during my first year at Yale. And later, he published his under-appreciated *magnum opus*, *War and Politics* (1973), while at the University of California, Los Angeles (UCLA) and the RAND think tank.

Klaus Knorr was developing his ideas on political economy and power, the basis of his insightful, though undervalued, early work in international political economy, *The Power of Nations: The Political Economy of International Relations* (1975). He later served as long-time Director of the Center of International Studies and Editor of the respected quarterly journal, *World Politics* at Princeton, to which most of my Yale IR teachers migrated in 1949. Knorr introduced me to international political economy, then an unknown branch of IR. He also taught me the importance of careful writing and rewriting in order to convey one's ideas with clarity: one day, when returning a paper that I had prepared for his seminar, he remarked, with genuine empathy, 'Michael, most people who read an article in a journal or a book, think that the author dashed it off quickly, in a single draft; that rarely happens; it usually takes several drafts to produce a polished scholarly paper or book'; it was valuable advice that I never forgot.

Percy E. Corbett, an older, respected Canadian specialist in international law and organization, moved from McGill to Yale before I did and stimulated my enduring interest in these branches of IR: he was the author of *Law and Society in the Relations of States* (1951).

As noted above, *Lasswell* moved to the Yale Law School in 1945. He co-authored (with a younger philosopher, *Abraham Kaplan*) a seminal work in political theory, *Power and Society: A Framework for Political Inquiry* (1950). And for many years thereafter he co-authored a myriad of works in an impressive collaborative project on law and society with *Myres S. McDougall*, a Yale luminary in international law. Fortunately, for a young Canadian graduate student, Lasswell offered a fascinating course to IR students who, like me, in admiration and awe, referred to our weekly sessions as 'drifting and dreaming with Lasswell'. It was his seminar that first made me aware of the psychological strand of world politics, to which I trace my research during the past half century on perceptions and decision-making in foreign policy crises.

Gabriel Almond, who became a major figure in comparative politics during the second half of the 20th century, at Princeton and later at Stanford, was then engaged at Yale in an original study of periodic mood shifts in American foreign policy.

Hajo Holborn, like Knorr, a non-Jewish voluntary 'refugee' from Germany at the onset of the Nazi regime, illuminated the 'International Relations of the Inter-War Period' for an eager and attentive student audience in his weekly seminar. Holborn, like Knorr, an empathetic teacher during my formative Yale experience, was one of the two most respected American authorities on modern German history; (the other, *Gordon A. Craig*, at Stanford, was, among other works, co-editor of *The Diplomats 1919–39* (1953) and *The Diplomats 1939–79* (1994), to which I contributed a chapter, 'Eban and Israeli Foreign Policy: Diplomacy, War, and Disengagement').

Regrettably, the most controversial member of the Yale group, Nicholas J. Spykman, was no longer teaching when I arrived: his provocative, geopolitical treatise, *America's Strategy in World Politics: the United States and the Balance of* Power (published in 1942, just after Pearl Harbor), argued, following Mackinder's 'The Geographical Pivot of History' and his concepts of 'Heartland', 'Rimland', and 'World-Island' [1904 and 1919], that the USA's 'natural' ally in East Asia was Japan, not China. It was a policy the USA pursued from 1949 onward, the year the Communists came to power in mainland China.

My years at Yale were intellectually stimulating. As noted, the IR faculty read like a blue-ribbon royal commission in a recently emerging field.

There were also several younger members of the Department of Political Science who became major figures in the discipline; and their courses were available to IR students. The three who stand out were: *Robert A. Dahl*, author of the classic, *Who Governs? Democracy and Power in an American City* (1961) and who became the acclaimed theorist of democracy of his generation, with many other respected works; *Charles E. Lindblom*, author of *Politics and Markets: The World's Political-Economic Systems* (1977), and *Inquiry and Change* (1990); earlier, Dahl and Lindblom jointly authored *Politics, Economics, and Welfare* (1953), ideas that were percolating while I was at Yale; and *Robert E. Lane*, author of a noted trilogy in political science, *Political Life* (1959), *Political Ideology* (1962), and *Political Man* (1972). I was also stimulated by one historian, *Ralph Turner*, author of a two-volume work, *The Great Cultural Traditions: The Foundations of Civilizations* (1941) that matched Toynbee's *A Study of History* (1947), in scope and quality, though not in influence.

Library of Congress (1947); The UN (1948)

My gratifying time at Yale included two unanticipated summers of research, one in Washington (1947), the other in New York (1948), both memorable incidents in my path to a life in academe. With youthful bravado, I was enticed by my closest friend at Yale, *Robert Crane*, a talented specialist in modern Indian history, to spend the summer of 1947 at the Library of Congress, gathering material for a history of modern India! Although it proved to be an abortive episode, it was a valuable, negative, learning experience—do not attempt an impossible research task!

The highlight of this premature research project was an unexpected invitation by a friend of Bob Crane, *Anup Singh* (1939), a Harvard PhD in Political Science, who was First Secretary of the Indian Embassy, to attend the flag-raising ceremony on the occasion of India's independence, 15 August 1947. Although unplanned, my reading of Palme-Dutt's *India Today* in 1944 and my premature project on modern Indian history in 1947 led, in due course, to the South Asia phase of my academic research, an immersion in the study of modern Indian history, politics, and foreign policy for two decades. In perspective, this phase, to be elaborated below, led to a substantial 'paper trail'—my doctoral dissertation on the Kashmir dispute, which became the first of my six books on South Asia and the first book by a Western scholar on *The Struggle for Kashmir* (1953), followed by

NEHRU: A Political Biography (1959) and four other books, and many articles on South Asia, mainly, India.

The summer of 1948, too, proved to be a valuable entry to the second long phase of my academic research, on Israel and the on-going Arab/Israel Conflict. As noted above, moved by the Holocaust, I worked as a volunteer research assistant to Abba Eban, more specifically, to his legal adviser, the erudite, sophisticated, charming, and empathetic *Dr. Jacob Robinson*. During the next three decades, Eban became a legendary figure as Israel's diplomat *par excellence*, as ambassador to the UN and the USA for a decade and, from 1966 to 1974, as Israel's foreign minister. He was an extraordinary orator, comparable to and often compared with Churchill, de Gaulle, and Adlai Stevenson, among 20th century political leaders, the most successful "Voice of Israel" in its entire history.

My principal task, for which my Yale studies were an invaluable training, was to prepare an analysis of the UN Commission on Palestine, the body that was created to implement UN General Assembly Resolution 181, the 'Partition Resolution' of 29 November 1947. It was challenging and rewarding, though I had no illusions about its potential practical utility in the Arab/Israel diplomatic struggles ahead.

ISRAEL: FORMATIVE YEARS (1949–51)

My first encounter with Israel lasted for almost two years. I lived in four places: first, for a month in Tel Aviv; then in a *kibbutz*, near the border with Syria, *Ma'ayan Baruch*, for six months; back to Tel Aviv for a year, during my brief experience with diplomacy; and, finally, in Haifa, on Mount Carmel overlooking the Mediterranean.

It was not an easy time, materially. The pervasive word that described one's daily life was *tsena*, rationing. Everything was in short supply, and a strict, war-like rationing system was in place, conducted with great efficiency by a successful immigrant lawyer from Montreal, a graduate of the McGill Law School, *Bernard (Dov) Joseph*. Coping with a desperate economic reality, nonetheless, generated the dominant traits of Israeli society in the years immediately after the War of Independence, 1948–49— equality and the bond that is created by sharing in a time of trouble and adversity.

Parenthetically, the dire economic reality also created a great divide in Israeli society in 1950–52, when Israel agreed, with great reluctance, to accept reparations from West Germany. In the graphic words of *David*

Horowitz, then Director-General of the Finance Ministry, 'We were in desperate economic straits. We looked into the face of possible collapse. Foreign exchange reserves were practically exhausted. Every ship was important, for the reserve of bread in the country [1950–51] was sufficient for one week only' (Interview with MB, 1966).

Yet the politics of Israel seemed to be oblivious of this grave economic crisis—there was an acute discordance between political behavior and the myriad of problems, internal and external, that confronted the new state. This discordance was poignantly reflected in an assessment by a talented and sensitive graduate student of economics at the Hebrew University of Jerusalem:

> Month by month the situation in our little country deteriorates, with very few rays of hope. We have had elections but they have changed nothing, except for further wearying the disillusioned multitude of politics and of vain promises and still more vain interparty squabbles. We have reached the brink of economic disaster and a shortage of supplies compared with which the situation in the spring and early summer [of 1951] was an age of plenty.
>
> Political discussion has degenerated into minor squabbles, and the larger issues of aim and ideology have taken on more than a tinge of mysticism. Above all, the pettiness and provincialism of it all, the endless talk and debate, make the stifling atmosphere more stifling still. And yet, the more advanced section of the people is no more critical of their fate and their leaders than the mute new immigrants. What these people do not realize is that audacity has given way to cynical bluff, that devotion has degenerated into blind acceptance of the leaders' word on the one hand, and into utter cynicism and exploitation of position on the other, and that there is no longer the will to achieve the impossible. (Dr. Meir Merhav, who later served as a senior member of the Bank of Israel Research Department and then was the stimulating Economics Editor of the *Jerusalem Post*: letter to Eva and Michael Brecher, 15 September 1951)

Ten days later, somewhat chastened by my skeptical response to his doomsday scenario, his negative disposition was reiterated with a different focus:

> The forces at work in Israel are much more complicated [than corruption and selfishness]: The difficulty for every thinking person is that there are no historical precedents for anything that is happening here. (Merhav letter, 27 September 1951)

The majority of those who experienced this period of acute scarcity and domestic political strife may—or may not—have known about the desperate economic and financial situation. However, the mood during my first encounter with Israel 67 years ago was less of impending disaster than of camaraderie, a seemingly natural commitment to sharing, with the unstated belief, 'we shall overcome'. There was no alternative (*ein breira*) to survival—it was only five years after news of the Holocaust had traumatized the world, especially the remnant of world Jewry, creating a belief that, in the end, after the blunders and squabbles alluded to in the cited lament and, most of all, by much pain and tragic losses—1% of the Palestinian Jewish community were killed during the 1948–49 War of Independence—Israel would survive. In perspective, despite all, it was the noblest period in Israel's history.

Phases of an Intellectual Odyssey

The first of three phases of a lengthy and continuing intellectual journey will focus on a selection of the literature on *Political Leadership* and the findings from lengthy interviews with *Political Leaders*: Nehru and his principal adviser on foreign policy, Krishna Menon, in India (1947–64), along with a brief discussion of the unresolved India/Pakistan conflict over Kashmir, a significant political consequence of the 1947 Partition of India; and a comparative assessment of the political record of the first four prime ministers of Israel, along with four prominent members of its second generation of political leaders.

The second phase in this multi-dimensional project concentrates on the *Arab/Israel conflict*, especially on *competing, often discordant, perceptions* by politicians, officials, academics, and advocates from principal adversaries, notably Egypt and Israel. This phase began in 1960 with preliminary research, in Israel, followed by a graduate seminar on the comparative analysis of foreign policy at McGill until 1969. The project gathered momentum, with further intensive field research in 1965–66 and was all-consuming until 1974, with partial involvement continuing until 1980. The findings from lengthy interviews with decision-makers and adviser in both Egypt and Israel, to be presented in the second book of this project, will contribute findings and insights into the Arab/Israel conflict, as well as the worldview of political leaders and officials of these adversaries—until their formal peace agreement in 1979.

The third, on-going phase, which began in 1975, has concentrated on the quest for theory and the presentation of systematic findings from case studies and aggregate data analysis of *international crises* and *interstate protracted conflicts* during the past near-century (late 1918–2016). This led to many books and articles by scholars from various states and universities associated with the *ICB* project, including my *Crises in World Politics: Theory and Reality* (1993), *International Political Earthquakes* (2008), and *The World of Protracted Conflicts* (2016) and, with my closest colleague in the continuing four-decade-old project, Jonathan Wilkenfeld, joint authorship of *Crises in the Twentieth Century* (1988, 2 Vols.), *Crisis, Conflict, and Instability* (1989) and *A Study of Crisis* (1997, 2000). Their updated findings will be reported in later books and articles of this project.

The three phases of this odyssey are linked intellectually but the areas of study and the duration of each phase were not neatly pre-arranged. They emerged in response to changing stimuli and varying concerns over time about *sources of turmoil* in the global system: from a focus on the *India/Pakistan conflict over Kashmir* (1951–53) and *Nehru's role in India's struggle for independence* and the creation of a stable, modern, liberal democracy during the first decade after the Partition of the India-Pakistan subcontinent (1955–66), with continuing interest until 1989; to the *Arab/Israel conflict*, in the 1960s and 1970s, on-going; and to a panoramic study of *conflict, crisis, and war* during the past near-century (since 1975).

This intellectual odyssey provides a framework for an assessment, in a current three-book project, of: (1) *political leadership and charisma*, notably those who profoundly shaped the political evolution of two regions, South Asia and the Middle East, specifically, India and Israel, since their Independence in 1947 and 1948, with special attention to the charismatic leaders, Nehru and Ben-Gurion; (2) the *dynamics and competing perceptions of the Arab/Israel conflict*; and (3) the myriad of findings on *interstate crises* and *protracted conflicts* in the 20th and early 21st centuries. This project will conclude with a candid assessment of the shortcomings in the current state of the field of IR. I begin with a brief report on encounters with a charismatic 20th century political leader of Canada, Pierre Elliott Trudeau, prior to his entry into active politics in 1965. This will be followed by the first phase of this intellectual odyssey, *South Asia*, primarily *Nehru's leadership role in India* and the politics of succession at the time of his death in May 1964.

Encounters with Pierre Elliott Trudeau

Pierre Elliott Trudeau was the first among many prominent political leaders whom I encountered over the decades, notably *Lord Mountbatten*, *Prime Minister Clement Attlee* and *Prime Minister Harold Wilson* (the UK); the first four prime ministers of Israel—*David Ben-Gurion, Moshe Sharett, Levi Eshkol,* and *Golda Meir* (1948–74); and, in India, *Jawaharlal Nehru*, the first and longest-serving prime minister and foreign minister (1947–64), and *Krishna Menon*, his closest foreign policy adviser (1947–62). There were many others—politicians, officials, intellectuals, academics, and journalists—whom I knew and interviewed, some who will appear later in this book.

Unlike all the other political leaders, however, my formative encounter with Trudeau occurred two decades *before* he entered politics in Canada. We met during a six-week student group discovery of Mexico in the summer of 1944. He was then 24 and had just completed a Law degree at the Université de Montréal, with great distinction. I was 19 and had just completed my second year in the McGill BA Honors program in economics and political science, with a minor in history. I had recently learned of my first academic award, the Alexander Mackenzie Scholarship for the highest-ranking student in Year 2 of the economics and political science Honors program.

I quickly discovered on the long train journey from Montréal to Mexico City that Trudeau was a talented, charming, sophisticated intellectual, strongly committed to a Roman Catholic worldview, which he had imbibed at the Jesuit-directed élite school for francophone Canadians, Collège de Brébeuf, in Montréal. Apropos, recent biographies of Trudeau have disclosed, from his voluminous personal archives, the extraordinary extent to which that worldview permeated his thought and influenced his behavior during his student years. Indeed, that pervasive influence continued even during his years of exposure beyond his studies in Montréal—at Harvard, the Sorbonne, and the London School of Economics (LSE), from 1944 to 1949.

Suffice it to recall one glaring incident: while studying in Paris, Trudeau still felt bound by the stricture that special permission from the Church was required for any Catholic wishing to read a book that was listed in the Church-ordained INDEX of prohibited books for the faithful. It is no less extraordinary that, later in life, Trudeau became the staunchest advocate of individual rights among Canadian intellectuals and politicians, first as editor of the leading French-language advocacy journal in Canada, *Cité Libre*, in the 1950s and 1960s, and then as prime minister of Canada. In 1982, he was the prime mover of Canada's 'Bill of Rights', the *Charter of Rights and Freedoms*, generally regarded as his greatest legacy to Canada. Trudeau's devotion to Catholic ideas and beliefs in his early years was unknown to me when we first met.

During the long train ride from Montréal to Mexico City (six days), during bus trips within Mexico, almost everywhere, we discussed, more accurately, we argued about everything: Pierre was then, and for the rest of his life, a committed Roman Catholic; I was then a Jewish agnostic. I become a committed atheist the next year in response to my discovery of the Holocaust (as noted above).

During WWII, Pierre flirted with the Right-wing *Bloc Populaire*. (Almost all young francophone intellectuals, it seemed, were drawn to the Quebec nationalist movement in the 1930s and 1940s, some briefly, and others for an extended period.) We exchanged ideas about ideology, politics and religion, Marxism, Communism, Fascism, Nazism, Liberalism, Democracy, the War, Canada, and Quebec—on every idea that engaged students in that era. We were in disagreement on many of these topics.

It was disquieting to discover, long before it was made known in several biographies of Trudeau, that, in the student phase of his life, Pierre Trudeau expressed views that were extremely reactionary: admiration for Marshal Pétain and the Vichy régime, which cooperated with the German occupation of most of France and its pervasive influence on Vichy Government behavior, including the dispatch of tens of thousands of French Jews to concentration camps and near-certain death or, at least, severe deprivation; indifference to the titanic struggle for the mastery of Europe and, ultimately, the world, between Nazi Germany, Fascist Italy, and imperialist Japan, on one side, and the Anglo-American-Soviet alliance on the other.

'This is a British war', he declared dismissively in 1944; and he was emphatically opposed to active participation in WWII by Canada, especially by the Quebecois. Yet almost 40 years later (1982), the young man with an exclusivist, narrow-minded, doctrinaire worldview in the 1930s and 1940s became the architect of Canada's *Charter of Rights and Freedoms*, one of the most comprehensive legislative expressions of liberal ideas in the western world. It was only when I read three superbly documented biographies of Trudeau's early years, drawing upon his voluminous and hitherto-closeted personal archives, that I realized the magnitude of the change that Trudeau exhibited from age 30 to 50: Stephen Clarkson and

Christina McCall, *Trudeau and our Times, Vol. I: The Magnificent Obsession* (1990); Max and Monique Nemni, *Young Trudeau: Son of Quebec, Father of Canada, 1919–1944* (2006); and John English, *Citizen of the World: The Life of Pierre Elliott Trudeau, Vol. I, 1919–1968* (2006). Moreover, while reading these splendid biographies I inevitably recalled my impressions of Pierre during that memorable first encounter.

Despite my unfamiliarity with the Jesuit ethos and Roman Catholic doctrine, it was crystal clear that there was an enormous gulf between the worldview of a young, Jesuit-indoctrinated Catholic devotee, who knew the truth and did not challenge any of its precepts, and a young, left-wing, agnostic Jew who, then and throughout his adult life was skeptical about all traditional religious beliefs. Further, I was already then a firm supporter of human rights, including the right to independence of all colonial peoples, who were perceived and treated by Western peoples as the inferior peoples of the Third World. During my first encounter with Pierre Trudeau in 1944, he did not exhibit the slightest inkling of empathy for, or support of, the right of non-Western peoples to independence and equal rights in the new world order that would emerge from the ashes of WWII.

Nonetheless, I recall a vague meeting of minds on some fundamental themes, or so it seemed then, but this may have been wishful thinking: the merits of Socialism as a set of ideas and values to guide politicians and intellectuals in their quest of a 'good society', especially in its Social-Democratic political form; the intellectual power of Marxism; and the high value of Democracy as a political system, and of human rights, especially, individual rights. We disagreed openly and profoundly on the value of religion, which I viewed as a major obstacle to human progress, as 'an opiate of the people'; Pierre espoused with passion his admiration for Roman Catholicism. For days, we talked and argued—and learned from each other, I thought then and later. It was for me a memorable encounter with an elegant, provocative intellectual who later became Canada's most charismatic and beloved public figure, as anyone who lived through the national trauma that followed his death in September 2000 would testify. I have reason to think, from a pithy remark by him 24 years after our first encounter that Mexico was a memorable encounter for him as well (see below).

Many years after our first meeting in Mexico, following a controversial and increasingly high-profile role as a Quebec intellectual—a professor of constitutional law at his alma mater and the provocative editor of the highly respected French-language journal, *Cité Libre*, especially his advocacy of human rights—he entered Canadian politics with high visibility in 1965, as Minister of Justice, along with two francophone colleagues, Jean Marchand and Gerard Pelletier, at the personal invitation of then Prime Minister and head of the Liberal Party, Lester Pearson. He succeeded Pearson in 1968 in an extraordinary display of charisma, widely remembered as 'Trudeau-mania'; and he remained Prime Minister until 1984, except for a brief nine-month period in opposition, in 1979–80.

To my regret, our paths crossed infrequently after 1944. Pierre moved on from his local educational milieu—Brébeuf and the Université de Montréal, as noted—to Harvard, the Sorbonne, and the LSE, a formidable combination of institutions of higher learning. I went on to Yale for my MA and PhD, then to Israel for two years, India for a year, and back to McGill—with visiting professorships at the University of Chicago (1963), the Hebrew University of Jerusalem (1970–74), Berkeley (1979), and Stanford (1980). My wife, Eva, and I met Pierre occasionally at social and cultural events. However, when he entered national politics in 1965, our paths rarely crossed. Yet I remember three incidents, the first of which made me realize that our 1944 long encounter was meaningful to him as well.

Soon after he became Prime Minister, Trudeau set in motion a national rethinking of Canada's foreign policy. To that end he organized a set of seminar-type meetings at his home in late 1968 with many segments of Canadian society—businessmen, trade unionists, journalists, and academics. I was invited to the scholars' seminar. When I arrived at Rideau Hall, the prime minister's residence, Pierre was standing at the door greeting each invitee with a personal touch. As we shook hands, he said to me with his engaging smile, 'Mike, do you remember Mexico'!

In the early 1980s, while he was Prime Minister, and Eva and I were living in Jerusalem most of each year, Pierre visited Israel and tried to locate me; so he informed me later. Acquaintances in the Foreign Office, who did not welcome my criticism of Israel's failure to come to terms with the Palestinian reality, in the concluding chapter of my book, *The Foreign Policy System of Israel: Setting, Images, Process* (1972), or my participation in the drafting of a very early manifesto advocating a two-state solution to the Israel–Palestinian conflict (1975) [both to be noted in a later volume], did not bother to inform him that I was in Jerusalem, around the corner from his hotel!

In early 1996, I wrote to Pierre from Jerusalem commending him for an intellectually superb response to then Quebec Premier Lucien Bouchard on the perennial issue of Quebec and Canada. He replied—it was during an upsurge of suicide bombing in Israel—'[U]nlike Quebec and Canada, Michael, you and all who live in Jerusalem have serious problems!'

Twenty-five years after our first encounter, Pierre Elliott Trudeau attained his longstanding, though not yet publicly known, goal of political leadership: he was elected leader of Canada's Liberal Party on 6 April 1968 and Prime Minister following its victory in Canada's general election on 25 June. His accomplishments were many and important, beginning with basic reforms of Canada's Criminal Code in 1967, as Minister of Justice, and most significantly, after 15 years of sustained struggle, the patriation of Canada's Constitution, the 1867 British North America [BNA] Act, on 17 April 1982, and the formal passage of Canada's Charter of Rights and Freedoms, which Trudeau aptly termed 'the people's package'.

Late in his long tenure as Canada's political leader [15 years], during his fourth period as Prime Minister, 1980–84, Trudeau launched a solitary 'peace initiative'. He was drawn to this short-lived (October 1983–February 1984) failed effort at global mediation by diverse sources: the urging of several trusted aides—Ivan Head, a Trudeau speech writer and head of the Trudeau-created International Development Research Centre, Robert Fowler, and Thomas Axworthy, a devoted Secretary to the Prime Minister; the low-key advice of former US Secretary of Defense Robert McNamara under Presidents Kennedy and Johnson, that 'old politicians simply become "ghosts"…and he should act while he still had a political life'; the pressure from several female friends; and a perceived replica of the 1962 Cuban Missile Crisis, triggered by a North Atlantic Treaty Organization (NATO) military exercise throughout Central Europe in October 1983, code-named 'Able Archer', perceived by the Soviet leadership as heralding a NATO first strike, which led to Soviet forces being placed on high alert.

Trudeau visited the leaders of the then known five nuclear weapons powers, China, France, the UK, USA, and USSR, aiming to persuade the superpowers to eliminate 'the fear of pre-emptive strike systems', to no avail. He realized the futility of his initiative when Prime Minister Thatcher informed him, 'one had to remember that things were growing again one year after Hiroshima', and China's paramount leader, Deng Xiaoping, expanding upon Mao Tse-tung's earlier reference to 500 million casualties, informed Trudeau that 'even though a nuclear war would leave two billion dead, "China would survive"'. There is no evidence of his influence on the superpowers' behavior. However, it is possible that Trudeau's peace initiative contributed modestly to the then emerging détente between the USA and the USSR, as evident in President Reagan's farewell 'Godspeed' on his peace mission as Trudeau set out to London, Paris, Moscow, and Beijing, and in the Reagan-Gorbachev 1986 Reykjavik breakthrough Summit Conference (based on the account by a Trudeau biographer, John English, 2010, 592–602).

The last time I saw Pierre Trudeau was during one of my daily long walks on Mount Royal, near his home, in November 1998: it was just a day before his 79th birthday and I indicated that, like many in Canada, I was looking forward to celebrating his 80th. He nodded. When I took the liberty of saying that many, including me, were waiting for a full-scale well-considered autobiography, clearly implying that a recent book containing his memoirs was deficient, he shrugged—as he often did when he was in disagreement or wanted to convey a non-committal response; and I never had the occasion to pursue this matter with him again. A few months later he suffered a terrible personal tragedy: his youngest son, Michel, disappeared in a fatal skiing accident in British Columbia. Pierre, from public photos at the time, was shattered. He never recovered from this personal trauma. He died almost two years later.

Trudeau was one of the most accomplished political leaders of Canada since its emergence as a quasi-independent state in 1867, though some found flaws in his controversial behavior and economic policy: historians of Canada rank him as one of the four or five most important prime ministers, though some accord him even higher rank. He was persistently vilified by Quebec separatists or, to use their euphemism, 'sovereigntists', because of his unconcealed and frequently reiterated primary identity with Canada from the 1960s onward; it was a visceral as well as an ideological conflict, highlighted by his use of the Canadian army to suppress what he and many Canadians regarded as open rebellion by the *Front Liberation de Québec* (FLQ), in 1971. He also incurred the hostility of the business community and criticism by some economists because of his Keynesian-type economic policy. But there was no dissension about his most far-reaching legacy, Canada's Charter of Rights and Freedoms, which became law in 1982. Admirers and critics alike regarded Trudeau as one of Canada's most illustrious and fascinating political leaders during the 20th century. Moreover, for some, he was also a prominent statesman of his era, though with few accomplishments in the domain of global politics because of Canada's (at most) middle power status. When he died in September 2000, he was lionized by the mass public of Canada in an unprecedented public outpouring of grief.

BEGINNINGS OF THE SOUTH ASIA PHASE (1951–53)

My first book, *The Struggle for Kashmir* (1953), an outgrowth of a doctoral dissertation, was an attempt to uncover the *basic and precipitating causes* of what became a protracted conflict between two new South Asian states, India and Pakistan, and the multiple early efforts by the UN and its *appointed mediators*, among others, to resolve this conflict by *mediation*. Then, after a long immersion, came an assessment of the Indian National Congress political leadership role during the crucial years leading to Britain's transfer of power in 1947 to India and Pakistan and Nehru's lengthy dominance of India's politics during the first 17 years of independence, presented in *NEHRU: A Political Biography* (1959). This was followed by a general work on newly independent states in South and South-East (Southern) Asia, with some overlap to 'old' states in Asia and 'new' states elsewhere, *The New States of Asia* (1963).

The fourth book in my initial research phase was an unplanned sequel to the Nehru political biography. India's pre-eminent leader since independence died on 27 May 1964. After a long period of uncertainty and a source of great concern among decision-makers, academics, journalists, and attentive publics over the issue of succession, both 'who' and 'how' the process would unfold, the process of choosing a successor was reconstructed and dissected in *Nehru's Mantle: The Politics of Succession in India* (1966).

The fifth book of this phase, *India and World Politics* (1968), explored the perceptions of independent India's first generation of political leaders through the worldview of Nehru's closest confidant on foreign policy issues during most of the period, 1947–62, V.K. Krishna Menon. The final volume of the South Asia phase examined the attitudes of India's political élite—cabinet ministers and an array of MPs in Delhi—in 1968, *Political Leadership in India: An Analysis of Élite Attitudes* (1969).

Bombay (May–June 1951)

Among the stimulating Indian politicians, academics, journalists, civil servants and leaders in business encountered in Bombay in May–June 1951, later known as Mumbai, at the beginning of my lengthy encounter with South Asia, the most noteworthy were:

Dr. *John Matthai*, recently returned to his position as a Director of India's pre-eminent Tata conglomerate, after serving in India's Cabinet as Minister of Finance, and later Director, State Bank of India
Minoo Masani, Personal Assistant to J.R.D. Tata and an articulate voice on the Right-wing of Indian politics
Frank Moraes, the talented editor of the *Times of India*
R.K. Karanjia, editor of the muck-raking, popular weekly, *Blitz*
D. F. Karaka, a well-known journalist and author of a sharply critical book on Nehru as India's leader; and
S. K. Patil, a long-time leader of the Congress Party in Bombay, who was to play a key role in the struggle for the political succession to Nehru in 1964.

Most of these interviews, along with stimulating discussions with faculty members at Bombay University and the Gokhale School of Politics and Economics in nearby Poona, concentrated on India/Pakistan relations, especially on their conflict over Kashmir. There was a notable consensus even then, only four years after the Partition of India, that the Kashmir dispute in all of its ramifications was the core problem of what became the India/Pakistan protracted conflict, now in its 69th year!

This was emphasized by *Dr. Matthai*, who revealed that, at all of the India/Pakistan conferences of leaders and senior officials he attended as a senior cabinet minister during independent India's earliest years, the supreme barrier to agreement was not any specific issue under consideration: not one of the tension-creating legacies of the 1947 Partition of India, notably control over the prized territory of the former princely state, Jammu and Kashmir, the primary cause of the first India/Pakistan war (October 1947–1 January 1949) and two other wars over Kashmir (1965 and 1999); not the distribution of the Indus river system canal waters, a rare case in this protracted conflict of a grave dispute that was resolved—in 1960; nor compensation for evacuee property and for refugees from the mass migration created by the Partition. Rather, the barrier to agreement was a pervasive atmosphere of distrust emanating from the conflict over Kashmir, which profoundly influenced the attitude and behavior of the Indian and Pakistani delegations on any disputed issue. Indeed, everyone encountered in Bombay and, later, in Delhi and Calcutta, and five years later, in Lahore, Karachi, and Peshawar emphasized that the struggle for Kashmir, then only four [and nine] years old, was the 'Gordian knot', the solution of which was the indispensable condition for a general relaxation of the existing tension and the attainment of a genuine rapprochement between India and Pakistan or, at least, a *modus vivendi*. So it remains in 2016, almost seven decades since its onset. (This first encounter with the India/Pakistan protracted conflict became a perennial research interest until the early 1970s.)

Bombay, later known as Mumbai, conveyed an impression of a city where East and West mingled in sharp contrasts, from the affluent British-inhabited enclaves of the city, to the unbelievable poverty and misery in large sections of Indian Bombay: no European or North American slums could compete with this human degradation. A welcome contrast was a discovery at that time of one of India's artistic wonders, the Ellora and Ajanta cave paintings in Hyderabad state, hailed by art critics in the West and East alike as comparable to classic Renaissance art and designated by UNESCO as one of the world's cultural treasures.

Delhi (June–July 1951, October 1951–February 1952)

During June–July 1951 and from September 1951 until February 1952, research on the attitude of India's political élite towards the Partition of the subcontinent and the ensuing conflict with Pakistan was facilitated by good fortune, in the form of a room for eight months in Constitution House, a New Delhi residence for Indian members of parliament. The prize, unrestricted access to the dining room, created an extraordinary opportunity to meet an array of MPs from across the political spectrum—politicians from the ruling Indian National Congress and all the major opposition parties—Socialist, Communist, and the Right-wing, nationalist Hindu *Mahasabha*, and several splinters from these parties, along with Independent MPs.

The myriad of interviews, reinforced by a plethora of English-language journals, daily, weekly, and monthly, provided abundant knowledge about the primary research focus at that time, the India/Pakistan conflict, with emphasis on the struggle for Kashmir, and India's politics more generally. Two themes became apparent quickly. One was that, in the summer and autumn of 1951 the hopes engendered by the Congress party's promises since the provincial election in the mid-1930s, before Independence, had practically evaporated, and the Congress was seen as a corrupt and inefficient organization, with the added negative traits of nepotism and maladministration—but that widespread dissatisfaction was still in a passive and negative stage. The second theme was that no political party at the time could pose an effective challenge to the Congress in the forthcoming (1951–52) general elections. Indeed, the widespread forecast was a Congress victory with about 70% of the vote and a Congress majority in all but three of the states [former provinces]. The primary reasons were twofold: the image and reality of Congress primacy in the struggle for, and attainment of, India's independence in 1947, and the *charismatic* quality of political leadership by Gandhi and Nehru, the former until his assassination in October 1948, and Nehru as the universally perceived successor to Gandhi although his status was not as exalted as Gandhi. Although his popularity had diminished somewhat, because of Government shortcomings, he remained the indispensable political leader of India in 1951, as he was viewed until his death in 1964.

Vale of Kashmir (July–September 1951)

During the course of many interviews in Srinagar, the summer capital of the former princely State of Jammu and Kashmir, I learned a great deal about the background and current conditions in Indian-controlled Kashmir, two-thirds of the State's territory, since the end of the first Kashmir War, on 1 January 1949, as well as the long-range plans for economic development and the prospects for the immediate future. Informative interviews were conducted with the Private Secretary to the Chief Minister, Sheikh Abdullah, the Director-General of Education, the Director-General of Information, the Secretary for Planning, the Constitutional Adviser to the Government, and a lengthy interview with Sheikh Abdullah, the *charismatic* Kashmiri leader for many years. These meetings, along with wide access to a multitude of documents on the pre-India-Pakistan independence phase of the struggle for Kashmir, supplemented by the abundant secondary sources on Kashmir and the Conflict in libraries abroad provided insights into the complexity of the Kashmir conflict and the sharply different attitudes of India and Pakistan to its Causes, as well as their rival conceptions and proposals for resolution of this primary tangible obstacle to agreement and mutually tolerable relations.

For Pakistan, the Kashmir issue was—and continues to be—perceived as one of life and death for many reasons. First, and most important, it represents a final test of the validity of the two-nation theory, which has long been the ideological *raison d'être* of Pakistan, namely, that Hindus and Muslims in the subcontinent constitute two nations, and that the partition of India was based upon this core principle. There are also important strategic and economic considerations. For all of these reasons, Pakistan could not yield to India on the Kashmir dispute and wanted resolution of the Conflict quickly. By contrast, India was in no hurry since it controls the most populous and fertile areas of the disputed territory since the Cease-Fire that ended their first Kashmir War at the beginning of 1949; and with each passing year the pro-India regime headed by Sheikh Abdullah appeared to be consolidated during the first four decades of this unresolved conflict. (This changed from 1989 onward, with a visibly active anti-India Islamist movement in Kashmir.)

Pakistan was determined to achieve a solution quickly and to compel India to accept the 1951 recommendation for a plebiscite by UN mediator, Dr. Frank Graham. Pakistan's case benefited from its simplicity and intuitive attractiveness: 'the Partition of the India-Pakistan sub-continent was based upon the recognition of the existence of two nations, Hindu and Muslim, and more than 75% of the population of the former princely state of Jammu and Kashmir is Muslim; *ergo*, Pakistan's claim to the entire territory of the former princely state is morally and legally unassailable'. India's case suffered from overemphasis on legality: the Maharaja of Kashmir, to whom the former ruler of the India subcontinent, Great Britain, granted exclusive right to determine his State's constitutional status at the time of the Partition of the subcontinent, chose integration with India: he signed the Instrument of Accession to India in September 1947, formalizing the legal status of Jammu and Kashmir as an integral part of India.

While India's case was juridically sound, this rationale was less powerful than Pakistan's emotive Muslim-majority claim. Moreover, Pakistan benefited from the valuable support of the USA and the UK, especially the former, which viewed Pakistan as a more reliable ally in the then flourishing global Cold War than non-aligned India, as expressed in India's policy on the Korean War, on Indochina, on the France/Vietnam War, and India's longstanding friendship with the Soviet Union and mainland China. The impasse remains in 2016.

Meaning of Kashmir

One high-visibility legacy of the 'end of empire' for Great Britain in South Asia was the conflict between the successor states, India and Pakistan, over the princely state of Jammu and Kashmir. For almost seven decades the relations between India and Pakistan have been characterized by profound conflict, a conflict that has found expression in persistent tension, mutual distrust and animosity, continuous propaganda, periodic economic warfare, and four outbreaks of war, in 1947–48, 1965, 1971, and 1999, and an ever-present threat of resumed military conflict between what are now nuclear-weapon states. The most high-profile issue in this Conflict has been the struggle for Kashmir, a highly strategic prize in Central Asia that has served as the principal obstacle to a mutual agreement, let alone reconciliation, between India and Pakistan.

The Kashmir dispute and the ensuing deadlock is, in the broadest perspective, a by-product of the policy of uncertainty regarding the Indian princely States bequeathed by Great Britain on the eve of its departure from the subcontinent in August 1947. In transferring authority to the successor governments of India and Pakistan, London granted the Princes *carte blanche* to decide their future constitutional status, the alternatives being accession to India or Pakistan or independence, the last of which would have meant Balkanization and utter confusion. In reality, the overwhelming majority of the 562 princely States had little choice because the factors of geographical contiguity and communal composition of their populations determined their decision. In fact, only three territorial conflicts emerged, namely, over Kashmir, Hyderabad, and Junagadh which, unlike all other princely domains, were characterized by a communal cleavage between the rulers and the bulk of their subjects. Yet it was Kashmir, with a Hindu ruler and a Muslim majority, the largest and one of the most populous of the pre-Partition princely States that was destined to become the critical issue between India and Pakistan.

Among the princely states, Kashmir alone borders on both countries, and its raw material resources are valuable to both of its neighboring giants. Moreover, it has a strategic location: Kashmir juts into the heart of Central Asia, its northern-most frontier being the point of convergence of Pakistan, Afghanistan, and the then Soviet Union, and China. To these material considerations must be added an ideological factor that sheds much light on the meaning of Kashmir and the intensity of the

India/Pakistan conflict. Stated succinctly, the issue is acute discordance between a secular state (India) and a state resting on religious foundations (Pakistan). Moreover, the territorial dimension of Kashmir is a crucial symbol for the internal politics of both India and Pakistan.

Indian leaders, especially Nehru, frequently emphasized the role of Jammu and Kashmir, the formal designation of this state, in the context of a secular–theological struggle in the new republic. Should a Kashmir plebiscite be held, and the predominantly Muslim population of the state (about 77% prior to 1947) vote for accession to India, the ideological foundation of Pakistan, namely, the two-nation theory, would receive a severe setback. Moreover, the forces of secularism in Indian politics would be vitally strengthened. By contrast, a popular choice of the Kashmiris to accede to Pakistan would be for the Pakistanis, the outside world, and the extremist Hindu groups in India a striking confirmation of the belief that Hindus and Muslims cannot live together in harmony. Of even greater human consequence, the outcome of the Kashmir dispute would have a profound effect on the social, economic, political, and physical security of the large Muslim minority in India (more than 140 million in 1947) and, in the early years after the Partition, of the considerable Hindu minority in Pakistan.

The stakes of Kashmir continue to be very high 69 years after the eruption of the protracted conflict between India and Pakistan: a *strategic location of great importance* in world politics; *control over economic resources of considerable value*; a *test of the relative strength of secularism and communalism*; and a *key to the security of the minorities* in both countries, especially the large Muslim community in India.

The history of India/Pakistan relations also reveals that the struggle for Kashmir has been—and continues to be—the most formidable barrier to a genuine *rapprochement* between the successors to the British Indian Empire. It has poisoned the atmosphere permeating all India/Pakistan conferences. Nor has its influence been negligible on their attitude to the UN, the Western Powers, the Soviet Union, China, and the Middle East. Finally, this tragic interstate protracted conflict exacerbated the relations between the Hindu and Muslim communities, and brought fear of the future to Muslims, Hindus, and Sikhs in Kashmir, who had learned to live together in cooperative endeavor and who provided until 1989 an experiment of relative communal harmony, in the communally hypersensitive subcontinent. In sum, the Kashmir impasse has acted as a cancerous growth gnawing at the political foundations of both India and Pakistan, preventing their accommodation and impeding the realization of their aspirations for economic progress, psychological security, and peace.

The Struggle for Kashmir *(1953): Contents*

Suffice it to note the dimensions of the still-unresolved conflict between India and Pakistan that were explored in *The Struggle for Kashmir* (1953): *Background*, in terms of the geostrategic, demographic, and historical settings of the dispute and the political constellation within Kashmir; the *Partition* of India in 1947 as it related to Kashmir—the tribal *Invasion* from Pakistan and Kashmir's *Accession to India* in October 1947; the *Importance of Kashmir* to the two successor states, India and Pakistan; several chapters on the UN dimension of this conflict—discussions before the *Security Council* in 1948, the *Role of the UN Commission* on India and Pakistan (UNCIP) in 1948–49, the *McNaughton Proposals* and the *Dixon Report* in 1950, and the *Graham Mission* from 1951–53. This project culminated with analyses of *Kashmir in Transition*, and *Consequences of the Dispute*.

Completion of the Kashmir project in 1952 and the beginning of what became a lifetime faculty association with McGill University the same year marked the end of the *Prelude to an Intellectual Odyssey*. This initial research experience in—and on—South Asia also paved the way for an intense involvement in a 25-year immersion in research on *Political Leadership and Charisma* in India and Israel, building on an earlier formative encounter (1944) with Canada's most compelling political leader in the 20th century, Pierre Elliot Trudeau. In essence, the India/Pakistan conflict over Kashmir catalyzed a pre-occupation for 15 years (1954–69) with India's political leaders, notably Nehru, and the challenge of succession to a charismatic leader in a democratic political system.

My South Asia phase, beginning with the India/Pakistan conflict over Kashmir, lasted from 1950 to 1969, with residual interest until the mid-1970s, culminating in a final assessment in 1989 of India's dominant political leader during the first 17 years of independence. As noted above, the cumulative findings on India's political leaders were presented in six books and many articles, notably a political biography of Nehru and an analysis of two leadership succession contests, following Nehru's death in 1964, and the death of his successor, Shastri, in 1966. That phase also analyzed India's nationalist movement culminating in independence in 1947 and the first decade of politics and IR, the Nehru era. During much of

Phase I, to which this intellectual odyssey now turns, research on political leaders and leadership also focused on the first four prime ministers and four younger political leaders of Israel, from 1960 to 1978.

CHAPTER 3

Political Leaders: India (1951–91)

IN QUEST OF JAWAHARLAL NEHRU (1955–1989)

Preparing the Way

The first of several large-scale research projects on political leaders in India was a political biography of Nehru, then one of the world's pre-eminent national leaders and international statesmen. It was made possible by a Travelling Fellowship from the Nuffield Foundation, based in Oxford, which facilitated 15 months of research in England and India.

London Phase (May–November 1955)

The UK part of a quest for insight into Nehru, the man and the leader, concentrated on the valuable collections of pre-India independence documents and papers and on interviews with many of the key figures who shaped and implemented British policy during the last phase prior to its transfer of power to India and Pakistan in August 1947. The library at India House, where India's High Commission (embassy) to the UK was housed, provided a valuable introduction to pamphlets and books on the India and Pakistan-to-be nationalist movements during the preceding half century. Chatham House, the home of the Royal Institute of

International Affairs, provided access to well-organized newspaper clippings on India dating back to the 1920s, a helpful chronological sequence of events, along with many articles on Nehru's perceptions and the political setting in India. A number of obscure publications were located at the Commonwealth Relations library, formerly the library of the British Government's India Office, and in the library of the School of Oriental and African Studies, University of London.

How to go about the task of interviewing persons who had made important decisions relating to India or had served in the subcontinent? There were no guidelines. Sustained by an intuitive belief that retired politicians and officials would welcome the attention of an inquisitive scholar, I wrote to approximately 75 politicians, senior officials who had been involved in the subcontinent, academics, and journalists, requesting an interview. The intuition turned out to be correct: virtually all consented to be interviewed. They spoke with revealing candor about many aspects of the controversial subjects of my research.

The most notable were: *Clement Attlee*, by then Lord Attlee, who provided interesting but unsystematic recollections from the vantage point of a prime minister (1945–51), including the crucial years culminating in the transfer of power and the partition of the subcontinent, 1945–47; and the *Earl Mountbatten of Burma*, who presided over, and profoundly shaped, the course of the Partition.

Interviews with Lord Mountbatten (November 1955)

Of all the individual actors in the drama of India's Partition and the coming of independence to India and Pakistan in 1947, one was unique—Lord Mountbatten. As the Earl Mountbatten of Burma, he was the last Viceroy of India, from March to August 1947, presiding over the Partition, and then Governor-General of the Dominion of India, August 1947–June 1948. At the time of my interviews (November 1955), he was Admiral of the Fleet, First Sea Lord, and Chief of the UK Combined Chiefs of Staff.

The first and enduring impression of him was of an exceptionally handsome man in his mid-50s. In his immaculate white naval uniform, his formal dress, or even on informal occasions such as these interviews, in his navy blue uniform, Mountbatten looked every inch the born leader of men. He was tall and erect, with a well-proportioned physique and strong, masculine features. His bearing and movement carried the imprint of a lifetime naval career and the pride of a man born to the highest rank of the aristocracy. He was polished, urbane, imperious, and completely self-controlled. Yet he was also serious and attentive to the questions posed, not stern or lighthearted, or adamant, as others noted. To some persons who had interviewed him and in biographies, his gestures and expression were consciously calculated to achieve the maximum effect. To others they were natural and intensely human. Both of these traits were apparent in these interviews. All agreed that there was a magnetic quality to 'the Admiral', as Lord Mountbatten was known to his devoted subordinates.

Mountbatten was acutely conscious of his place in history and acted his role with supreme self-confidence: he had been Supreme Commander, Allied Powers (SCAP) for Southeast Asia during WWII, then Viceroy of India, and was now Head of the British Combined Chiefs of Staff. From the outset of the two lengthy interviews he displayed a shrewd insight into men and affairs and displayed formidable powers of persuasion. He was certain that all his decisions relating to the Partition were wise; the alternative, he contended, would have been more chaos, more violence, more human suffering. Others, I among them, are not convinced and remain so almost seven decades later.

One of Mountbatten's traits, also discernible among most of the public figures and political leaders I interviewed over several decades—in England, India, and Israel—is a difficult-to-conceal streak of vanity: it seemed to be of great importance to them to ensure that their version of significant and controversial events be given the widest possible publicity. In this case, the interviewer in 1955 was a young (30-year-old), unknown Canadian academic engaged in a research project that might never be completed or published, while the person being interviewed was a commanding figure with world recognition and visibility, who had left his mark in war and peace. Throughout the interviews, I sensed that it was important for him to place on the record once more his interpretation of the wisdom of his decisions on the Partition of India eight years before.

How then to assess Lord Mountbatten's role, positive and negative, in the cataclysmic events of 1947 that culminated in the partition of India and its fallout, the creation of the two largest, most populous, and most powerful new states in Southern Asia, accompanied by horrendous human consequences? Mountbatten and the Partition have been largely forgotten almost seven decades since that upheaval. Nonetheless, they merit attention because, in 1947, he was a compelling and controversial figure, whose role was central in the timing and consequences of the Partition, a momentous event in 20th century history and world politics, the beginning of the end of the British Empire and, one might argue, the beginning of the end of Western colonial rule in Asia and Africa.

Lord Mountbatten's tenure as Viceroy of India was the shortest in the history of the British *Raj*, but he stayed on as Governor-General of India until 21 June 1948. He arrived in March 1947 when India was aflame with communal riots. His mission was to supervise the transfer of power from the UK to two new Dominions, India and Pakistan, a task requiring statesmanship of the highest order. The mission was accomplished five months later, but the price was high—a million dead and 15 million Hindus, Muslims, and Sikhs who were forced, or in fear felt compelled, to leave their ancestral homes. Whether any other course of action would have reduced the human suffering or have magnified it continues to be the subject of conjecture. The fact remains, however, that the climax of Mountbatten's mission was accompanied by the gravest outbreak of communal violence in the 4000-year-old history of the subcontinent.

Yet he was acclaimed by the leaders and people of India alike, the recipient of popularity, affection, and respect. The basic reason must be sought in the peculiar psychological atmosphere of India at the time. The struggle for independence had been long and arduous. Many Indians doubted British sincerity even as late as the spring of 1947, despite Prime Minister Attlee's unqualified pledge to transfer power, which he recalled with typical understatement during my interview with him in 1955. When at last Independence came, Mountbatten was its carrier, the symbol of a promise fulfilled and the personification of the best qualities of the British *Raj*.

Moreover, unlike most of his predecessors as Viceroy, he was gifted with a common touch. He mingled freely with Indians at all levels, showed a keen interest in their problems and sympathy with their aspirations. And was he not a prince in fact, cousin to the King, George VI. It was this unusual combination of qualities and status, along with his role as the bearer of independence, that endeared him to many Indians. He was an arresting figure, a man of irresistible charm. He could do no wrong. His appearance and manner seemed to give visible expression to this idealized self-portrait.

Mountbatten was a man of many talents: military commander, administrator, and statesman. He was, too, a superb showman on the public stage, highly articulate and gifted with a sense of timing. His personality was forceful and dynamic, his energy seemingly irrepressible, his capacity for work enormous. To many who observed him in the months before Partition, his greatest asset—and liability—was his habit of making important decisions swiftly, in the opinion of many, too swiftly. Of his capacity for leadership, a colleague remarked: 'No man could get us out of a mess more quickly, or into one, than Mountbatten' (an interviewee who requested anonymity).

One of his least 'finest hours' as a military commander, long remembered in Canada, was the disastrous Allied raid from England on the Normandy coastal town, Dieppe, on 19 August 1942: the one-day toll was 2000 prisoners and a thousand dead, including 68% of the Canadians and 20% of the commandos who had landed on the French coast. In the words of his official biographer: 'With the possible exception of the partition of India, no episode in Mountbatten's career has earned him as much harsh criticism as the raid on Dieppe' (Ziegler, *Mountbatten*, 1985, 186).

He approached the problem of Indian independence as if it were a military campaign. Most revealing was a calendar hanging on the wall behind his desk: inscribed in large, black print were numbers and below each, 'Days Left to Prepare for the Transfer of Power'. When D-Day arrived, the surgical operation was performed. He drove his staff and himself mercilessly, for the deadline had to be met: it was. Critics of his role in implementing the Partition Plan in 1947 argued then and later that India paid an exorbitant price for his military approach—bifurcation and the enormous number of casualties. Nevertheless, Indo-British friendship after Partition must be credited largely to Mountbatten's handling of the transfer of power. In terms of British interests, it was a brilliant achievement, the skillful execution of a policy of withdrawal. Mountbatten's diplomacy at the time won rich dividends for Britain.

The first November 1955 interview with Mountbatten had clarified many important points about the enormously complex process of the transfer of power and the end of empire, the Partition, and the consequent transformation of South Asia. Yet not all of the questions prepared for the interview had been explored. Sensing my concern, he ended the interview by offering another session: 'I am off to America for meetings. I will be away for ten days. Please arrange a date with my ADC.'

The second interview was no less rewarding. Mountbatten was in excellent form. He answered all the questions, crisply and with admirable clarity. As in the first interview, he showed no doubt about the wisdom of his skillfully executed plan for the transfer of power—quickly; for him, there was no other way.

In the course of my two lengthy, informative, and insightful interviews in November 1955, Lord Mountbatten filled in some of the hitherto unknown aspects of his tenure as the last Viceroy and, immediately after, as the last Governor-General of India (1947–48). He also contributed much insight into the personality of Gandhi, Nehru, Jinnah, leader of the All-India Muslim League since the 1930s and the last Governor-General and first President of Pakistan, and Sardar Patel, the dominant organizational figure in the Indian National Congress for many years before Independence, who shared power with Nehru in their *duumvirate* during the early years of Independence, from August 1947 until Patel's death in late 1950.

The second interview ended on an especially positive note: Mountbatten, nonchalantly, or so it seemed, asked, 'Mr. Brecher, would you like a letter to the Prime Minister?' It was not easy to control my excitement at the thought of what this would mean for my book project, as indeed it was. In response to '[T]his would be most helpful; thank you', the letter arrived a few days later, just as my family and I were preparing to leave for India. [This gesture has enabled me to answer the question posed over the years by skeptical colleagues and curious students: '[H]ow was it possible for a young Canadian assistant professor to get to Jawaharlal Nehru, then at the height of his prestige and influence on the world stage, as Gandhi's successor, India's Prime Minister, and a leader of the emerging non-aligned movement (the Afro-Asian Bandung Conference was held in 1955)?' Put simply, the answer was good fortune!]

Since this was my first experience with systematic interviews of (mostly) prominent politicians, officials, academics, and journalists, it was necessary to devise a technique that would stimulate the memory of the persons being interviewed eight to nine years after the events (1946/47–55), encourage candor, and, at the same time, permit me to retain most of what was being recalled and communicated. Thus I went to each interview solely with a set of questions prepared in advance, by topic. I did not take any written notes during an interview, even when it lasted several hours, for example, my two interviews with Mountbatten in London in November 1955.

I sensed that taking notes during an interview would have a negative effect on the free flow of words by the person being interviewed. I rarely did more than one interview a day. Then, solely guided by my questions, I would allow memory to do the necessary. The technique, though demanding, sometimes exhausting, worked! When I had succeeded in reconstructing the interview, as close to verbatim as possible on the main points, I made my reconstruction available to the person interviewed, as a matter of courtesy, with the request that he/she correct any errors, insert any points that I had omitted, and indicate whether or not I had the person's permission to use the interview material, including verbatim quotations, in my manuscript. All of the interviewees responded favorably; that is, they checked the accuracy of my reconstruction of their remarks and made corrections, additions or deletions—very rarely; and, with very few exceptions, they granted permission to use the interview material as I saw fit, though some requested the omission of their name in any direct quotations; the latter was accomplished by a footnote designation, 'Related to the author in London in 1955 by a person who wishes to remain anonymous'.

In an effort to acquire some insight into Nehru's educational experience in England, I visited Harrow and Cambridge. The Master of the Headmaster's House at Harrow arranged a tour of the school, along with conversations with persons who could recreate, with some success, the atmosphere of one of England's élite private [public] schools when Nehru was there for two years, from 1905 to 1907, at the age of 15–17; then to Cambridge until 1910; and, finally, to the Inner Temple until 1912. I also perused old issues of the *Harrovian*, but, to my regret, they contained little of value. So too with Trinity College, Cambridge, except that my brief stay at both institutions deepened my appreciation of the legacy on his outlook. A valuable personal source was *Sir Walter*, later Lord, *Monckton*, a fellow student of Nehru at Harrow, much later Constitutional Adviser to the Nizam of Hyderabad, including the period of its crisis with India in August–September 1948.

By the time my wife, Eva, and I left England, on 1 December 1955, with Leora, then three and a half, and Diana Rose, six weeks old, I had succeeded in preparing a detailed outline of the book and had acquired substantial knowledge from archives and interviews, on the basis of which I could proceed with further inquiries in India. As in England, my research was divided between documentary materials, many of them available only in Delhi, and interviews with a large cross section of knowledgeable Indians. My task was made much easier by my letter of introduction from Lord Mountbatten to Nehru. Indeed, it was the Mountbatten letter that paved the way for extraordinary access to archives and interviews in India.

Entrée *to Nehru (December 1955)*

Two days after our arrival in Delhi, I phoned *M.O. Mathai*, Special Assistant to the Prime Minister and an envied and feared gatekeeper for Nehru, whose devotion to India's leader was acknowledged by all. I introduced myself as a Canadian academic, author of *The Struggle for Kashmir*, now engaged in research for a political biography of Nehru—and the bearer of a letter to the Prime Minister from Lord Mountbatten. The response was immediate and friendly: 'Come to my office tomorrow morning at 11.00 and let me know how we can be of assistance in your project.' The gatekeeper had opened the gate!

I prepared a brief, precise memo for Mathai, specifying the items that would be helpful:

1. one or more interviews with the Prime Minister;
2. an opportunity to spend time with him during one of his visits to the countryside;
3. access to some private papers of Nehru over the decades;
4. access to the archives on the nationalist movement from 1885 to 1947; and
5. a signal to Congress Party leaders and MPs from all parties, conveying the view of the Prime Minister's Office that cooperation with me in interviews would be welcome.

Mathai assured me that my requests would be arranged, as indeed they were. Moreover, with the formal approval of Nehru, access was granted to various unpublished papers of great research value. Among them were:

papers acquired thus far for a projected seven-volume History of the Freedom Movement;
confidential files of the British Government of India Home Department Political Section from 1919 to 1947; and
around 250 unpublished letters by and to Nehru between 1920 and 1945, with colleagues and English and American friends setting forth his attitudes to many issues, domestic and foreign, of great public importance during that period (they were published later, in 1958, as *A Bunch of Old Letters*), and a large collection of then still-confidential *Fortnightly Letters*, which Nehru wrote to the State Chief Ministers since Independence.

In addition, the President of the Indian National Congress in 1956, U.N. *Dhebar*, gave me permission to peruse the party archives from 1912 to 1956, including reports of the annual sessions, presidential addresses, correspondence among the party leaders, miscellaneous pamphlets, and the valuable collection of press clippings on Nehru diligently maintained from 1946 to 1956. And Dr. *Syed Mahmud*, an intimate friend of Nehru for 40 years, gave me permission to use extracts from their substantial unpublished correspondence. Taken together, this was a treasure, a researcher's 'good fortune'.

While waiting for my requests to materialize, I replicated the interviewing technique devised in London. I wrote to approximately 150 Indians: politicians, Nehru family members, parliamentarians, officials, academics, economists, and journalists. Almost all responded favorably. I prepared clusters of questions to tap the knowledge of each interviewee about some aspect of Nehru's life, ideology, and leadership. This meant the Indian National Congress from the time Nehru entered Indian politics, in 1920, his relationships with his domineering, devoted father, *Motilal Nehru*, a respected nationalist leader and lawyer, *Mahatma Gandhi, Sardar Patel, Subhas Bose*, Nehru's rival for leadership of the Congress in the 1930s, Socialist politicians, Communists, Hindu nationalists, and others.

The large number of persons interviewed in 1955–56 in England and India constituted the oral research part of the task of illuminating *Jawaharlal Nehru* as a man and as a political leader and statesman. To tap the knowledge of Englishmen who had made and implemented crucial decisions during the last phase of the British *Raj*, in London and in New Delhi, and the knowledge of prominent Indians of that era who made, implemented, and commented on key decisions during the last phase of the struggle for independence and the first nine years of independence provided an array of insights into the central Indian figure of that era and the focus of the planned political biography. Fortunately, the pivotal interviews with Nehru on 6 and 13 June 1956 were taped, and my notes of the later interviews with him, in December 1958 and December 1963, were preserved.

Discovery of the Indian Village (January–February 1956)

While waiting for the promised interviews with Nehru and a several-day tour with the Prime Minister, as well as access to archival materials, I decided 'to discover India' on my own. I traveled around India by second-class train, sleeping bag in hand. Every second day I descended from the train to visit a nearby village, to try to acquire a sense of the way of life and the pervasive poverty in rural India—and an understanding of the magnitude of the problem of moving a traditional society and underdeveloped economy into the 20th century. Wherever I stopped, I found someone with enough knowledge of English to make possible indirect conversations with villagers, mostly poor peasants, the vast majority living below the poverty line, suffering from malnutrition, harsh conditions of employment, pitifully low wages, without access to health care and often the most elementary conditions for survival, including clean water. It was a journey that created a powerful, grim human dimension to the academic concepts, 'Third World' and 'underdevelopment' or, more generously, 'developing society'.

The discomfort of spending most of a month in a second-class Indian railcar, with a sleeping bag, seemed almost like indescribable comfort when compared to the intense visual pain resulting from near-daily exposure to the harsh reality of Indian village life in 1956 and for millennia past. Only after this journey through the countryside did I begin to understand the reality of poverty in the Third World and the tasks confronting Nehru and all other political leaders of nations only recently emancipated from colonial rule.

Interspersed with my visits to many villages, I also stopped in cities and towns and conducted interviews for my project which were not feasible in the capital. Starting in Delhi, I journeyed through Uttar Pradesh (the United Provinces, or UP) to Allahabad, Nehru's birthplace, and the holy Hindu city of Benares (now, Varanasi), where many of the great festivals of Hinduism are celebrated, often by millions of pilgrims. From there I continued on to Santiniketan, forever associated with the great Indian poet of the 20th century, Rabindranath Tagore, who founded a unique university there to blend the cultures of East and West; Nehru's daughter, Indira, later the prime minister of India as Mrs. Indira Gandhi, attended Tagore's university in Santiniketan starting in 1934. I spent a few days in Calcutta and the nearby countryside, observing that poverty in the slums of that great center of Bengal's rich and proud culture was not significantly different from that in villages not far from the metropolis.

From Calcutta I proceeded to Waltair, where I conducted a seminar for faculty members and students at the University of Andhra Department of Political Science, and then to Madras (later re-named Chennai), the largest urban center in south India. I also paused in Bangalore, Poona, Bombay, and Nagpur before returning to Delhi.

During this tour, I had the benefit of interviews with about 30 persons who had known Nehru well at different stages of his life. Among the most senior were:

Dr. *B.C. Roy*, the long-serving then Chief Minister of Bengal;
Morarji Desai, then Chief Minister of Bombay, later, Prime Minister, the two most powerful State politicians at the time;
Sri Prakasa, then Governor of the State of Madras, who knew Nehru since his early days in Allahabad;
Dr. *Sitaramayya*, the very knowledgeable official historian of the Indian National Congress and, later, Governor of Madhya Pradesh; and
V.P. Menon, the right-hand adviser to Sardar Patel on the princely states who, in that interview, reflected on the Nehru–Patel relationship with candor and insight.

In Bombay, I interviewed:

S.K. Patil, the dominant Congress leader in Bombay;
Minoo Masani, Executive Assistant to J.R.D. Tata, both of whom I had met in Bombay in 1951; and
Krishna Nehru Hutheesingh, the younger of Nehru's two sisters.

Various scholars at Bombay, Calcutta, and Andhra universities and the Gokhale Institute of Economics and Political Science offered thoughtful ideas on many facets of my project.

In Bombay and Madras, as well as Delhi, upon my return, I benefited from discussions with many journalists who had observed Nehru for some years, including:

A.D. Gorwala ('Vivek'), a prominent publicist;
Frank Moraes, editor, *Times of India*;
Prem Bhatia, *The Statesman*;
Shridharani, *Amrita Bazar Patrika*;
Srinivasan, *The Hindu*; and
Eric da Costa, editor, *Eastern Economist*.

Rationale of Nehru Project

Before presenting an assessment of Nehru's record as a leader of the Indian nationalist movement in the 1920s, 1930s, and 1940s, his role in the formative period of India as an independent state (1947–58), and his role in the wider world during his lengthy tenure as Prime Minister and External Affairs Minister, from 1947 to 1964, I think it appropriate to provide a rationale for this research project. One goal was to try to illuminate the conflicting forces at work in a nationalist movement about which little was known in the West at that time. Another was to attempt to shed some light on the puzzle of a relationship between the pre-eminent and the second most influential leader of that movement, Indian nationalism, who were bound together by the powerful bond and aspiration of a common objective, India's independence, but who seemed to represent the polar alternatives of tradition (Gandhi) and modernity (Nehru) in the Indian nationalist movement and its predominant political expression, the Indian National Congress. Why focus on Nehru, though providing glimpses of men who crossed the Indian stage during those decades, including Churchill and Roosevelt, Attlee and Mountbatten, Stafford Cripps and Lord Halifax, and, within India, Sardar Vallabhbhai Patel and Subhas Bose, and Mohamed Ali Jinnah, apart from Gandhi and Nehru?

My earliest formulation of 'why the Nehru book' was set forth 60 years ago in my *report to the Nuffield Foundation* which launched the project with a Traveling Fellowship for 1955–56:

> 'The political life of Jawaharlal Nehru had attracted my intellectual interest for a decade, from 1945 to 1955. As the most articulate spokesman of Indian nationalism in the struggle for independence, Nehru had already emerged as one of Asia's heroic figures. As the first, long-serving Prime Minister of the Republic of India (1947–1964), he set the pace and the direction of the experiment in which an ancient society was attempting to adjust to the 20th century and was transforming itself by democratic means. As the leading exponent of neutralism/non-alignment in foreign affairs, Nehru had earned both praise and opprobrium. His diverse roles within India, as Gandhi's principal political disciple in the nationalist movement and as the commanding figure in the goal of refashioning Indian society merited, I thought, a comprehensive and critical evaluation of the man and the political leader in an era in which he was playing a vital role. Yet no significant book on Nehru's life, thought and leadership had been attempted by a Western scholar.'

'More generally, I was impressed by the unique importance of *political leaders* in the newly-independent states of Asia and visualized this project as a potential exemplar on the role of leadership in the quest for political stability and economic development, on democratic foundations. Moreover, a study of Nehru presented the challenge of using the political biographical method as an approach in political science.'

'From afar I had followed closely Nehru's emergence as one of the leading statesmen of his generation and the remarkable spectacle of India's renascence, politically, economically and culturally. My first opportunity to observe his leadership and the new India occurred during an extended study tour of India in 1951–52. At that time, I was principally interested in the problem of Kashmir. Nevertheless, I was able to begin preliminary work on the Nehru study by interviews with prominent Indians. After my return to Canada in the spring of 1952 I devoted much time to Nehru's voluminous writings, both autobiographical and his musings on Indian history. By the end of 1954 I had exhausted the potential of research on Nehru while in Canada and had become convinced that an extended return to India, as well as a period for research in the U.K. would be necessary if this project were to bear fruit.'

The second venture in providing a rationale for the Nehru project took the form of an interview published in an Indian magazine, *Link*, in November 1964, five years after my political biography of Nehru had appeared and six months after Nehru's death.

Q What was it that led you to select Jawaharlal Nehru as the subject of a biographical work?

A There were two principal reasons. One was his extraordinary personality, of which I had become aware as a university student. The other was his unique leadership role in the Indian nationalist movement and his towering position in independent India. Nehru's nationalism was interlinked with internationalism and economic welfare. He had a vision of a vigorous new India which could be created after independence. His was the voice of youth, of progress and modernity he represented liberal and democratic strands of thought in renascent India.

Nehru combined within himself so many traits of India in the 1930s and onward that he was an ideal figure around whom one could weave the complex and fascinating drama of India's struggle for independence. This is not to say that he was the dominant personality in the movement; he was not. But he spoke and acted in a way which communicated more readily to non-Indians. These were two distinct but related facets of Nehru, the national leader and the voice of emergent, modern India. Together they made him a charismatic, youthful, and heroic figure.

Q You were attracted to him because he represented the modern in India and spoke the language which the West could understand. But is it not precisely this which at times made Jawaharlal Nehru feel out of place in India?

A Nehru considered himself a unique blend of East and West, the impact of his upbringing in India and his education in England. Unlike Gandhiji, he was not a product of the mainstream of Indian life. But he had a remarkable feel for the aspirations of the most inarticulate sections of Indian society, the peasant masses. Both Gandhiji and Nehru appealed to the peasantry, but whereas the Mahatma made them conscious of their past, "Panditji" invoked a vision of the future which could be theirs. Gandhiji appealed to their spiritual and moral beliefs; Nehru projected an image of the tangible material changes in their lives which independence could bring. In that sense there was a natural harmony between them; their appeal was complementary. In the pre-independence period Gandhi was certainly the preeminent Indian nationalist leader. And yet Nehru stood apart from all other national leaders because of the quality of his personal leadership.

I also knew that this would be a fascinating but demanding exploration of social forces, political leadership, the personality of charismatic and less charismatic leaders engaged in one of the momentous political dramas of the 20th century, the future of what had been the 'crown jewel' of the British Empire, the Indian subcontinent.

In sum, what was the rationale for a political biography of Nehru? As will be evident, it comprised multiple intellectual sources and aspirations.

At the turn of the 20th century, Western Powers held sway in Asia almost without challenge, except for Japan and Thailand. Then, new ideas and social forces came to the surface, inducing change among the ancient peoples of that continent. The result, until the 1960s, was an unfinished Asian Revolution, worth studying not only for its human interest, but also for its insight into *political leadership* and because it shattered the traditional *relations between Asia and the West*. The Nehru project was an attempt to view that revolution in its Indian setting.

The phenomenon to be investigated was multi-layered and complex. Many persons played a notable role. But only Jawaharlal Nehru linked the years of promise and fulfillment, of nationalist agitation and national reconstruction. This made Nehru an admirably suited focus to serve as the binding thread in an analysis of modern Indian history and politics. Thus the technique of biography was utilized to shed light on events, ideas, and movements. At the same time, the Indian non-violent revolution was highlighted as the setting for an Asia-centered study of political leadership.

My political biography of Nehru set forth four objectives. One was *clues to the* tortuous *course of modern Indian history and politics*. If it succeeded in *making Nehru more intelligible*, to admirers and critics alike, it would, hopefully, serve a second goal. If this project provided *insight into the role of the outstanding individual in history*, it would accomplish a third goal. Finally, it aimed at *contributing to the understanding of the state of mind among 'the uncommitted billion'*.

ENCOUNTERS WITH NEHRU (1956–63)

These encounters will be presented in several broad strokes:

(1) an account of a *three-day tour of the countryside* with the prime minister in March 1956;
(2) the most salient sections of *interviews* with Nehru in June 1956;
(3) my *portrait of the man*;
(4) my *assessment of Nehru as an intellectual*;
(5) an *interview in 1958*;
(6) an *interim assessment of Nehru's roles as the leader of India and as a statesman*, in 1959;
(7) a farewell interview in 1963;
(8) *thoughts on the day Nehru died*, 27 May 1964; and
(9) finally, my *re-assessment of Nehru in 1989*, his centenary year.

Tour with Nehru (March 1956)

It was dark and pleasantly cool that March 1956 morning when I drove through the deserted streets of the capital toward Palam Airport, later, Indira Gandhi Airport. To the surprise of everyone, Nehru was late in arriving, just a few minutes; but even this was a rare occurrence, for the Indian leader was typically Western in his punctuality.

After brief, formal introductions, we boarded the luxurious Viscount which had been purchased recently for his official travels and headed south to Hyderabad City on the first lap of our journey. The flight was swift and uneventful. Nehru withdrew immediately to the private compartment which served as bedroom, sitting room, and office during his travels within India and abroad. There he passed the time in one of three ways: dictating letters, minutes, and memoranda; reading official files or a book which had lain by his bed in Delhi, neglected for want of time; or resting his weary mind and body. On this occasion, he slept throughout the two-hour flight which followed a week of conferences with the American, French, and British Foreign Ministers who had descended upon the capital in rapid succession. His penchant for sleep while traveling was well known.

Presently we found ourselves at Begumpet Airport on the outskirts of Hyderabad City, in central India, where the local élite had gathered to pay their respects to the uncrowned king of the Indian Republic, including the aged Nizam of Hyderabad. After the usual garlanding ceremony, with the ubiquitous photographers surrounding the Prime Minister, we were herded into a caravan of old American cars for the short trip to the railway station. A large crowd patiently awaited the arrival of their hero. As his open car approached the entrance, a mighty roar went up, 'Pandit Nehru *Ki jai*, Pandit Nehru *Ki jai*' ('Hail Pandit Nehru, Hail Pandit Nehru'). Unlike the throngs in totalitarian states, this was a spontaneous crowd expressing genuine affection for India's first citizen. Being accustomed to this adulation for the past 25 years, Nehru took it in his stride, smiling to the crowd and reciprocating their warm greeting with the traditional *Namaste* salutation—holding his hands together palm to palm and moving them toward his forehead.

Further evidence of this hero-worship was provided during the lengthy journey by car along the dusty roads of rural Hyderabad. At one large village a crowd of 10,000 had gathered to greet the Prime Minister. As our caravan rounded the bend, they broke into a frenzied run toward the opposite side in order to get another look at him. The race for a *darshan* was like an instinctive, compelling drive, a craving for association with an exalted man, however brief. Throughout the journey there was a mumble among the crowds along the route, which was translated for my benefit. 'We saw him, we saw him,' they were saying in ecstasy to their families. In the evening, on the return journey, the road was again lined with masses of admiring people.

Watching this scene and others like it in the next few days recalled to memory some passages in a vivid portrait of Nehru published anonymously in 1937:

> *Jawaharlal ki jai!* [Hail Jawaharlal!].... From the Far North to Cape Comorin he has gone like some triumphant Caesar, leaving a trail of glory and a legend behind him. Is all this just a passing fancy which amuses him ... or is it his will to power that is driving him from crowd to crowd? ... What if the fancy turns? Men like Jawaharlal, with all their great capacity for great and good work, are unsafe in a democracy.... His flashes of temper are well known. His overwhelming desire to get things done, to sweep away what he dislikes and build anew, will hardly brook for long the slow processes of democracy. ... His conceit is already formidable. It must be checked. We want no Caesars. (*The Modern Review* (Calcutta), 62, November 1937, 546-7)

The purpose of this critique was to persuade the Indian National Congress not to re-elect Nehru for a third successive term as President of India's then pre-eminent political party. The author was Jawaharlal Nehru!

Most of the characteristics mentioned in this remarkable, candid self-analysis remained with Nehru for the rest of his life—his command of the crowd, the actor's finesse in the center of the stage, mass popularity, prestige, influence, impatience, and the like. Some of these traits were tempered by time and experience: his outbursts of anger became less conspicuous, and he acquired a greater measure of tolerance and sympathy for the failings of others. Aware of his autocratic tendencies, he strove successfully to curb them lest India revert to the condition of benevolent despotism, which he abhorred. Few men with these talents could have resisted the inducements to exercise dictatorial powers.

Lunch was an informal affair in the Prime Minister's private car, very modest by any standards. To those known to favor a traditional Indian cuisine, he said in a good-natured tone, '[Y]ou vegetarians go off to that side', while one aide and I joined him for a mixed Indian/Western meal. Unlike Gandhi, Nehru had no fads regarding food. After lunch and conversational pleasantries, Nehru retired for a brief nap. At that point, there occurred an amusing but rather significant episode. One member of the group suggested a change in the itinerary so as to reduce the Prime

Minister's discomfort. For half an hour the pros and cons were weighed with due solemnity. 'Why not do it without bothering him?' I interjected. 'Oh no,' was the sober reply. 'He has already seen the itinerary and might become irritated by any change.' Finally, the great decision was made—to 'let sleeping dogs lie', even though the change would have been wiser. At last, we arrived in Naziabad for the conference of the *Bharat Sevak Samaj* (National Service Organization). Ostensibly, this was the primary purpose of the tour, though the meeting with *Vinoba Bhave*, a revered Gandhi-like figure in rural India, was far more important.

Nehru spoke twice in the afternoon, first to the delegates who had come from all over India and later to about 100,000 peasants who had trudged from surrounding villages to see and to hear their hero. He was in excellent form, speaking in his typical conversational manner. The scene then shifted to the huge throng of peasants waiting for a *darshan* of 'Panditji'. There they sat, passive and quiet, stretched out as far as the eye could see. They had assembled early in the morning and had waited patiently for six hours or more in the burning heat: it was well over 100 F.

To observe Nehru talking to his people made it possible to penetrate the intangibles of his popularity. There he stood in his typical pose, bent slightly forward as he surveyed the audience, his hands now resting on the podium, now gripping the microphone, sometimes folded behind him, with a crumpled handkerchief tucked up his right shirt sleeve. He was not a natural orator and rose to great heights only on rare occasions, such as on Independence Day and the death of Gandhi. His voice was soft and relaxed. He did not rouse his listeners by thundering pronouncements. He talked to them like a teacher to his pupils, showing them the errors of their ways, pointing out the proper path of conduct, stressing the need for discipline, hard work, unity, tolerance, and faith, drawing on the inspiration of Gandhi and the freedom struggle, painting a picture of the India of the future, pledging himself to their welfare, calling for rededication to the cause of a good society.

Candor and spontaneity were the outstanding qualities of his speech. He talked as he thought and felt at the moment. He thought aloud, sharing his ideas as they developed. His words flowed as in a stream of consciousness and therefore into endless side channels. He came to his main points very slowly and indirectly, his words reflecting the variety of thoughts and emotions which filtered through his mind as he spoke. The result was a rambling, verbose, repetitive, and, very often, woolly speech, especially in the last few years. In fact, in the decade after 1947, less than a dozen of his speeches were prepared statements. By contrast, in the 'thirties and early 'forties, his important speeches were thoroughly prepared and were models of clarity, such as his presidential addresses to the Indian National Congress in 1929, 1936, and 1937. Later, however, the pressure of time, combined with the practice of almost daily speeches, made spontaneity inescapable.

The tour also revealed Nehru's penchant for reading. Books were a constant companion on his travels before Independence. It was comforting to have books with him, he used to say, even if he could not read them all. During this particular outing from the capital, he was absorbed by Dr. Oppenheimer's *Science and the Common Understanding*. The literature of science was his favorite reading, almost a passion with him. As he remarked over lunch: 'Where I differ from Indian Socialists is that I have a scientific background and am more aware of the impact of science on social evolution.' He was also a great admirer of English poetry: a collection of Keats was always close by. The lack of time was part of the price of power and responsibility. Yet he found time for reading, almost daily for a half hour or more at the end of a day and while traveling.

Despite the arduous road journey, the Prime Minister showed no signs of fatigue, partly because of the rejuvenating process resulting from direct contact with the masses and partly because this excursion to the countryside was in the nature of a holiday when compared with his normal schedule in Delhi. Not that Nehru was, in principle, averse to holidays. Prior to Independence, he loved to wander in the hills and valleys of Kashmir or in the Kullu valley of Himachal Pradesh or in the isolated splendor of the Himalayas viewed from the hill stations of the United Provinces (Uttar Pradesh). But the demands of public office pressed him forward relentlessly, with little time for leisure and relaxation. It was his bountiful good health which enabled him to maintain his furious pace of activity. Apart from the good fortune of an extended interaction with the Prime Minister, the most vivid recollection of three days with Nehru was the insight it provided into the extraordinary chemistry between a political leader and his mass public.

Interviews (June 1956)

The two interviews with Nehru, on 6 and 13 June 1956, were held in his spacious office at the Ministry of External Affairs, which he occupied throughout his long tenure as Prime Minister and Minister of External Affairs, 1947–64. They ranged over a vast tapestry—his views on:

Gandhi
Partition of India
Non-Violence
Preventive Detention
The Press
India's Achievements since Independence
Economic Planning, Democracy and India's 'Hope Level'
Land Reform
Socialism
China
Population Control
Foreign Policy, War, and Non-Alignment
World Federation
The USA and the Soviet Union
Kashmir and India/Pakistan Relations
Bandung Conference (1955), Israel, and the Arabs
India and the Commonwealth
Centralization of Power
Communalism and the Protection of Minorities
'After Nehru'
Good Society

From these two lengthy interviews, the following extracts provide enduring insight into the worldview of Jawaharlal Nehru at age 66, almost nine years after India's independence.

On Gandhi and Non-Violence

Michael Brecher (MB) On many occasions, as related in your Autobiography and elsewhere, you found yourself profoundly disconcerted by Gandhi's decisions. Yet, ultimately, you followed his course of action. I find it difficult to understand this apparent duality.

Nehru Primarily, it was my lack of understanding of, well, what he called his inner voice. He would go on a fast. I didn't understand that—and I don't understand it still. Again, he referred to the Bihar earthquake [1934] and said that it was because India had the sin of untouchability. I didn't understand that and I don't understand it still. But, on the political plane, and I would say also to a considerable extent on the moral plane, he attracted me a great deal. Also, it's always difficult to describe a man who is rather unusual and a tremendous personality, and who gave an impression of enormous strength and inner reserves of power.

Now, I don't think, myself, that I have changed my mind at all about violence or non-violence during the last 35 years.... I should imagine, indeed, that in the early twenties ... I was much more powerfully influenced by him; in fact, to the extent, if I may say so, that my mind was sort of under his—not under his control, that's not right, but still more so than I was a few years later when I started questioning about violence and non-violence.

On the Partition of India

MB What were the circumstances which compelled you to accept Partition, particularly in view of your dedication to a united sub-continent all during the Freedom Movement?

Nehru Well, I suppose, the compulsion of events, and the feeling that we couldn't get out of that deadlock or morass by pursuing the way we had done; it became worse and worse. Further, a feeling that even if, somehow, we got freedom for India, with that background, it would be a very weak India, that is, a federal India with far too great power in the federating units.... A larger India would be weak and would have constant troubles, disintegrating pulls; and, also, the fact that we saw no way of getting the freedom too—in the near future, I mean. And so we accepted this, we said, let us build up a strong India. And, if the others, the Muslim League leaders and those who do not want to be in it, well, how can we and why should we force them to be in it?

MB Would you say, in the perspective of 1956, that the partition of India was inevitable?

Nehru The partition of India became inevitable, I should say, in less than a year before it occurred. It wasn't inevitable till the last year.

MB Could you recall for me, very briefly, the crucial acts or sequence of events which, in your opinion, sealed the issue of a divided or united India?

Nehru I don't think that preceding the war [World War II] they [the British] had any clear ideas about partition or, indeed, wanted it. But obviously throughout that period, and long before, the British Government's policy, as the policy of any such governing authority in a colonial territory, was to weaken the national movement. And the major way of weakening it was to play up the Muslim League and other dissident elements.... I think now, looking back, that Partition could have been stopped if the British Government's policy had been different, about a year or, say, eighteen months before the partition.

MB From what you say, Mr. Prime Minister, it would appear that in your opinion the onus for the partition of the subcontinent must rest ultimately on the then-existing Government of India.

Nehru Yes the chief men here.

On India's Achievements Since Independence

MB What do you consider to be the significant achievements of independent India since 1947?

Nehru First, the Indian [princely] States, the absorption of the Indian States into the Union of India. Secondly, our meeting the tremendous problems following Partition, including the, well, not only the killing, etc., but in a sense a kind of rebellion... And then the third biggest thing was, I think, our dealing with the refugees, a pretty big task, and seven or eight million coming over in two or three months' time, a tremendous task, not only then but in subsequent years. Then, broadly, our general economic rehabilitation, with big schemes (the Five Year Plans). And finally, something that I think is bigger than all, the community schemes, the Community Development projects, which are really, I think, revolutionary in their context.

On Socialism

MB I know of your own socialist convictions dating back to the 'thirties, but why was [the Congress Party's official] move to socialism taken only last year; why not earlier or why not later?

Nehru We [had] talked about socialism throughout, and as long ago as twenty-five years the Congress said that the chief industries, heavy industries and basic industries should be owned and controlled by the State.... The Congress, being a vast organization, had all kinds of people in it, anti-socialists, socialists....In consideration, really, of many of our senior colleagues, who didn't like to go that far, we didn't press it.

On China

MB I wonder if you could tell me briefly your basic impressions during your tour of China in 1954.

Nehru My major impression was one of the enormous basic strength of the Chinese people. Of course, even in the old days [his tour of China in 1939] I had that sensation but it was spread out. They are amazing workers and they work together and that itself gives strength. And now, with a centralized government, it gives them really a terrifying strength, I may say, these masses of people all working together and each person capable of working hard. The average Chinese is a harder worker, certainly, than the average Indian.

MB One question that has often been raised is whether it would be correct to say that there is in reality a peaceful economic and cultural competition between India and China?

Nehru There is no competition as such, but it is, perhaps, inevitable for people to compare, from time to time, the progress made because the two countries are alike in that they are big, with large populations, industrially undeveloped and also very ancient countries. We have many similar problems.

On Foreign Policy, War, and Non-Alignment

MB What do you consider to be of primary importance in making decisions in foreign affairs? Is it considerations of power or material factors, or is it, rather, ideological urges?

Nehru Ideological urges obviously play some part, though not so much the ideological urges of the individual. However, in the final analysis, all foreign policy concerns itself chiefly with the national interest of the country concerned. National interest can be seen in two ways, that is, rather narrow national interest, temporary national interest and most people see it that way—or a long-term view of national interest, which may well lead one to the conclusion that a country's national interests are served, let us say, by peace in the world, or by friendship with other nations, or by the well-being of neighboring countries. So it becomes an intelligent long-term interest . . . enlightened self-interest.

MB Would you sum up briefly the primary considerations which give rise to the policy of non-alignment?

Nehru During the last thirty years, I should say, that is, in the Indian National Movement, we gradually developed a foreign policy of a kind, though we were not a Government. Secondly, apart from our desire for peace, which is there, is our feeling that peace is absolutely essential for our progress and our growth. And if there is war, big or small, it comes in the way of that growth which is for us the primary factor. Thirdly, with the coming of nuclear weapons, war seems to us—and seems to most people everywhere—as extreme folly. War is sheer folly. One may say, of course, 'what are we to do if some mad person or some mad bull comes in and we have to deal with him?' That is a different matter; that is, if some mad country attacks you, you must defend yourself, and if you have to defend yourself you have to be prepared to defend yourself. That is true, but, apart from that, war should be ruled out. It's only a measure of fear that comes in the way, that the other party might take advantage of us if we do this or that.

MB Would you say that a state which can remain non-aligned with either bloc in time of peace can also remain non-aligned if the Great Powers are at war with each other?

Nehru I do not conceive of any kind of, let us say, invasion or attack on India, not because of other countries' love of India but because it will bring them no profit and it will only give them trouble, whether it is a world war or any major conflict of that type. India does not come into the picture. Of course, if it takes place it is obvious that the people of India will fight that attack and defend themselves. But why not have friendly relations, for when there is no particular inducement to attack, there is less likelihood of attack. I would say that non-alignment is a policy which is nationally profitable for any country.

MB I wonder how one should distinguish non-alignment from the concept of a Third Force.

Nehru Non-alignment is a negative word and only partly explains the position. What is much better is a positive policy for peace. You talk about a Third Force. That simply means you are trying to create another force to counter the forces or as a balancing factor but you are thinking still in terms of force. I think that this thinking in terms of force really puts you in that vicious circle of force.

On the USA and the Soviet Union

Nehru Take the two most powerful countries in the world today, the United States and the Soviet Union. I think that the conflict between them in the past few years has been essentially due to political reasons, not communist or anti-communist, the main reason being two Great Powers whose national interests appear to come into conflict.

I don't think that they are as terribly far apart as they themselves or other people imagine. I think there are quite remarkable similarities between them despite their different systems. And I am inclined to think that the gap between them will lessen. And it might even lessen with fair rapidity once the present climate of fear and war is removed.

On Kashmir and Indo-Pakistan Relations

MB In view of the Pakistani rejection of your proposal to negotiate a solution of this problem on the basis of partition along the cease-fire line, where do we go from here?

Nehru There are only three ways of dealing with the Kashmir problem. One, if you like, is war. We rule it out. The others are a legal approach, legal and constitutional, or, if I may use the word, a practical approach, not quibbling about legal points and taking things as they are.... If you want a practical approach to this problem, my practical approach would be governed, first of all, by no war of course. Secondly, by accepting things as they are, in the main, because any other approach leads to some kind of conflict.

MB What makes Kashmir so important to India? Does it have any implications for India's efforts to establish a secular state and to maintain communal harmony in this country?

Nehru Yes, that is probably the most important aspect of it....We have never accepted, even when Partition came to India, the two-nation theory, that is, that the Hindus are one nation and the Muslims are another.... I say we cannot accept that because once we accept that nationality goes by religion, we break up our whole conception of India.... When Kashmir joined India... it was very important for us because it helped our thesis of nationalism not related to religion. If the contrary thesis were proved in Kashmir, it would affect somewhat—I don't say it would break up India but—it would have a powerful effect on the communal elements in India, both Hindu and Muslim. That is of extreme importance to us that we don't, by taking some wrong step in Kashmir, create these terribly disruptive tendencies within India.

MB If Pakistan withdraws all its forces from Kashmir and fulfills all its obligations under the UN resolutions, as India interprets them, would India then be prepared to reconsider the question of a plebiscite under international supervision?

Nehru I cannot rule out a plebiscite under any conditions.... But if you put this question to me, that if every condition is fulfilled, then am I to refuse a plebiscite? I say no.

We have always attached great importance to one factor in a plebiscite, that is, we have said that if there is a plebiscite, it should be a fair political plebiscite and not one in which wildly religious passions are roused.

Many people think and say that the Kashmir problem is a major problem which comes in the way of good relations between India and Pakistan. That is true, in a sense, but not basically true. What I mean is this: the Kashmir problem is a result of other conflicts between India and Pakistan, and even if the Kashmir problem were solved, well, not in a very friendly way, those basic conflicts would continue.

MB What are these basic conflicts?

Nehru I should say, basically, they are ideological. And we go back again to what I was just talking about, this business of the two-nation theory: under no circumstances whatever, even from the view of the narrowest national interests, do we wish to interfere in Pakistan. We want them to be an independent country and a flourishing country.

MB Is it possible to secure an agreement in principle on the entire gamut of disputes between the two countries? Many people refer to this as a package deal.

Nehru We have no objection at all to considering all the issues.

On the Bandung Conference, Israel, and the Arabs

MB Would you sum up briefly your view of its significance, [the Bandung Conference] in terms of the renaissance of Asia?

Nehru There was a psychological feeling of commonness, in spite of our differences, common objectives, common—if you like—adversaries. And that in itself gave one a feeling of strength and created a feeling of comradeship and friendship among those countries. Practically, as you know, nothing much was decided.

MB There is one aspect of the Bandung Conference which perturbed many people and that was the exclusion of one sovereign Asian state, namely, Israel.

Nehru Conditions were and still are that the Arab nations and Israel don't sit together. And one is offered this choice of having one or the other. It is not logical, my answer, but there it is. When the proposal was made for Israel to be invited ... it transpired that if that were done the Arab countries would not attend ... Our outlook on this matter was based on some logical approach. Our sympathies are with the Arab nations in regard to this problem. We felt that logically Israel should be invited but when we saw that the consequences of that invitation would be that many others would not be able to come, then we agreed. Our approach, obviously, if I may add, is that it is good for people who are opponents to meet.

On India and the Commonwealth

MB What were the considerations which induced India to remain in the Commonwealth?

Nehru In all the statements I made previously I said that India must be independent and an independent republic. We did not consider or rule out any kind of association with England or the Commonwealth. ... We decided that there was absolutely no reason why we should break an association which didn't come in our way at all, legally, constitutionally, practically, in any sense, and which merely helped us to co-operate in a measure, consult each other and maybe influence others.

The positive benefits are, I say, that it is always a good thing for a number of countries to be on friendly terms of consultation. They accepted us as a republic. It does help us in conferring with a number of important countries and, through them, to influence world affairs to some extent.

On 'After Nehru'

MB [T]here are many who wonder where to look for the safeguards that the policies and programs associated with your leadership will be continued, in particular, socialism, democratic institutions, the secular state, and non-alignment in foreign affairs.

Nehru Well, that is a very long question! At the same time, the policies I have encouraged, advocated, sponsored, have not been just individual policies. They have, vaguely and broadly speaking, the backing of the masses in this country. My chief business, in so far as the people are concerned, has been, if I may use the word, to speak to them as a schoolmaster, to try to explain things to them in as simple a language as possible. For the rest, well, really, one does one's best and one doesn't worry too much about the future. But I don't think it is possible in the future for the mass of the people to be taken away, far away, from their moorings.

On the Good Society

MB It would be appreciated if you were to sum up very briefly what, in your view, constitutes the good society.

Nehru Broadly speaking, apart from the material things that are necessary, obviously, a certain individual growth in the society. I do believe that ultimately it is the individual that counts. The idea appeals to me without belief, the old Hindu idea that if there is any divine essence in the world every individual possesses a bit of it ... and he can develop it. Therefore, no individual is trivial, and he should be given full opportunities to develop—material opportunities naturally, food, clothing, education, housing, health, etc. I'm not at all concerned about the hereafter. And I am not prepared to deny many things. I just don't know! I do believe in certain standards. Call them moral standards; call them what you like, spiritual standards. They are important in any individual and in any social group. And if they fade away, I think that all the material advancement you may have will lead to nothing worthwhile. There is the religious approach. It seems to me rather a narrow approach with its forms and all kinds of ceremonials. And yet, I am not prepared to deny that approach. If a person feels comforted by that, it is not for me to remove that sense of comfort. I don't mind. Whatever raises a person above his normal level is good, however he approaches that, provided he does not sit on somebody and force him to do it. While I attach very considerable value to moral and spiritual standards, apart from religion as such, I don't quite know how one maintains them in modern life. It's a problem.

Portrait of the Man

Nature and circumstance were kind to Jawaharlal Nehru. He was born into the Kashmiri Brahmin community, one of the most aristocratic sub-castes in the Hindu social system. His father was a distinguished and wealthy barrister, modern, urbane, highly cultivated and lavishly generous. As an only son—and the only child for eleven years—Jawaharlal was the focus of concentrated affection. He had, too, the advantages of the leisure and education of an English aristocrat in the secure atmosphere of the Edwardian Age—private tutors in India, Harrow, Cambridge and the Inner Temple. When he was drawn to the political arena soon after his return to India, his path was eased by the guidance and support of his father and Gandhi. Nehru recalled this head start in a modest portrait of his past seen almost forty years later:

"My growth to public prominence, you know, was not by sharp stages. And if I may say so," he added dryly, "I began at a fairly high level." (MB Interview, New Delhi, 30 January 1958)

Nehru was also favored with a strikingly handsome appearance, both by Indian and by Western standards. Pictures of him at the age of 20 or 60 reveal the slim, chiseled features which stamp the Kashmiri Brahmin. The later ones reveal much more: expressive eyes, sometimes pensive or sharp with irritation or gay and self-satisfied and, at other times, intent and alight with resolve; the high, full temples suggestive of two of Nehru's outstanding qualities—stubbornness and intellectual curiosity; the wide mouth and sensuous lips which pouted shamelessly during moments of ill-temper; the soft-molded chin; and the long, delicate fingers. His smile was captivating, at times disarming. His face was oval-shaped and his profile classic Greek, making Nehru one of the most photogenic statesmen of the 20th century. He exuded the magnetic charm which swiftly won individuals and crowds alike. His straight back and good posture expressed the vigor and youthfulness for which he was justly famous. With years and especially since 1956, the lines of age began to score his face. Nevertheless, in his late 60s he remained an unusually attractive man.

The benefits of aristocratic background and education were not without price. Security was accompanied by an overweening paternalism which hindered his growth to self-reliance. This tendency to depend on a strong, decisive, and older man became a marked feature of Nehru's character in his adult life. Even before the death of his father in 1931, he had already transferred this dependence in large measure to Gandhi, who served as guide, counselor, and father-confessor in matters both political and personal. It was not until his early 60s that Nehru emerged completely from the shadow of the two men who exercised more influence on his character than all other persons. Thus, despite his enormous power and prestige, he often exhibited a lack of confidence about the right course of action. In part, this was due to the intellectual in Nehru who saw all points of view and therefore hesitated to act boldly lest he destroy that element of 'good' which he thought all viewpoints possessed. But in large measure, this indecisiveness can be traced to the circumstances in which his character was molded.

Other elements in his background helped to shape the character of Nehru. Alone among Indian nationalist leaders of his generation, he was a true aristocrat. Nehru detested the waste and iniquities of the caste system, but he could not escape the indelible mark of his caste origin. He remained a Brahmin with everything that this status connotes.

His education in the West also set him apart from his colleagues in the Indian National Congress, a solitary figure in a middle-class, tradition-minded General Staff, guiding a petty bourgeois and peasant army.

Although he accepted the stern discipline imposed by Gandhi and functioned as a member of a team, until Gandhi's assassination in January 1948, Nehru's approach to strategy and tactics revealed the Western rationalist. This made Nehru alien in his own society, a Hindu out of tune with Hinduism, 'a queer mixture of the East and the West, out of place everywhere, at home nowhere', as he wrote in his autobiography, *Toward Freedom* (1942, p. 353). In this respect, his was merely an extreme case in a whole class of young, Westernized Indian intellectuals. In his later years, Nehru acquired a deeper appreciation of Indian history and philosophy and enriched the bases of his subsequent thought and action, as evident in his *The Discovery of India*, written during his long wartime imprisonment at the age of 55.

From his father Nehru acquired an intense pride frequently asserted in his public life. Here lay the root of his resentment against British rule—for Nehru's *initial response to politics was emotional, not intellectual.* Anything that smacked of racialism produced instinctive anger, as the behavior of Great Britain and France in the Suez War of 1956 amply revealed. So too did rampant discrimination in the Union of South Africa. His volatile temper, too, moderated. He was quick to anger, but his outbursts were usually short-lived, and he rarely bore a grudge against those who experienced his momentary fury.

Nehru was a most affable and charming man. Indeed, he had the gift rare among statesmen of inspiring genuine regard and affection from persons ranging the whole spectrum of political opinion at home and abroad. But an inner quality of aloofness prevented him from reciprocating, even with colleagues of long standing. His early life in Allahabad strengthened a natural reticence and so did a British public school education. 'Yes,' he wrote to Dr. Syed Mahmud, an old friend, on 24 November 1933, 'we did not discuss personal matters. You ought to know me sufficiently to realize that I never discuss them unless the other party takes the initiative. I would not do so even with Kamala [his wife] or Indu [his daughter, Indira]. Such has been my training' (unpublished Nehru-Mahmud correspondence).

Nehru's natural reserve made him feel uneasy in the company of a few, detached, almost withdrawn from those about him. But he was not so in the presence of a crowd. There his personality was transformed. He became alive, relaxed, uninhibited, as if infused with the collective energy of the group. He never lost himself completely, for the aristocrat in his makeup prevented a complete fusion with the mass. He was in the crowd but never of it, stimulated, but not absorbed.

For 35 years, he was the idol of the Indian masses and élite, second only to Gandhi and, after the Mahatma's assassination in 1948, without peer. They literally adored him, with a vivid affection and hero worship. From distant villages they came in thousands to hear him, more to see him, to have a *darshan* (visual communion) with their beloved 'Panditji', successor to the Mahatma, champion of the oppressed, symbol of the new India of their vague dreams. They did not understand everything he said, but no matter. He came to talk to them, to inspire them, and to make them forget, even for a little while, their misery and their problems. And he, in turn, felt a bond with the masses. Their faith touched his vanity, giving him a sense of power—power to alter the grim poverty which they had always known. But most of all, they provided him with an inexhaustible source of energy which enabled Nehru to maintain his incredible pace of work.

Remarkable indeed was the mutual impact of Nehru and the crowd. They seemed to transmit waves of energy to him by virtue of their presence and their constantly expressed faith in his leadership. The larger the audience, the more exhilarated he felt, the more determined he became to persevere in the face of great odds. By periodic tours and almost daily speeches before crowds, large and small, his storehouse of energy was constantly replenished, not depleted. He, in turn, transmitted his buoyant enthusiasm and irrepressible optimism to the masses, maintaining the precarious 'hope level' which enabled them to press ahead in the long, difficult task of improving their way of life.

No one recognized this unusual emotional link between Nehru and the masses better than the Prime Minister himself: 'Delhi is a static city with a dead atmosphere,' he declared in a speech to an audience of sophisticated urbanites, in November 1952. 'I go out and see masses of people, my people, your people, and derive inspiration from them. There is something dynamic and something growing, with them, and I grow with them. I also enthuse with them.' [As evident in the preceding section, I witnessed the extraordinary chemistry between Nehru and the Indian people during a three-day tour of the countryside with the Prime Minister in March 1956. That visit also provided personal insight into his complex character.]

Nehru as an Intellectual

Nehru was not only the charismatic leader of India's urban intellectuals and, second to Gandhi, the beacon of light for India's peasantry in the struggle for independence. He was also an intellectual, for whom ideas were an important instrument in the nationalist movement. The clearest expression of this dimension of Nehru the man were the three major books composed by him behind the prison walls during the 1930s and 1940s: *Glimpses of World History* (1934–35), *Toward Freedom: The Autobiography of Jawaharlal Nehru* (1942), and *The Discovery of India* (1946). Nehru's books were not scholarly, nor were they intended to be. He was not a trained historian, but his feel for the flow of events and his capacity to weave together a wide range of knowledge in a meaningful pattern give to his books qualities of a high order. In these works, he also revealed a sensitive literary style.

Glimpses of World History is the most illuminating on Nehru as an intellectual. The first of the trilogy, *Glimpses*, was a series of thinly connected sketches of the story of mankind in the form of letters to his teenage daughter, Indira, later a prime minister of India. It is rambling and repetitious, introspective and 'romantic'. There are errors of fact and dubious interpretations. It lacks objectivity, for it was not written with an ivory tower mentality. Yet it revealed Nehru's shifting moods. It is, then, uneven in quality and perspective.

Despite its polemical character in many sections and its shortcomings as an impartial history, *Glimpses* is a work of great artistic value, a worthy precursor of his noble and magnanimous *Autobiography*. The canvas is as large as the record of humanity; the strokes are sweeping and multi-colored. There is a sure grasp of detail, yet a breadth of outlook that distinguishes it from the standard history. This is no dry, scholastic tome. The author was deeply involved in his story, freely contributing personal judgments viewed from his own world outlook. It can best be described as cultural history, though there is no lack of political events. It is, too, a human document, a projection of Nehru the man and seeker of truth on the stage of societies in motion.

From the early civilizations of the Tigris-Euphrates valley and the Far East, through the Greek world and ancient India, on to the empire of Ashoka in the 3rd century BC, the period of the Ch'in and the Han dynasties in China, the story of Rome from its ascendancy to its utter collapse, the emergence of Islam—on and on the reader is taken on a voyage of discovery of the story of humankind as seen by a sophisticated hybrid of East and West.

India, of course, occupied a significant place in the chronicle, but the range was vast. The Maya civilization was treated with respect and sympathy. The Crusades occupied a separate letter, as did the exploits of Genghis

Khan, the travels of Marco Polo, the Renaissance, the Reformation, the Dutch struggle for freedom, the kingdoms of Malaya, and the English Revolution of the 17th century. As befits the atmosphere, the Moghuls were treated at greater length, but so too was the Enlightenment, the French Revolution, and Napoleon. There was a letter on the American Revolution, another on the industrial transformation of Europe and the West, the Hundred Years' Peace from 1815 to 1914, still others on the unification of Italy and Germany, the Chinese Revolution of 1911 and beyond, and the emergence of Japan as a modern state.

The literary giants of 19th century Europe were sketched with understanding, as were the implications of Darwinism and Marxism. The Irish Revolt, the Turkish Question, the Russian Revolution, WWI, and the Turkish Revolution under Ataturk also fell within his purview. A number of letters dealt with the Middle East, the emergence of nationalism in the Arab world, and the reawakening of India under the inspiring leadership of Gandhi. There was a disproportionate emphasis on the modern period, the rise of Fascism in Italy, the victory of Nazism, the developments in Russia after the Revolution, the collapse of the League of Nations, the Japanese onslaught on China, the Great Depression, the disarmament problem, the emergence of America from isolation, and, finally, the 'Shadow of War'. Altogether, there were 197 letters, of which about 50 dealt with the first 30 years of the 20th century.

What made *Glimpses* original and unique was its Asia-centered orientation. The imbalance in historical writing was redressed. Europe and America were placed in the perspective of world history, and the reader was made aware of the fact that the history of non-European peoples is not merely an extension of European culture overseas. There is much light on Nehru himself in these letters, both the man and his philosophy. There is evidence of humility and of deep devotion to his family and Gandhi, for whom respect and admiration merge with affection, indeed love. His theory of history, as exhibited in this book, was an amalgam of the 19th century belief in perpetual progress, the crucial role of 'the great man', and sociological analysis of groups in motion, with a strong infusion of Marxist ideas. These three strands permeate his approach to historical change throughout his life.

The *leitmotif* of Nehru's thought and action at that period of his life was the global struggle for freedom. In this sense, *Glimpses of World History* was a milestone in his developing political outlook, embodying in its purest form his internationalist idealism. The central focus of attention was the world stage, and India was but one of the many battlefields. The most notable feature of Nehru's outlook in the early to mid-1930s was the combination of revolutionary goals with purist Gandhian non-violent methods. Two characteristics of his letters to his daughter did not change—an optimistic strain and the attraction of struggle: 'Life would be dull and colorless but for the obstacles that we have to overcome and the fights that we have to win.'

Interview with Nehru (January 1958)

The setting for this interview was a year of turmoil and disquiet for Nehru following a period of relative calm, a year of continuous crisis that tried his faith as no other time since the aftermath of Partition (1947). First was the storm of the States Reorganisation Commission (SRC) which undermined the foundations of Indian unity—riots, violence and bloodshed, tension between Sikhs and Hindus, threats and squabbling in many parts of India. For Nehru this upheaval was a bitter personal blow.

Amid the reverberations of SRC came the Hungarian Uprising and the spectacle of Soviet repression. This, too, was an event for which he was unprepared. Had not the Russians loudly trumpeted their support for 'peaceful coexistence', non-intervention, and the *Panch Shila* (Five Principles) during the tumultuous reception accorded him in Moscow only 16 months earlier? How could they violate their pledge with such impunity? Did this not make a mockery of the 'Geneva spirit' of 1955 which seemed to offer the prospects of a new era in IR? The decline of faith in Soviet sincerity was coupled with a mixture of anger and sadness as the British assault on Suez unfolded. Was this not a symbol of Western Imperialism reborn? The deep wounds of the past, which had healed so slowly, were now reopened by what he considered to be a dastardly act against a weak, non-white people asserting its rights.

A few months later, the Indian general elections brought a new source of anxiety. The Congress was returned to power at the Center and in all but one of the States. The results, however, were not entirely reassuring. The Communists had come to power in the state of Kerala through the ballot box, and though they secured only 35% of the vote, they had broken the Congress monopoly of political power.

India was also confronted with an economic crisis, the most alarming since independence. On the one hand, floods and drought played havoc with food production, causing serious hardship in many parts of the country and had depleted the slender reserves of foreign exchange. At the same time, the Second Five-Year Plan, launched with high hopes of success a year earlier, was in jeopardy unless the staggering sum of $1.4 billion could be raised abroad as loans or gifts. The specter of failure on the vital economic front began to haunt Indian minds.

The effect of these *international* and *domestic crises* on Nehru was profound. His buoyant spirit and vivid enthusiasm of earlier years were less in evidence since 1956. The 'new' Jawaharlal was less confident about the future, less exuberant, and less temperamental than the 'old'. He mellowed a great deal. His outbursts of anger and irritation were much less frequent. He was inclined to be more patient and more tolerant of human failings. An air of almost philosophical calm appeared to have descended upon the mercurial Indian leader.

Another result of 'the year of crises' was the beginning of disenchantment with Nehru's political leadership. The masses continued to adore him. But in the vocal section of India's population, questioning and critical voices multiplied. Some focused on his vacillation during states reorganization, others on his initial rationalization of the Soviet onslaught on Hungary; some commented on his alleged inability to put the Congress house in order; and still others were dissatisfied with his handling of the economic problem. Since then he was not accorded such widespread adulation. The conviction of indispensability ebbed. Indeed, it became fashionable for intellectuals and middle-class Indians openly to criticize him. No longer did he climb the stairs to his office in the Ministry three at a time. He moved more slowly and reacted less quickly than the Nehru of old. The river of time, which seemed to stand still for him mentally and physically until a relatively advanced age, moved at a rapid pace from 1957 onward.

The change in Nehru's mood, the decline in popularity, the ageing process in recent years—all this became apparent from interviews with well-informed Indians, from the press, and from the atmosphere of India. Most of all, they emerged from another lengthy interview with the Indian Prime Minister in January 1958.

When I was ushered into his office in External Affairs, he was standing behind a huge neat desk poring over some papers. My first impression was that age had caught up with him, that he had begun to look elderly. He was a handsome man still, but no longer with the youthful appearance in 1956, less than two years earlier. The lines on his face were more pronounced, the eyes seemed sadder, and the general expression was one of fatigue.

He moved slowly to his seat, placed his hands under his chin and turned to my list of prepared questions. A sword-like letter-opener in his left hand served as a diversion while he thought aloud in his usual manner. This time, however, he spoke more slowly and softly, with longer lapses for thought. He seemed fidgety throughout the hour-long interview. At times, he moved forward and stared straight ahead as he spoke. At other times, he sat back in his chair while his mind wandered back to the great events in his growth to public prominence. His monologue added little to the known record, but it was a moving performance, an intensely human self-analysis by an extraordinary person.

He swung his chair to the side and ran his fingers through his fringe of white hair. There was a pensive, withdrawn expression on his face as he searched out the past, the long, eventful road to his position of eminence in India and the world at large. After what seemed like an unusually long silence, a slight, almost embarrassed smile appeared, his eyes lit up, and the glow of pride transformed his expression of fatigue. One could almost observe his memory at work, with an endless flow of impressions, of persons and places and experiences in the molding of his character and outlook—and the molding of independent India.

He began, somewhat self-consciously, by referring to the special position he occupied at the outset of his career by virtue of his father's prominence and Gandhi's fondness for the young man. 'At that time I didn't think very much about myself,' he said. 'We were so involved in the struggle, so wrapped up in what we were doing that I had little time or inclination to give thought to my own growth.' His words exuded warmth, sincerity, and humility. They were simple words, gentle words, gently spoken in an honest portrait of his past.

Certain landmarks were deeply rooted in Nehru's memory. The first to be mentioned was *Jallianwalla Bagh*—the Amritsar Massacre in 1919, the effect of which had been feelingly described in his autobiography. Along with this, 'my visit to the villages'—his discovery of the peasants in 1920— and 'my first close contact with Gandhi'. In 1920–21, 'I lived my intensest,' he continued, referring to the first civil disobedience campaign. Then came prison, 'a period with no peaks of experience'. Despite the sharp change from a life of activity and fulfillment, 'I adjusted very well. I have that capacity, you know. I was much less agitated than my colleagues by events outside; there was nothing I could do about it so why get involved. I was interested, of course, but I adjusted very well to the changes which prison brought.'

Later, he returned to his prison experience. As he talked freely, he conveyed more poignantly than anything he had written the lasting effects of the nine years of enforced isolation from the outside world. 'I did a lot of reading and writing,' he remarked casually. He also learned the art of self-discipline and used his time to think through the next phase of the struggle for Indian freedom. There was no hint in his words of anger at his captors, nothing to suggest that his experience had produced resentment. A Gandhian spirit of forgiveness seemed to permeate his attitude as he reflected on the lonely days and nights behind the walls. But he had not forgotten them.

The next milestone was the Lahore Congress in 1929 'which remains vivid in my memory'. Understandably so, for this was the year Nehru came of age politically, the first time he was elected Congress President. Suddenly he remembered his European sojourns in 1926–27, 'which gave me time to think, to broaden my outlook, to see India from afar, to think on life itself. Until then I was so involved in Indian affairs that I had little time to think about the broad world or about life's problems in general'.

Nehru had moments of doubt, but his deep belief in the ability and desire of India and the world to solve their problems dispelled misgivings. *Caste* would gradually fade away, he said, though the process would be slow. So too with *economic development* which might proceed less quickly than he and others would like. Although tired and seemingly aware that he may have entered the final stage of his public life, Nehru showed that he retained a determined faith in the future.

Little time remained, for he had dealt with his early life at leisure. But he seemed oblivious of the clock and began a discourse on the world situation. I asked if he had reason to feel optimistic in the light of the preceding year. 'There are some hopeful features,' he began, seizing upon the brighter side of the picture. 'Take *Hungary*, for instance. The events of 1956 show that *Communism*, if it is imposed on a country from outside, cannot last. I mean to say [one of his characteristic expressions] if Communism goes against the basic national spirit, it will not be accepted. In those countries where it has allied itself with nationalism it is, of course, a powerful force, as in China; in Russia, too. The events in *Suez* also brought out an important fact. It is no longer possible for strong, former colonial powers to return to areas they once ruled.' His discussion of Suez underlined the continuing influence of *Colonialism* on his thought.

He then turned to *Eastern Europe*. He seemed convinced that the Russians would ease their grip on the entire area 'once this wretched Cold

War is ended. Once, perhaps, Eastern Europe was of benefit to Russia, economically and strategically. But now well, look at Hungary and Poland. It is a major cost to the Russians; strategically, it is of little value, and they have lost a great deal in world opinion. They will give it up, but not as long as they feel threatened'. The Soviets still labored under the psychology of siege, Nehru appeared to believe at the beginning of 1958. 'As Khrushchev said to me, "for forty years we have had to defend ourselves." They have never had a chance to settle down. If only they were allowed to do so, this fear would give way and then they could give up their hold on Eastern Europe.' This remark provided insight into the point of departure for Indian policy making regarding European problems and Nehru's attitude to the *Cold War* which he clearly regarded as a great evil.

This was further clarified by his observations on *military pacts and Western policy*, particularly the idea of bargaining from strength. 'I cannot see the value of a military approach to these problems. This approach can no longer solve any problems. Besides, I do not see why some people in the West think the Russians are out to conquer other peoples. They are not interested in this. It is only when a neighbor is hostile that they try to weaken it. The Russian people want peace. So do the Americans. In fact, *they are so similar, the Russians and the Americans.* If only they could agree to end the Cold War.'

On the *world situation in general* he made the following comment, more revealing of his personality than the subject itself: 'Viewed logically, there is much to be pessimistic about, but looked at in a human way there is a good deal to be optimistic about.' By this he meant, as he later elaborated, that people everywhere were yearning for peace and that the force of public opinion in all lands would make itself felt, as the awful consequences of nuclear war became understood, and they were now understood by thinking people everywhere. On this note, the interview came to a close.

Nehru had aged since I last saw him, briefly, in Ottawa a year before. He also seemed mellower, more troubled, more tired. But the most vivid impression was a quality of deep sincerity, a human touch which breathes warmth and tenderness. Throughout the interview I felt that here was a sensitive man who had succeeded in absorbing the shocks of life without coarsening his mind, character, and personality.

Interim Assessment in Nehru: A Political Biography *(1959)*

In my assessment five years before his death—the conclusion of my political biography—I noted several contributions of Nehru in the *struggle for independence*. One was to prevent the national movement from becoming egocentric: as Gandhi remarked, Nehru 'made us accustomed to looking at everything in the international light, instead of the parochial'; and more important, he made the world conscious of India and its urge to freedom. A second contribution was to infuse social and economic content into the meaning of *swaraj* (self-rule, independence), to give the movement a materialist (non-spiritual) and socialist orientation. A third was to enlist the active support of the young Westernized Indian intelligentsia and young people generally for the Congress Party cause. In performing this role, Nehru made another, indirect contribution to the Congress: he offered militant and radical youth a satisfying alternative to communism, to the benefit of nationalism. And through his pledge of far-reaching land reform, he supplemented the traditionalist appeal of Gandhi to the rural masses of India. Finally, the purity of his public life, his honesty, and his aversion to corruption served as a model in a movement that was affected by various motives and impulses. Taken together, these contributions formed an impressive record. Gandhi's role in the attainment of independence was undoubtedly greater, but he lacked Nehru's vision, both international and social.

Of Nehru's leadership since independence, my 1959 assessment cited four basic achievements in the domestic arena: *political stability* and *democracy*, the *Five-Year Plans*, a *secular state*, and *social change*. In the *political sphere*, he provided the basic philosophy of a *constitution* for the Republic of India, through his Objectives Resolution in December 1946. He created the beginnings of a pattern of democracy through free elections in 1951–52, 1957, and 1962. He nourished the *central place of parliament* in India's political system. And he established a *strong, stable government* in the largest and most populous new state in the Third World. Against this must be set inefficiency and widespread corruption in the public service. The blame for this state of affairs rested largely with him, for Nehru was an inept administrator.

As for *economic development*, national planning was a significant instance where an idea was translated into reality. And the credit belongs entirely to Nehru. Against this must be set the glaringly inadequate land reform program throughout his tenure as Prime Minister. For more than 20 years he had preached the necessity of revolution in the countryside, but he did not practice what he preached. The inadequacy of land reform revealed one of Nehru's weaknesses as a political leader: the gap between words and deeds was often wide.

Perhaps his most notable accomplishment was the creation of a *secular state*. To Indian Muslims, he was a rock and a shield. His contribution in this regard was twofold: to ease the transition to greater mutual trust between Hindus and Muslims and to embody the secular ideal in the Indian Constitution. He also maintained a continuous onslaught on the ideas of communalism. As for *social reform* proper, his most notable achievements were the formal abolition of untouchability and the enactment of the Hindu Code Bill.

The pillars of India's *foreign policy* in the Nehru era were: *anti-colonialism* or, in more positive terms, active support for all peoples in Asia and Africa who were striving to eliminate foreign rule; *anti-racialism*; *non-alignment* with the power blocs, not in the negative sense of neutralism but in an active, dynamic positive assertion of independent judgment and decision on all issues, taking each on its merits; the *recognition of Asia as a new force* and the rights of Asian states to decide the issues of direct concern to them; *mediation*, with a view to relaxing international tensions and creating an atmosphere conducive to India's economic development; and the *creation of a no-war area in the Third World*. As for Nehru's influence, I termed him the philosopher, the architect, the engineer, and the voice of his country's policy toward the outside world.

India's outstanding achievement in that domain was to provide leadership in the political awakening of Asia after centuries of colonial rule, and Nehru was the most articulate spokesman for this urge to reassert Asia's place in the global system. It began with his sponsorship of Asian Relations conferences in Delhi in 1947 and 1949 and culminated in the historic Afro-Asian Conference in Bandung in 1955, the forerunner of the Non-Aligned Movement, institutionalized at Belgrade in 1961 and beyond. Moreover, Nehru predicted that the superpowers would come, more and more, to resemble each other in the future. For many, his was a genuine voice of peace.

Nehru's *weaknesses* as a *political leader* were apparent from the outset. Among statesmen of his era, he was perhaps *the supreme individualist*, a man who felt compelled to do things himself. This was true during the struggle for independence when, by his own admission, Nehru as Congress President also 'functioned often as a secretary or a glorified clerk'. This was also true of Nehru as Prime Minister. His *attention to trivia* was startling for a man in his position. He also insisted on handling his vast correspondence personally, with the result that he wrote thousands of letters a year. And on the *minutest affairs of party and government* he had to be informed.

Nehru held an array of positions of responsibility in the Government and the Congress Party. From 1947 to 1964, he was Prime Minister and Minister of External Affairs, as well as Head of the Atomic Energy Department. Since 1950 he served as Chairman of the Planning Commission. From 1951 to 1954, he also held the time-consuming post of Congress President, and throughout the period, he served on the party's Working Committee. On various occasions, he filled a gap created by the death or resignation of a Cabinet colleague.

Thus, much more than temperament was responsible for Nehru's all-embracing direction of affairs. Apart from the myriad of formal portfolios and responsibilities, Nehru was acutely conscious of his place in history and *was driven to act in all spheres so as to hasten the attainment of his goals*. For another, he had never forgotten the disappointments of the 1930s which led him to write, '[O]ne must journey through life alone; to rely on others is to invite heartbreak.' Moreover, Nehru was essentially a Westerner in his intellectual makeup, and an *impatient* one at that. He became easily annoyed at evidence of inefficiency or an unruly audience and felt constrained to put things right. Lack of order and organization irritated him, as did the Indian indifference to time. Thus in his mission to transform Indian society, he felt obliged to act at every level.

He was also the last hero of the freedom struggle. For the masses, he alone seemed to offer the promise of a higher standard of living. The effect was to place Nehru on a pedestal, to rely on him for guidance, direction, and decision. Colleagues and subordinates felt the necessity of consulting him on a host of issues which should never have reached the desk of a Prime Minister, partly because they did not want to risk incurring his displeasure by making a decision that might be objectionable to the 'P.M.', partly because he had set the pattern by involving himself in matters beyond his normal jurisdiction. Members of the Congress High Command had been in the habit of consulting Nehru for 30 years or more. In sum, a combination of *his self-image as indispensable to the attainment of his ambitious goals* for India, domestic and international, and a *deep-rooted dependence of his colleagues and aides* on his leadership and ultimate decision-making authority in virtually all matters important and trivial had *profound negative consequences for the working of all branches of India's administration and the Congress Party*, and probably on Nehru's health: the burden for India and for Nehru was too great.

Apart from his shortcomings as an administrator and the gap between words and deeds, his *gravest defect was indecision*. Moreover, he was completely lacking in ruthlessness. Ever the quintessential democrat, he had a compulsion for universal consent; he also revealed a tendency to yield to pressure. Moreover, he was a *bad judge of character*. Loyalty to old colleagues often outweighed sound judgment. Finally, during more than a decade in power, he *did not train a successor or a group who could assure continuity* in policy 'after Nehru'.

While this litany of shortcomings seemed formidable, I termed them the *weaknesses of a giant*. Nehru was *India's unifier* at a time of great stress, during the ghastly riots and killings which accompanied the transfer of power in 1947. He *laid the foundations of a genuine parliamentary democracy*. He *fashioned the machinery for planning* and instilled the idea that therein lays the path to material progress and national power. He *emphasized* the significance of *individual rights*, as expressed in the new constitution. He *secured widespread acceptance of the ideal of a secular state*. He restored India's faith in itself and its place in the international system. And he had begun the arduous task of social change. Overall, Nehru had *set in motion forces for long-term social, economic, and political change*.

Last Interview with Nehru (December 1963)

Five months before Nehru's death, during a brief research visit to New Delhi, I had a final meeting with the Prime Minister. I did not anticipate a formal interview, as in 1956 and 1958, for I had requested a very brief courtesy visit, but it turned out to be another engrossing substantive interview.

When I entered his office at External Affairs on the evening of 13 December 1963, I was struck by what many Indians knew and about which they spoke candidly to me, namely, that Nehru's health had deteriorated markedly. Time itself was bound to take its toll for an active man in his mid-70s. Moreover, much had happened to try his faith, optimism, self-confidence, and equanimity.

To many this was in part a consequence of the trauma resulting from the war with China in October–November 1962 which, for Nehru and Krishna Menon, his devoted aide, then Defense Minister (see below), and most Indians was a shocking betrayal of India's friendship with China since the Communist regime came to power in 1949. Added to the sense of betrayal was the reality of a severe military defeat, the shattering of Nehru's dreams about peace in Asia based upon the widely cited *mantra*, 'Hindi-Sini bhai-bhai' (India and China are brothers). The trauma of China's invasion and humiliation, both personal and national, had shaken India's national leader. Economic stagnation at home, more intense factionalism within his own Congress Party, the loss of India's prestige in the councils of the world—all this must have accentuated a growing despair in his capacity to transform his ancient land into a 'good society'. There was also by then medical knowledge of a grave illness.

When I was ushered into the Prime Minister's office at ten minutes to six in the evening, he rose from his chair, smiled a little wanly, shook my hand, without the vigor of the past, and welcomed me graciously to India once more. He thanked me for my latest book, *The New States of Asia*, published a few months earlier, but added quickly, 'I regret I have not read it yet'," and then returned to his chair where he sat in a relaxed and informal mood throughout our conversation.

I introduced the conversation by inquiring whether he had jotted down notes and musings over the decades which he intended to make public one day, like his letters to his daughter that appeared in his first book, *Glimpses of World History*. His reaction was a soft-spoken remark: 'I have no jottings or notes to speak of; I have not had time to keep them.' He did, however, refer to a batch of old letters which 'I have been intending to go through for some years but have not found the time to do so.'

There was a casual but effective shift to an entirely different theme, namely, the forthcoming *Congress of Orientalists*. 'What can I say to the Orientalists?' he asked modestly, when I reminded him that he was expected to open the proceedings.

The unexpected informal interview that followed fell into the three broad categories: *domestic affairs, foreign policy*, and *Indo-Pakistan relations*.

I asked first to what he would ascribe the *marked decline in the rate of India's economic growth* during the preceding two years. The principal cause, he answered quickly, was the failure of the agricultural sector to fulfill its expectations. He also made reference to the abrupt and substantial diversion of resources to defense in the wake of the Chinese invasion in the autumn of 1962, and, in a passing reference, to rising population as well. I seized this opportunity to remind him that, during our 1956 interviews, he had dismissed the *population problem* as an economic myth and asked whether he was still of the same view. It was a measure of flexibility in his thinking that he now acknowledged the crucial place of population growth in the economic scheme of things. He then explained at some length the efforts being made by the Indian government to arrest the population spiral—though I added that there did not seem to be a sense of urgency in this important issue.

I then asked whether *untouchability* was less evident in the country as a whole, after paying due respect to the legislative attempts to eradicate this malaise of Indian society. He acknowledged that it remained a regrettable feature of the Hindu social order but tried to differentiate among groups within the untouchable community. Indeed, so alert to the privileges granted to some groups of 'dalits' that there was powerful opposition from more depressed castes for a share in the spoils! He did not, however, really come to grips with the question, though he evaded it skillfully.

I asked the Prime Minister whether *peasant lethargy* was not the real root of India's economic problem. He agreed firmly and then referred to *panchayati raj* (people power) as a conscious effort to galvanize the rural masses into cooperative effort and a sense of purpose. When I referred to the depressing picture portrayed by Kusum Nair's book, *Blossoms in the Dust*, he interjected that, while it was accurate for some parts of the country, it should not be taken as an authentic portrait of rural India as a whole.

On this theme he then digressed at length. He pointed to the contrast between those districts that had experienced the modernizing consequences of industrialization, such as the lower parts of Bihar and Bengal, and those which remained relatively isolated and backward, such as the southeast portion of the United Provinces (Uttar Pradesh) and the northern half of Bihar. Of some interest was his reference to the marked progress of small-scale industry in the Punjab. Along with this reaffirmation of his deeply held view that modern industry and technology would roll back the frontiers of a traditional society, he referred time and time again to the critical role of education as a catalyst to basic social and economic change. We did not get into the declining quality of India's *educational system*. However, I am certain that he would have responded that at this stage of India's development the sheer number of young boys and girls in schools is the most important aspect of the process.

I recalled to his attention his observation in 1956 that India would be able to do away with *preventive detention* in less than a year and remarked that, by coincidence, I had arrived just when the law was being extended to 1966. He did not seem bothered by the bluntness of the question and once more noted that this law was rarely used except in time of emergency and against anti-social elements. When I responded that the Defense of India Rules could accomplish these purposes as well, he said, 'Much better, but we do not plan to keep this indefinitely.' I pressed for further clarity on this point, and he noted that 'we do not know what the Chinese will do'. It seemed to me, I retorted, that using this criterion one might retain the Defense of India Rules indefinitely, at least until the territorial problem were solved, and added that the sense of emergency was no longer evident in the country. At last, he declared that within a year he hoped that these Emergency Rules might be removed.

On the prospects for a *solution with China*, he was noncommittal but seemed hopeful, almost wishfully thinking, that the Chinese would at some stage accept the Colombo Proposals offered soon after the end of the India/China War by a group of well-disposed neutrals *vis-à-vis* the India/China conflict, notably Egypt, Burma, and Ceylon [later, Sri Lanka]. There was no doubt in my mind that he was anxious to negotiate the problem to a mutually acceptable solution, but pride and national prestige—and Indian public opinion—prevented this without the Chinese agreeing to the Colombo bases for a settlement. There was to be more on China later.

I referred to *corruption* and to the character of the *bureaucracy*, which seemed to many devoid of contact with, and sensitivity to, the needs of a developing society. He remarked this was certainly true of the pre-1947 bureaucracy that was essentially concerned with law and order and with the most senior members of the civil service after 1947, but he hastened to add, 'They are doing their work most efficiently.' More encouraging for him was the belief that the newer members of the service were much more attuned to the problems of India in transition.

I referred to the widespread allegations of '*licence raj*' (bureaucratic rule) and asked whether the likely abuses of greater freedom for the private sector would not be compensated by more rapid growth. He disagreed firmly and remarked: '[W]e gave them their head a few years ago and are still suffering the consequences.' I was left with no doubt that as long as he was at the helm, the commitment to Democratic Socialism and the special place for the public sector would be guarded against major encroachment by private enterprise—unless the changed circumstances of a weaker India, more dependent than ever on Anglo-American military and economic support, make it necessary to yield to the pressures for a wider arena for foreign private capital which may spill over to the benefit of indigenous private enterprise.

In the realm of *foreign policy*, I asked first for his views of Chinese motives in the NEFA (India's North East Frontier Agency)–Ladakh border war in 1962. He responded quickly that he surmised China wished to persuade the peoples of Southeast Asia that it alone was a major Power in the region and that India was not in any sense its equal. He added, sadly, 'And they have accomplished this.' No other Chinese aims were mentioned, a revealing insight into Nehru's view of this event.

I then asked whether *non-alignment* could any longer be a feasible foreign policy for India in the light of China's invasion, American and British military aid, and the recent entry of the US Seventh Fleet into the Indian Ocean. He reiterated his faith in non-alignment, though with less enthusiasm, pointing out that it retained its validity as the basis of India's policy to matters in dispute between the USA and the USSR. I then reminded him of his remark six years ago that the USA and the USSR were likely to come closer together and asked what would happen to non-alignment if this process continues much further. He smiled and answered, 'The closer they come together, the less scope there is for non-alignment.' As for the Seventh Fleet affair, he said, 'I do not like this act but a protest would accomplish nothing,' and then he added, 'The reports that one of their ships is carrying nuclear weapons chips away further at non-alignment.'

What in his judgment was at the root of the *Soviet/Chinese squabble*, I asked. 'Basically their interests have clashed,' he answered. 'It is not primarily ideological. Of course, ideology plays a role, much more so than with other states.' He then went on to observe that the Chinese Communist position was much more in line with Leninism than was Khrushchev's Russia. 'This', he added, 'was due to the fact that Russia had passed through the early difficult phase of her revolution', and 'had toned down, I am pleased to find', while China was still in the throes of its revolutionary fervor. I was struck by his further assessment of China, namely, that he could not see how it would soon emerge from its state of underdevelopment because of a massive persistent food problem accentuated by a steady increase in population which required substantial food imports year by year. He seemed to be linking this problem with the negative economic effects of the Soviet/Chinese imbroglio.

Time was moving, and papers were rapidly accumulating on his desk, so I plunged quickly into the morass of *Kashmir and Indo-Pakistani relations*. 'The Kashmir dispute seems to go on forever, Mr. Prime Minister. Do you see any hope for a settlement in the near future?' It was obvious that he did not—at that time. When I referred to the six rounds of India-

Pakistan negotiations during the preceding winter, he noted, somewhat irritably (this was the only moment of irritation in the whole interview), 'Why, they made impossible demands!' 'You mean the whole [Kashmir] Valley?' I asked. 'Much more than that; they asked for all of Kashmir except for two small districts!' Was there no other basis for negotiation, I asked, that is, an Indian counter-offer? He remained silent long enough to suggest disinclination to go further into the matter. He was also annoyed by the fact, as he said, that 'the Pakistanis were unwilling to talk about anything else except Kashmir, and there are many other problems between us'.

I referred to my recent experience in Karachi when there was a widespread expression by prominent Pakistanis that the crux of the Kashmir dispute was 'India's unwillingness to reconcile herself to the partition'. 'That is not so,' he said, 'all groups in the country, even the communalists, accept the fact of the partition.' Then, disturbingly, he remarked, '[T]he Pakistani people do not think this; only the politicians think so.'

The Prime Minister rose to signal the end of what had become, for me, another interesting interview. My impression of Nehru at the close of 1963 was of a man who was aging but was by no means aged. Throughout the hour-long discussion, he was alert, fluent, lucid, and utterly relaxed. He fingered a flower, smoked a cigarette; indeed he was much less fidgety at six o'clock in the evening in 1963 than he was in the forenoon in 1958 when I last interviewed him. When I thought of the incredible schedule that he maintained in Bombay a few days earlier, laying foundation stones, opening one institute or another, I could not but wonder how long a man of his age [74] could sustain the pressures and demands placed on him, almost literally around the clock. One other impression was that here was a man who would not step down from the pinnacle of power. He seemed urgently aware that time was slipping away, that much remained to be done, and he had, quite naturally perhaps, created an image of his own indispensability in this, India's, time of crisis.

Our final exchange remained fixed in my memory because of its poignancy. As I was about to say farewell, I informed the Prime Minister that my family and I were planning to return to India in August 1964 for a year of further research and that I looked forward to the pleasure of meeting with him again. He paused for a moment and replied, sadly, '*August is a long time away, Mr. Brecher.*' This jolted me, for the Nehru of a few years ago would never have attached such importance to so short a period of time. I sensed then that this would be our last meeting; it was. Nehru died on 27 May 1964.

Further Interim Assessment (November 1964)

Six months after Nehru's death, I elaborated on some of the themes in my 1959 interim assessment during an interview in Delhi:

Q How exactly would you describe the quality of his leadership?

A It is very difficult to put this into words; it is something intangible, the magic of charisma, a quality found rarely in history. Both Gandhi and Nehru possessed it in abundance. Nehru had an indefinable power to inspire confidence and affection from the rural masses and the urban middle class through sheer force of personality. He placed within their reach the prospects of a good society through such ideals as social reform, mass welfare, individual liberty, democracy, progress through rational planning, and reconstruction of the whole fabric of Indian society. He was an indispensable link between diverse groups of a society in transition. He was the focal point of the complex of aspirations and expectations that filled the mind of India in the years immediately before and after independence. Gandhi did not live long after independence; and in the decade after India became free Nehru's was the dominant role in Indian public life. A political biography of Nehru, therefore, provided the key to an understanding of India in motion.

Q As his biographer can you suggest what aspects of his life and work have not yet received adequate attention?

A The definitive work on Nehru is yet to be written: a final assessment could not be done in the midstream of his career. Only now is it possible to contemplate it. However, such a work will depend on a careful study of the personal and other papers relating to almost 50 years of his life in the service of India. It may take years to sift and digest all the available materials.

Q What is your impression of the image of Nehru in India today?

A Returning to India after some time I have observed undue emphasis on the last three, unhappy years of his life, almost in total disregard of the preceding 40 years of dedicated service to the nation. There is a tendency to minimize Nehru's positive contributions and to focus attention on the setbacks of the last three years. I hope that when a dispassionate final assessment of Nehru's role in modern Indian politics and history comes to be written, this gross imbalance will vanish.

Q To what do you ascribe this exaggerated stress on the last three years of his life?

A For one thing, India did not maintain its earlier rate of economic progress between 1961 and 1964. There was, too, the shattering setback of October 1962 [the war with China].

The *idea of economic progress through rational planning* is one of Nehru's lasting contributions. The *nurturing of* the political system of *parliamentary democracy* is another. The concept of *scientific spirit* as an essential element of progress is a third. And for more than a decade Nehru achieved the unique feat of *world influence without power*. Regrettably, there is a tendency to relegate these contributions to the background in the difficult days of the transition after Nehru. (*Link* [New Delhi], 14 November 1964)

Nehru and Shastri: Nehru's Mantle: The Politics of Succession in India (1964, 1966)

The Nehru era ended with high drama, a succession contest that tested the stability of India's democratic political system, to which Nehru was committed long before Independence and which he nurtured with care throughout the 17 years of his tenure as prime minister. Democracy emerged triumphant from both the high-stakes Nehru succession contest (1964) and the second challenge to political stability within 19 months, following the death of Nehru's successor, Lal Bahadur Shastri, in January 1966. I witnessed the second contest, and for both I received extraordinary cooperation from all the contestants and, in fact, virtually all the senior Congress Party leaders at the time.

Political Succession: Universal Problem

The issue of succession is central to all political systems: it is an inevitable consequence of Time and Mortality. The appearance of youth or vigor and the illusion of permanence, often combined with fear of the unknown, may shroud the issue for a decade or more. But ultimately political pressure, ill-fortune, disablement, or death compels attention to the questions, who and what will succeed the existing leader and the configuration of power: the political élite and often the populace as well cannot escape this responsibility. In essence, the stability, welfare, and progress, sometimes even the continuity, of the polity depend upon a successful process of succession.

The problem of succession is thus not unique to the contemporary world; it is as old as the history of political organization. However, it was accentuated by two striking characteristics of the 20th century: *Gerontocracy* and *Charisma*. The list of elderly men, many of whom wielded political power for lengthy periods, in some cases extending back to the 1920s, constitutes an extraordinary club.

Some old *democratic leaders* stepped down from the summit of power more or less voluntarily, such as Canada's longtime Prime Minister, Mackenzie King at 73, in 1948; Churchill at 80, in 1955; West Germany's Adenauer at 87 and Israel's Ben-Gurion at 76, in 1963; Jamaica's Bustamante at 82, in 1967; and South Africa's Mandela at 80, in 1999.

Many died without an *effective* challenge to their power. Some were *leaders of communist regimes*: Stalin at 74, in 1953; Ho Chi-minh at 79, in 1969; Mao Zedong at 82, in 1976; Tito at 87, in 1980; and several post-Stalin communist leaders, notably the USSR's Brezhnev at 75, in 1982; North Korea's Kim Il-Sung at 82, in 1994; and China's Deng Xiao-ping at 92, in 1997. Others who died without an effective challenge to their power, dominated *non-Communist or anti-Communist authoritarian regimes*, monarchical and republican, for lengthy periods: Spain's Franco at 82 and Nationalist China's Chiang Kai-shek at 87, in 1975; Kenya's Kenyatta at 89, in 1978; several Arab rulers: King Ibn Saud of Saudi Arabia at 72, in 1953; King Hassan II of Morocco at 70, in 1999; Sheikh Zayed of the United Arab Emirates (UAE) at 86 and Palestine's (the Palestine Liberation Organization's [PLO's]) Yasir Arafat at 75, in 2004; King Fahd of Saudi Arabia at 84, in 2005; Sheikh Jaber Al-Sabah of Kuwait at 79, in 2006; and Pope John Paul II at 84, in 2005.

A few elderly democratic leaders died in office, notably India's Nehru at 74, in 1964, and Israel's Eshkol at 73, in 1969, or were incapacitated—Israel's Sharon, by a brain hemorrhage and coma at 77, in 2005 (he remained in that state until his death in 2014). Others, both authoritarian and democratic leaders, resigned voluntarily, were compelled to resign, retired, or were voted out of office: Finland's Mannerheim at 78, in 1946; Italy's de Gasperi at 72, in 1953; Syngman Rhee of South Korea at 85, in 1960; Khrushchev at 70, in 1964; de Gaulle at 78, in 1969; Portugal's Salazar at 81, in 1970, after a brain hemorrhage and coma two years earlier; and Fidel Castro of Cuba, in 2008, after 49 years in power. Two were assassinated, Trujillo of the Dominican Republic at 69, in 1961, and Israel's Rabin at 73, in 1995.

Here, then, is a microcosm of the mid and late 20th and early 21st centuries: the club of Old Men represents all continents, most types of political system, virtually all races and cultures, great, middle, and small powers, and economies in various stages of development.

Based upon their age at the time they left the summit of power, the oldest among this group was Deng at 92, followed by Kenyatta at 89, Adenauer and Tito at 87, Pope John Paul II at 84, Kim Il-Sung and Mao at 82, Churchill and Mandela at 80, Ho Chi-minh at 79, Ben-Gurion at 76, Nehru and Stalin at 74, and Ibn Saud at 72. Some of these Old Men exercised power, in whole or in part, through *charisma*.

That gift of power through extraordinary personality traits extends beyond the gerontocrats to another significant club, nationalist revolutionaries of Asia, Africa, and Latin America, not all of whom left the political arena when they were old. Thus to the charismatic Old Men must be added once-younger charismatic leaders of the Third World: Sukarno (until his ouster from power in Indonesia in 1966) and, perhaps, Prince Sihanouk, though no longer in power, in his 80s, in Asia; Gadhafi, Nasser, Nyerere, and Nkrumah in Africa; and Castro in Latin America. In most Third World states, many political leaders who vacated the pinnacle of power were neither old nor charismatic. Yet the problem of succession remains. The evidence thus far indicates a pre-eminent role for a military *coup* as a mechanism of political change.

A peaceful and orderly succession to an individual leader who had dominated the politics of his own country since independence has occurred in only a few new states, notably Israel (Eshkol after Ben-Gurion, 1963) and India (Shastri after Nehru, 1964). (The succession to Mandela in South Africa in 1999, too, was orderly, but he was in power for only five years.)

In both cases, the former leader was a gerontocrat with charisma in abundance. But there were two vital differences: the succession to Ben-Gurion was incomplete: he resigned as Prime Minister in 1963 but did not withdraw from the political arena; and second, few doubted the capacity of Israel's democratic system to survive the passing of Ben-Gurion from the political scene, but many had profound misgivings about India's democracy without Nehru.

In the India case, the magnitude of India's domestic pressures and centrifugal tendencies, the narrowness of its democratic infrastructure at that time, Nehru's dominant role in Indian politics for 17 years, and the uncertainty about the Indian political élite's ability to achieve a smooth succession without shattering the system and its rules of behavior had created grave fears in India and abroad about the future of Indian politics. This was one reason for exploring the succession to Nehru in depth. Another was the intrinsic interest in the drama itself and the light it would shed on the principal forces and actors in Indian politics in 1963–64 and beyond. A study of the succession in India seemed important also because the process of selection would have far-reaching consequences for the distribution of political power in the first year of the post-Nehru period. Fourth, it would provide insight into the last phase of Nehru as a political leader. And finally, it could reveal some of the inner workings of the governing Congress Party in what was then a democratic one-plus party system. In sum, the research project on the successions to Nehru (1964) and Shastri (1966) arose out of concern for the future of India's democracy and intellectual curiosity.

Long years of study led to a natural interest in the last phase of the Nehru era and the fascinating web of men and forces in Indian politics that were responsible for the succession to India's towering leader since independence. The initial aim was to confine research to the Shastri succession to Nehru in May–June 1964. However, Prime Minister Shastri died suddenly in Tashkent in early January 1966, hours after the conclusion of the USSR-brokered Indo-Pakistani summit conference, which formalized the end of their second war over Kashmir. India was again confronted with the challenge of succession, twice within 19 months. Was the pattern of 1964 likely to be repeated or would the actors and the forces they represented respond differently? If the latter, what changes in behavior would take place, and what would these changes presage for the working of India's political system in the future? These and related questions prompted a return to Delhi to observe, document, and analyze the second succession.

There are various ways in which a political process as complex as the succession to Nehru and Shastri could be explored. One viable method is to construct an elaborate analysis of the drama and its background, based upon a series of related functional questions, and then to examine the main consequences of the successions for India's political system. *When* did the process begin, that is, at what point did the struggle for the succession enter the mainstream of Indian politics? *What* were the main interlocking developments in Nehru's declining phase that led to the decision in favor of Lal Bahadur Shastri and, later, to the decision in favor of Mrs. Indira Gandhi, Nehru's daughter, as the successor to Shastri? *Who* were the key actors and what forces did they represent? And finally, what ideas and institutions legitimized the process of decision and the decisions? An attempt to answer these questions is made below, in the discussion of the background to the succession struggle and the key actors, and in the comparative analysis of the two succession contests that follows.

Preparing the Ground

As early as the spring of 1963, Congress leaders began to prepare the ground for an orderly succession to Nehru, in light of: three prestige electoral defeats in by-elections to the *Lok Sabha*, the lower house of India's parliament; the debacle of the border war with China; a food shortage; an unsuccessful Third Five-Year Plan; a severe drain on India's foreign exchange reserves; and unmistakable evidence of a steady deterioration in Nehru's health. The response was a far-reaching purge at the highest level of the Congress Party.

The 'Kamaraj Plan', named after its official author, the Chief Minister of Madras and the foremost Congress leader in south India, was simple yet revolutionary: a dozen senior Congressmen in government, six Cabinet ministers and six Chief Ministers, were to resign their posts and assume full-time organizational work in order to revitalize the party. The key persons chosen to take the path of renunciation were: the two leading candidates to succeed Nehru: Morarji Desai, Finance Minister, with a powerful base in Bombay state, where he had served as Chief Minister before moving to the Union Cabinet, and Lal Bahadur Shastri, Home Minister, with a strong base in the Hindi heartland state, Uttar Pradesh, along with a lesser candidate, Jagjivan Ram (Transport and Communications), S.K. Patil (Food and Agriculture), a key figure in the ensuing struggle over the first succession, and two influential Chief Ministers, Kamaraj himself, and Biju Patnaik (Orissa), the initiator of the Kamaraj Plan. Nehru was persuaded of the Plan's multiple benefits at a meeting of the Congress Working Committee on 24 August 1963.

The role of the Kamaraj Plan in the final stage of the Nehru era merits attention in this report for two reasons: first, because its effects on the succession to Nehru were fundamental; and second, because I had the good fortune of interviewing all the major figures in the drama, albeit a few months later. Morarji and Shastri, a lesser contestant, Jagjivan Ram, and an influential minister, Patil, were deprived of direct power and patronage—they were removed from the Cabinet, the political body that would furnish the next Prime Minister, and were relegated to the party's enlarged Central Parliamentary Board. No less important, Morarji, who, as the second-ranking member of the Cabinet, would have become Prime Minister on 27 May 1964, when Nehru died, and would have been in a strong tactical position in the struggle for succession during the next six days, was deprived of this advantage. A third consequence was to add Gulzari Lal Nanda to the candidates for successor to Nehru: he succeeded Shastri as Home Minister and replaced Morarji as number two in the Cabinet. Finally, the Kamaraj Plan heralded the shift of decision-making regarding the succession from the Cabinet to the Congress Party's supreme body, the Working Committee.

Key Actors

There were two crucial, informal bodies that managed the succession to Nehru: the *Caucus* or *Syndicate*, and the much larger *Grand Council of the Republic*. The Syndicate was formed at a quiet gathering of Congress leaders in Tirupathi, Andhra Pradesh, in early October 1963. Present were: K. *Kamaraj*, Chief Minister of Madras; *Atulya Ghosh*, Congress Party leader in West Bengal; *Sanjiva Reddy*, Chief Minister of Andhra Pradesh; Nijalingappa, Chief Minister of Mysore, and present by telephone, *S.K. Patil*, Bombay City party leader and inveterate rival of Morarji Desai. The Syndicate's first choice for party president was Shastri. If he declined, or Nehru was unreceptive, Kamaraj was to be requested to assume the post. The real aim was to exclude Morarji from this key position.

The Caucus/Syndicate played a dual role in the struggle for the succession. One was to serve as the coalescing agent for diverse interest groups which viewed Shastri as the most effective protector and transmission belt for their specific interests—regional and State, institutional and organizational, ideological and electoral. The other was to channel these complementary interests into a concentrated thrust and to manage the mechanics of a tranquil selection, through the device of consensus. However, the influence of the Syndicate in the outcome was limited, certainly in the view of Shastri himself, then prime minister: '[E]ven if these gentlemen [the Syndicate] had done nothing, a large majority, at least 80 per cent, of the Congress Parliamentary Party, would have voted for me. I knew that. I did not speak to anyone about it; I sensed this support' (MB Interview with Shastri, 10 April 1965). His assessment may have under-rated the contribution of the Syndicate and may have exaggerated his majority, but it was basically correct. The decisive factor was the clear majority for Shastri in the three key institutional groups, the Working Committee of the Congress Party, the State Congress Party machines, and the Congress Parliamentary Party (CPP), superimposed on the relatively inarticulate but known choice of Shastri by the mass public. The role of the Syndicate was to give political form to that national preference. However, it also prevented the succession struggle from becoming disorderly, with danger to the unity of India and the Congress, and to the stability of the political system.

The consensus in favor of Shastri was also evident in the supreme, informal institution in Indian politics in the early 1960s, the Grand Council of the Republic, which emerged from an enlarged Congress Working Committee on 31 May 1964, four days after Nehru's death. What made the Grand Council powerful was its unique membership, namely, all the crucial wielders of influence in Party and Government: the 19 members of the Congress Working Committee; the 13 Chief Ministers who were not members of the highest executive organ of the Congress Party; 2 representatives of the CPP; most of the 8 members of the Cabinet who were not included in those three groups, and a few special invitees, like Krishna Menon and U.N. Dhebar, a former Congress president. The Council's membership varied, then, from 40 to 46, the combined Congress-Union Government-State Governments' élite.

A glance at this membership reveals the enormous concentration of power represented on the Grand Council. Apart from the four key institutional interest groups—Congress Working Committee, Chief Ministers, Cabinet, and CPP—there were spokesmen from every State; indeed, more than one from each State, except Jammu and Kashmir, Kerala, Mysore, and Rajasthan. The Caucus (or Syndicate) that managed the two successions was there in full, as were all who contested the succession, and prominent individuals outside the institutional network. Thus, the Center and the States, the Congress Party and the Government, and diverse factions, groups, and ideological tendencies were all present, making the Grand Council a combined authority-power summit in the Indian polity. It was small enough to permit effective deliberations yet sufficiently representative to give its decisions the quality of finality and likely acceptance by India's *attentive publics* and *mass public* as well.

The actors in the first, Nehru, succession contest (1964) may be summarized as follows: *Kamaraj*, the astute kingmaker; *Shastri*, the retiring king-in-the-making; *Morarji*, the proud, eager candidate; *Nanda*, the aspiring non-contestant; *Jagjivan Ram*, the frustrated politician; *Indira Gandhi*, the grief-stricken daughter of Nehru and recipient of caring attention; and the President of India, guardian of constitutional continuity and conscious of history in the making. Others, like *Atulya Ghosh*, *Patil*, *Reddy*, and *Patnaik*, Congress leaders in Bengal, Bombay, Andhra Pradesh, and Orissa, respectively, were the key lobbyists in the contest, with *Chavan* and the Chief Ministers the main objects of their courting; and *Krishna Menon*, Nehru's devoted long-term foreign policy adviser, who had fallen from grace as a result of the border war with China, now an interested onlooker.

Others interviewed about the first and/or second succession were:

Sheikh M. Abdullah, longtime Chief Minister of Jammu and Kashmir
General J.N. Chaudhuri, Chief of Army Staff
L.K. Jha, Secretary to the Prime Minister (Shastri)
R. Karanjiya, Editor, *Blitz*
K. Malaviyya, former Cabinet minister and left-wing Congress leader
Mrs. V.L. Pandit, Nehru's sister
Dr. S. Radhakrishnan, President of India
L.P. Singh, Special Secretary Home Ministry, later, Home Secretary
Raghunath Singh, General Secretary CPP
Cabinet members, others than those noted above
Many MPs, civil servants, and political analysts
Other members of the Nehru family
Officials in the Ministry of External Affairs
Access to Morarji Desai's personal correspondence 1952–56
Access to Nehru's unpublished letters

The most valuable sources for research into the two political succession contests were my unrestricted interviews with almost all of the Congress leaders throughout the drama of the second, as well as the first, succession contests. These oral encounters were not deep, except for the 17-hour taped interviews with Krishna Menon (see below), which covered many topics other than the two Succession contests. However, by then, my political biography of Nehru during his lifetime (1959) provided extraordinary access, without which my analysis of the two political successions would have been shallow. All the key actors, some of whom I interviewed frequently and at length, were insightful on the dynamics of succession, without régime change, in a stable and functioning democracy, on two occasions within 19 months.

The most noteworthy feature of the interviews was the candor of the participants and onlookers in (sometimes lengthy) interviews. No questions were embarrassing. Seemingly, no information of value was concealed from an academic inquirer, who was the fortunate recipient of recollections about politically significant developments that were to test the ability of my interlocutors to cope with the challenge of traumatic change and uncertainty and to shape the future of India's political system; it was a reception without constraints of any kind.

At 9 a.m. on 2 June 1964, 5 days and 19 hours after the death of Jawaharlal Nehru, the CPP met in extraordinary session in the Central Hall of Parliament and unanimously elected *Lal Bahadur Shastri* the party leader. Seven hours later, *President Radhakrishnan* invited Shastri to form a new government. With that act the succession to Nehru was complete. (A comparative analysis of the two succession contests and their implications for India's political system, prepared soon after the second succession, is presented below drawing upon my *Succession in India: A Study in Decision-Making*, also published as *Nehru's Mantle: The Politics of Succession in India*, both 1966.)

Findings on Succession to Nehru (1964)

Several themes are evident from an inquiry into the six-day struggle for succession to Nehru. The *first* was *Morarji Desai's haste in declaring his availability for the office of Prime Minister*, in violation of a cardinal informal rule of India's political system.

More important were the *contrasting strategies* of the *Shastri and Morarji camps*: the former relied heavily on the organizational wing of the

Congress Party and lobbied quietly; the latter sought support in the CPP and pressed the case for an unfettered secret election by the CPP—and pursued these aims with conspicuous vigor. A closely related theme in the process was the *abortive struggle between the CPP Executive* and the *Congress Working Committee*, representing the two long-competing wings of the Party, for the right to play the decisive role.

A third finding relates to the *strategy of the Left*, moving in haste from an alignment with Morarji, a long-established leader of the Congress Party's Right Wing to the more comfortable position of supporting Nehru's daughter, *Indira Gandhi*, and then *Gulzari Lal Nanda*, all in an effort to block Shastri's path. Even more opportunistic was the *strategy of Jagjivan Ram*, first in backing his former rival, Morarji, then in throwing his weight behind Mrs. Gandhi, and finally proclaiming himself a candidate. There was, too, *Nanda's contradictory behavior*, a seeming disinterest in the post of Prime Minister, which only thinly concealed an eagerness for the prize: if there was any strategy at all, it was in creating the appearance of an active Head of Government and, second, offering to serve as a compromise candidate in order to break the impasse and maintain party unity. Only Mrs. Gandhi's role was somewhat obscured by personal tragedy and the utterly passive nature of her involvement in the succesion process, apart from indicating her support for the continuation of the interim arrangement, that is, Nanda as Prime Minister. Was that out of conviction, ideological or other, or was it, as some suggested, part of a strategy to succeed her father a few months later? Her goal remained unclear.

An academic's inquiry also revealed the operation of *basic forces* in the *Indian polity*. One was *Regionalism*, as expressed in the composition of the *Syndicate* (*Caucus*): it was a coalition of South, East, and West, the non-Hindi-speaking coastal regions of India. Another, closely related force may be termed *State Autonomism* and Parochialism. There were various forms in which this was manifested. Most important was the pivotal position of the *State Congress Party machine* in the all-India configuration of political power. Regarding the first succession, its impact was twofold: first, the individual role of State Chief Ministers in shaping the decision of the Grand Council of the Republic, as invitees to the enlarged Congress Working Committee meeting on 31 May 1964, and second, the influence of State chiefs deriving from their known control over blocs of votes in the CPP. State loyalty as a criterion of political action was apparent in at least two major developments: *Maharashtra*'s antipathy to Morarji for the events of 1956 which, apart from any other consideration, would have denied this large bloc to the Gujarati leader; and the reported revolt of members of *C.B. Gupta*'s faction in *Uttar Pradesh*, rejecting his support for Morarji against a 'local son', Shastri. The latter may not have been in their faction, but the historic primacy of Uttar Pradesh's influence in the Congress, as well as in the Union Government, with all the patronage and pride that this entailed—all this, they thought mistakenly, would be better safeguarded with Shastri than Morarji, an outsider.

Factionalism is another basic force in India's political system, at all levels. Closely linked to this is the interpenetration of *personal and group rivalries in State and Union politics*. Illustrative was the split in the *Bihar* State Congress, the *Sahay* faction backing Shastri, and the *Jha* faction, Morarji; so too in Uttar Pradesh, with Gupta supporting Morarji, and Tripathi backing Shastri; and in *Madhya Pradesh* as well. A curious result of this linkage between the two levels of politics, as noted earlier, was the dilemma confronting *Malaviyya*, a self-conscious leftist, under pressure from left-wing legislators in *Bihar*, whose faction in the State Party was befriended by Morarji.

The interplay of *differentiated* and *specific interest groups* in the struggle for the succession was another notable feature of the process. There were *institutional interest groups* at work, such as the *All-India Congress Working Committee*, the *CPP Executive*, and the *Pradesh (State) Congress Committee* leadership. There were also *associational interest groups*, more or less well organized for political activity: the caste type (*Untouchables*, supporting *Jagjivan Ram*); communal (*Muslims*); MPs from each State, who met as a distinct interest group; and factional groups within the State Congress leadership and their extensions to the State parliamentarians. *Occupational interest groups*, labor or entrepreneur, do not appear to have played a role in the process as such, though moneyed interests, especially in Bombay and Gujarat, reportedly invested substantial sums in the outcome.

The outstanding *non-associational interest group* in the process, in fact, the newest in the political system, was the *Caucus* or *Syndicate*, really a committee of Chief Ministers and their allies at the Center. Another was the ideological Left. And the press and pundits acted throughout as a cohesive interest group in the background and during the six days supporting Shastri as the most suitable man to succeed Nehru.

There are other facets of the process which merit attention. One is the *attitude of Nehru to the succession* and the related issue of *his preference*, if any. Another is the *reasons for the choice of Shastri* among the politicians and the populace. A third is the explanation of *Morarji's behavior*, especially his withdrawal from the contest. There is also the intriguing question of *the Army's role* in the brief interregnum. More important is the part played by the *Syndicate* in the decision. One must examine as well the *reasons for a tranquil succession*. And, finally, there is the issue of *constitutionality*.

The attitude of India's charismatic leader to the perennial question, 'after Nehru, who?', was steadfast to the end: he resisted all pressures to name a successor or even to train a group to ensure the continuity of his policies. Those who bore him animus merely trotted out the familiar, 'après moi, le déluge'. But the reasons were much deeper, as one would expect from a character as complex as Nehru. First was a genuine belief in the democratic ethic. Second, and closely linked to this, was his profound faith in the ability of India's political system to meet the test of an orderly succession. Not only did he not consider it his task to arrange continuity; the attempt to do so might cause irreparable harm to the fabric of constitutional democracy—and this was a cherished value in his vision of India. No less germane was a tendency to denigrate the role of a future leader, the product of two strands in his makeup: the Marxist residue in his philosophy led him to attribute change and progress primarily to the 'masses', not the élite; and his own experience gave him the comforting assurance that he had laid the foundations for modernity and secularism; these he considered irrevocable. This became apparent as early as 1956, when he remarked about the future: 'All this trains, educates people, makes them think in a particular way and drives all of them forward in a particular direction. Now, some of them [successors] may stop the pace, not going in that direction or they may make it faster. But I don't think it is possible in the future for the mass of the people to be taken away, far away, from their moorings' (MB Interview with Nehru, March 1956).

While Nehru's views on his successor remained open to question, those of Shastri's peers did not. They discerned five distinct *assets* in *his political and personal makeup: first*, he came from the Hindi-speaking heartland, *Uttar Pradesh*, like Nehru, and, at that time, it was inconceivable that anyone from a non-Hindi-speaking area could be Prime Minister; *second*, his *political reputation* was *unblemished* and he had no known enemies; *third*, he had *vast administrative and organizational experience*, having held an array of elective positions in the Party and the Government, from that of Secretary of the Allahabad Congress Committee to Union Home Minister; *fourth*, he was *a centrist* by ideological conviction and temperament, a conciliator and a man with an open mind, who would not split the

Congress or the country; and, *finally*, he combined the *qualities of ability and genuine humility, with a natural ambition* effectively concealed by *gentility*.

Perhaps the most striking characteristic of the first succession contest was its smoothness. On the surface, this may be explained by Congress President Kamaraj's skillful direction of the enterprise and the Syndicate's sense of purpose. But there are more basic factors to be noted. First, *decision by consensus* was not new to the Congress tradition; in fact, it was an established part of Congress decision-making. Voting was virtually unknown in the proceedings of its Working Committee, and while a formal ballot was taken at meetings of the larger All-India Congress Committee, the result was invariably unanimous for the record, after divergent views had been aired. Second, the appearance of unanimity, smoothly reached, was an admirable instrument for the perpetuation of Congress power. There was, too, *a deep concern about external opinion* and a genuine desire to demonstrate maturity in handling a potential domestic political crisis. But most important was the *pragmatic outlook* of almost all members of the Congress élite. All were formally committed to Socialism, yet they mean different things, and few understand the term or its implications. And the ideological component in their behavior was minimal. They were adaptable to the powerful currents carried by India's interest groups; none was highly motivated ideologically. As Prime Minister Shastri later remarked, '[T]here are no ideological differences between the factions, they are all personal; therefore, there are no compelling factors to lead to an open split.' Thus, it was relatively easy to close ranks once the man with a clear majority was known. In this particular process, the actors, the managers, and the electorate (CPP) were conspicuously free from the divisive force of ideology. In the largest sense, a great polyglot party flushed out its groups, who contested maturely for the prize of office; it was a good omen for the future political stability of India.

As for the issue of *constitutionality*, the forms were meticulously maintained. Within two hours of Nehru's death, the President of India swore in the ranking member of the Cabinet as Acting Prime Minister. On 2 June, the CPP elected a new Leader, and the same day he was invited to form a government. This government was duly sworn in on 9 June. Constitutional propriety was maintained throughout. Moreover, the procedure of election and the involvement of the Congress President were in order.

Succession to Shastri (1966)

The forces that shaped the outcome of India's second succession contest (1966) were not identical to those responsible for the Shastri consensus, though they were strikingly similar in terms of institutional interests. To use a lock metaphor, the *succession to Shastri may be likened to a safe with a complex combination*: the head of the Congress Party at the Center (Kamaraj), plus 12 of the 14 Congress Chief Ministers, plus (reluctant) support by the Syndicate, plus an overwhelming majority in the CPP, plus a compulsion to keep Morarji out, plus concern about the 1967 general elections. Only *Mrs. Gandhi fit that combination in 1966*, and Kamaraj knew its composition. Stated in different terms, Mrs. Gandhi was the key to the second succession, and Kamaraj deftly unlocked the door. It was a brilliant feat of political management.

As in the first succession contest, there was a sophisticated interplay of *institutional interest groups*, notably the All-India Congress Party Working Committee, the Chief Ministers' club, and the CPP Executive. But *associational interest groups* were marginal, except for factions: organized and communal groups played no role. The second succession was managed by a few people, but they represented powerful forces in the Indian polity—region, state, and party organizations.

As for the behavior of the main actors in the second succession: the principal player was Congress President Kamaraj, whose dexterity and skill in manipulating others in the game command respect. Yet his strategy remained obscure during the first five days. To accomplish this it was necessary to persuade or cajole other power centers in the Party.

First and foremost was the Syndicate, whose influence flowed from control over a substantial bloc of votes and the prestige acquired in the management of the first succession. Kamaraj knew of its disunity on all possible candidates. Instead of applying the tactic of direct assault, he resorted to encirclement, using the Chief Ministers' club as his instrument.

Morarji Desai's behavior in the early days was a mixture of caution and disdain for the political game. Indeed, he revealed a desire for the crown but no strategy to achieve it.

Mrs. Gandhi's strategy, too, can be deduced from deeds and words. This time, she was keen from the beginning of the game and saw no reason why she should not be Prime Minister. As one member of the Grand Council observed, in her view, only the Nehrus are fit to govern India. Yet a shrewd political instinct led to caution: she did not push herself forward and never formally declared her candidacy. She did not canvass for votes or even for support in the power centers of decision. She entered the contest only four days after the game began.

The behavior of *Chavan*, former Chief Minister of Maharashtra and then Defense Minister, was similar to that of Mrs. Gandhi: he was keen but cautious—and was never an active player in the game.

Nanda's strategy was simple: to maintain the *status quo*, for continuity would assist his claim to the succession. However, his lack of popularity at all levels of politics and the widespread view that he would lose to Morarji in a secret ballot dislodged him from the succession game.

Two Succession Games: A Comparison; Nehru's Mantle: The Politics of Succession in India *(1966)*

Viewed in terms of political dynamics, the succession to Nehru—and Shastri—may be likened to games. Both in 1964 and in 1966 there appeared to be a multiple choice, but in reality there were only two players: Morarji Desai and the anti-Morarji Coalition; the role of all other individual actors must be seen as impinging upon, deflecting, blurring, and crystallizing the two real constants in the game. Yet *the decision process differed in India's experience of political change at the summit.*

The proper designation of the 1964 game is 'Morarji vs. a United Front'; in 1966, it was 'Morarji vs. the Pack'. This contrast derives from the different setting in which the games were played and highlights revealing differences in play-acting and decision-making by political leaders. It was the psychological atmosphere and the manner in which the object of play—the Prime Ministership—became accessible that explains the change in environment and actions of the political players.

Long before Nehru died, the Congress Party élite had pondered the issue of succession with concern and disquiet. The gradual decline in vigor and health of India's charismatic leader had the political compensation, however, that steps could be taken to fill the vacuum, if not directly by him, then by careful planning by party leaders. And those preparations were made, with skill and finesse, from October 1963 onward: a powerful coalition came into being, the Syndicate, headed by Kamaraj, and with it an agreed choice, Shastri.

In perspective, Shastri was the partial recipient of Nehru's mantle. Thus, a combination of fear of the collapse of the political system, widely shared and genuinely felt, time to prepare the ground, a coalition to direct the play, a pre-eminent player, and the perceived charismatic leader's approval determined the flow of events, the character, and the outcome of the game.

How different was the setting of the second succession contest, only 19 months later. Fear had given way to self-confidence because India's political system had demonstrated ability of a high order in filling the void caused by Nehru's passing. Nor were the 'eyes of the world' upon the political leaders, partly because of preoccupations elsewhere, notably the *coup* in Nigeria, partly because the death of Nehru was viewed as the end of an era and that of Shastri was not, and partly because of the precedent of stability in 1964. There was, then, no sense of urgency or uncertainty in filling the vacuum. The suddenness of Shastri's death was a further variable, for little if any thought had been given to 'after Shastri, who?' and no preparations had been made for this contingency. Apart from the lack of time, the coalition of 1964 had eroded. Finally, the successor to Nehru had not lived long enough to transmit, by word or deed, his mantle to any other political leader, for he was too busy establishing his own claim to primacy.

The result was a *change in the set of rules* and in the *decision process*, though the players were identical, except for the departure of Shastri. In the first game, there was one smooth and relatively frictionless phase of decision-making between Wednesday afternoon, 27 May 1964, when Nehru died, and Sunday morning, the 31st, when the Grand Council accepted the consensus principle, leaving the decision, in effect, to Kamaraj and the Caucus/Syndicate. Morarji challenged the united front briefly, but he displayed self-imposed restraint, both on Sunday morning and again on the following evening when he yielded to the Congress President's judgment of the consensus.

In the second game, two phases were evident. The first was a struggle of wills among the anti-Morarji forces. The second phase took the form of an open contest between Morarji and the Coalition, pragmatically united behind Mrs. Gandhi, from 16 to 19 January 1966. It was the 'struggle of wills' and the 'open contest' which explains the difference in the *duration* of the games, three and a half days in the first, almost nine days in the second succession process.

Decision-making in the two games can also be compared in terms of the power centers through which the decision had to pass before it was consummated. In 1964, there were only two 'circles of decision'. The core group was the Syndicate, including Kamaraj, which had made its choice before the game began. In 1966, the process was much more complex and difficult. Four 'circles of decision' can be discerned. The core was *Kamaraj* himself, with a clear and firm choice, though he may have wavered in the direction of *Chavan* when unanimity still seemed possible. The second circle was the disunited *Syndicate* which could not agree on any candidate and did so only when faced with a *fait accompli*. The third power group was the *Chief Ministers' club* which, partly on its own and partly under Kamaraj's gentle prodding, played an autonomous role in the process. And finally, the *CPP* had to be convinced in a secret ballot. In size, these four circles followed an ascending order, 1, 4, 12, and 526 members.

Some reflections on the *forces* at work in the two games merit attention. As noted earlier, several enduring forces in Indian politics were manifested in 1964: Regionalism, State Parochialism, Caste Identity, and Factionalism. To what extent were these evident in 1966?

Regionalism was certainly displayed in the attitudes of a number of players.

State attachments were no less apparent in the calculations of the four power centers of decision.

Caste plays a major role in State and local politics but is marginal at the all-India level; there is no evidence that it operated in either succession contest, except insofar as it was intertwined with Factionalism, which was present in both.

There were several differences between the two succession games. To begin with, Shastri was the pre-eminent candidate in 1964, whereas Indira Gandhi *emerged* from a process of elimination in 1966. Mrs. Gandhi owed her triumph to three persons: Kamaraj, for superb management of the game; her father, for providing the name and mantle; and Morarji, for pressing the issue to a secret ballot.

The role of the Syndicate declined in the interim between the two successions. In essence, the myth of its power was drastically undermined, if not shattered, by the events of mid-January 1966. Erosion of its members' influence had already taken place during Shastri's brief tenure of office. And their inability to block Mrs. Gandhi and, even more, their disunity during the crucial game dramatized their decline in the attentive public view.

Kamaraj was the principal figure in both successions, but the second was infinitely more complex: there was no pre-eminent candidate; the Syndicate opposed his choice, and consensus had given way to contest.

Thus the Congress President's achievement as 'kingmaker' (or 'queenmaker') was of a higher order. His success in the second game was partly due to the sustained cooperation of the Chief Ministers, whose role was far more conspicuous than in 1964. Indeed, they replaced the Syndicate as the Congress President's principal pillar of support. More important, the role of the State leaders confirmed and strengthened the trend to decentralization of power in the Indian Union, vividly demonstrated in decision-making over *food* and *language policy* at the time.

A curious feature of the 1966 succession was the *inconsequential role of the Congress organizational leaders in the States*; rather, it was the *State governmental leaders* who occupied the center of the stage.

Another difference between the two successions was the *role of the CPP*: in 1964, it was a mere rubber stamp for a decision reached by the Party's Working Committee; in 1966, it exercised the franchise in a secret ballot. For three days, it was the principal object of attention, as both camps canvassed furiously for support.

Stated in other terms, the second succession game legitimized decision-making by overt intra-Party conflict. This, too, was Morarji's contribution to the developing pattern of Indian politics.

The Military played no role whatsoever in 1966. Nor was there any talk or rumor of its involvement, as there was in 1964. There was also no organized conclave of Muslim MPs, and the role of the Left was less vocal than in the first game.

A final noteworthy comparison was the set of criteria applied by the actors in assessing the qualifications of the different candidates. Shastri was chosen partly because of Party interests—he was considered the leader most likely to unify and strengthen the Congress, but much thought was also given to 'national interests'—who would serve India most effectively in a time of trouble. In 1966, however, the latter consideration was *never* raised, except by Morarji; not once was it mentioned in any interviews and discussions with members of the Coalition. The only concerns appeared to be 'to beat Morarji' and 'to win the 1967 general election'. In that sense, the second succession contest was much more a Party affair.

The *similarities in the two successions* were fewer in number, but they are no less important. One was *tranquility*, which indicated *an instinctive and intellectual grasp of the rules of the Congress game*. It was the mythology and tradition of 'Mother Congress' that provided both the ballast for a tranquil process and the framework for peaceful competition among and within the key interest groups—the Working Committee, the Chief

Ministers' club, the CPP, and the Syndicate—with a commitment by all not to destroy the symbol or the substance of unity. Another similarity was *maturity* and *resilience*, accentuated in the second succession game by the contrasting method of political change at the summit in India's counterpart in Africa—a *coup* in Nigeria.

In both successions, too, *constitutional propriety* was demonstrated. The President filled the vacuum within hours and later appointed as Prime Minister the person elected as Leader of the CPP, though the election was unanimous in the first and contested in the second. Finally, the Congress élite managed both processes; they were largely leadership decisions, but the leaders spoke for large and well-defined constituencies.

In sum, *half a dozen conclusions* emerge from this comparative analysis of succession games and the Indian political system. *First*, the *effective duration* of a succession game in India is about 72 hours. Whatever the date fixed for completion of the game, that is, the secret ballot in the CPP, the *play was confined to three days*; beyond that the 'rules of the game' would be broken or distorted. *Second*, in an intra-Congress game over succession, *the value of party survival overrides personal ends*; the bargaining process is sophisticated and never exceeds the bounds of party interests. *Third, the party president performs vital functions*: moderating influence, good offices, mediation, and pivot of the communication network. Other things being equal, he predisposes the game to a consensus outcome. *Fourth, political change at the summit of the Congress Party was routinized in India*; future succession games, if centered on the Congress, would follow the paths set by the first two and lead to acceptable outcomes to ensure continued stability. *Fifth, the all-India segment of the Indian political system is stable, mature, sophisticated, and resilient*. Its survival potential is high, in the absence of overwhelming disturbance of the system from outside, notably massive invasion or unremitting economic crisis. *Finally*, the successions in 1964 and 1966 exhibited *an impressive democratic process*, conducted in full public view, domestic and foreign, with no qualms about revealing the lobbying and bargaining throughout.

This was evident in the extraordinary candor displayed by all of the major participants in the two succession games. As one member of the Syndicate, West Bengal's Congress leader, *Atulya Ghosh*, exulted immediately after the (second) succession—to Shastri: 'Last time we did it by consensus because of our inferiority complex. The British and American newspapers had cried so long, "after Nehru, who?" and so we yielded to it. There is no need of this any longer. We are politically mature' (MB

Interview with Ghosh, January 1966). It was clear 50 years ago that *India's political system was as stable and mature as any democracy in the world.*

Nehru as a Political Leader: Final Assessment (November 1989)[1]

Three decades had passed since I presented an initial appraisal of Nehru's political leadership—in my 1959 political biography. He was then approaching 70, and I was a young scholar [34] on a long voyage of discovery.

As noted in that early assessment, one of Nehru's *weaknesses as a political leader* was that the gap between words and deeds was often wide. That *gap between rhetoric and action*, in marked contrast with the other charismatic leader encountered during this intellectual odyssey, Israel's Ben-Gurion [see below], revealed something even more profound about Nehru—a tendency to shrink from radical deeds. In Nehru's case, this trait was partly because of the basic liberal makeup of the man, compared with Israel's much less tolerant founding figure, and partly because of the experience of awesome violence and disorder attending India's Partition in 1947. In short, Nehru was an indecisive leader, and Ben-Gurion, the epitome of decisiveness.

Perhaps Nehru's *most notable accomplishment* was the creation of a secular state. To Indian Muslims, he was a rock and a shield, in sharp contrast to Ben-Gurion's indifference to the social, economic, and educational welfare of Israel's large Palestinian Arab minority, approximately 20% of Israel's population.

As for Nehru's influence in the domain of foreign policy, I termed him the philosopher, the architect, the engineer, and the voice of his country's policy toward the outside world. In this domain, too, there was a marked contrast between Nehru and Ben-Gurion. Israel's charismatic leader had to share primacy in the conduct of foreign policy by the *yishuv* [Jewish community in Palestine] during the 15 years preceding statehood (1933–48) with Moshe Sharett, his appointed Head of the Political Department of the Jewish Agency for Palestine, and during the first eight years of independence, with their sharply competing perceptions and policy preferences toward Zionism's and, later, Israel's principal adversary, the Palestinians. Moreover, Ben-Gurion did not match Nehru's unchallenged leadership in India until the end of his life; he was ousted from the pinnacle of power in Israel's political system—Prime Minister and Defense

Minister—seven years after he had compelled the resignation in 1956 of his primary political colleague for more than two decades, including eight years as Foreign Minister (to be elaborated below).

Nehru's outstanding and enduring achievement in foreign policy was to provide leadership in the political awakening of Asia after centuries of colonial rule. And he was the most articulate spokesman for this urge to reassert Asia's important place in the global system. It was crowned at the historic Afro-Asian Conference in Bandung, Indonesia, in 1955, the forerunner of the Non-Aligned Movement. In the largest sense, Nehru spoke for a large part of the Afro-Asian world, as one of the few voices of sanity in a world of cold war and ideological conflict between East and West. For many, his was a genuine voice of peace, notwithstanding his one lapse, his forced annexation of Portugal's tiny but longstanding colonial territory, notably, Goa, in 1961.

In that respect, his peace-oriented counterpart among Israel's political leaders was the second-ranking figure in the then pre-eminent political party, *Mapai*, Israel's Labor Party, during most of the first three decades of independence, not Ben-Gurion: Moshe Sharett was the genuine *voice of peace* throughout his tenure as *de facto* Foreign Minister of the Jewish community aspiring to statehood, from 1933 to 1948, and as Foreign Minister of Israel from 1948 to 1956, including a brief period as Prime Minister (1953–55). Ben-Gurion, by contrast, was the voice of *violence* as the path to achievement of a viable peace with the Palestinians.

Moreover, Nehru was completely lacking in ruthlessness, another fundamental difference between the two charismatic leaders, Nehru and Ben-Gurion. Ever the quintessential democrat, Nehru had a compulsion for universal consent, partly due to an instinctive playing to the gallery, a desire to please the crowd, the ultimate basis of his political power. Nehru also revealed, before and after independence, a tendency to yield to pressure. Moreover, he was a bad judge of character. Loyalty to old colleagues often outweighed sound judgment. In all of these dimensions of effective political leadership, Ben-Gurion's record was conspicuously superior to his Indian counterpart.[2]

Notwithstanding these shortcomings, my assessment in 1959 was that, while this litany of failings seemed formidable, they were the *weaknesses of a giant*. Nehru was India's unifier at a time of great stress, during the ghastly riots and killings which accompanied the transfer of power to India and Pakistan in 1947. He laid the foundations of a genuine parliamentary democracy. He fashioned the machinery for planning and instilled the idea that therein laid the path to material progress and national power. He emphasized the significance of individual rights, as expressed in the new Indian constitution. He secured widespread acceptance of the ideal of a secular state. He restored India's faith in itself and its place in the international system. And he had begun the arduous task of social change. Overall, Nehru had set in motion forces for long-term social, economic, and political change. In sum, Nehru had fashioned the elements out of which a new India could emerge. It was too early to be certain about the outcome, for the process of change had barely begun during the first 12 years of independence (1947–59).

During Nehru's twilight years and, especially, when he died in May 1964, many political leaders and attentive publics in democratic states had profound misgivings about India's democracy in his absence. The magnitude of India's internal pressures and centrifugal tendencies, the narrowness of its democratic infrastructure, and Nehru's diminished status following the debacle with China less than two years before his passing created grave fears about the future of Indian politics.[3] However, as noted above, the Congress Party élite demonstrated impressive ability in achieving a smooth political succession in 1964 and again in 1966, when Nehru's successor, Shastri, died, without shattering the democratic political system and its rules of behavior. There was extensive bargaining and lobbying, but no coup or cabal. The two successions, I wrote at the time, augured well for the future of Nehru's political legacy.[4]

Did an appraisal of 1959 require change in the light of the last five years of Nehru's leadership (1959–64) and the half century of the post-Nehru era, and if so, how?

The shifting sands of time and the evidence uncovered by later works on modern Indian history have not altered the essence of my interim assessment of Nehru's contributions to India's struggle for independence.[5] It remains true that he was the indispensable link between Gandhi's backward-looking traditionalism and the modern, future-oriented outlook of the new Indian intelligentsia whom he mobilized to active service in the Congress cause. He was, too, the voice—and *conscience*—of the *Indian nationalist movement* in the conflict of the 1930s and beyond between liberal and progressive forces, on the one hand, and the Nazi-Fascist alliance, on the other. As the leader of the left-nationalists—within and outside Congress—he was, as noted, the hope for *land reform* among India's peasants, awakened by Gandhi but eager for material change after centuries of oppression by an entrenched landed gentry. He was, as well, the *catalyst to pre-independence thought about economic planning*, through the National Planning Committee of the Congress in 1938–39. Among the nationalist leaders of his generation, he was the *most committed to a political system based upon universal participation in the political process through free elections at all levels of government*. And in that system, he was determined to enshrine the *array of individual rights* of classic liberalism. Through these roles Nehru made a crucial contribution, second only to Gandhi, to the attainment of independence. No less important, they created the foundations of the Republic of India.

Nehru's legacy was even more striking in the domain of *political institutions*. While others, notably Ambedkar, drafted the new, impressive Constitution of the Republic, cumbersome and complex as it is, Nehru profoundly influenced its philosophy and thrust in the deliberations of the Constituent Assembly.

More important, the Indian National Congress, transformed by Gandhi into a mass party from 1920 to 1947, became, in the Nehru era, the *primary instrument of political stability, national unity, and institutional continuity*. From 1951, when, in the aftermath of Patel's death, Nehru achieved effective control of the party machine, until 1964, he shaped the Congress to win all national and most state elections and to mobilize mass support for the new modernizing policies of economic planning, industrialization, limited land reform and social change, the reorganization of the states along linguistic lines, and the enlargement of the domain of science, through the creation of advanced institutes of technology and a critical mass of scientists in atomic energy and related fields.[6] Congress *Raj* continued for 25 years after his death, following a brief interlude of opposition (1977–80), though its image was tarnished by his daughter's experiment in authoritarian rule (1975–77) and the decline of values, efficiency, élan, and achievements under his grandson's tenure in the late 1980s.

In that context, an erroneous interpretation of the political successions to Nehru and Shastri as Congress leaders in the 1960s fostered the myth that Nehru and not, in reality, Indira Gandhi, strove to establish a political dynasty in India. The attitude of independent India's charismatic leader to the perennial question, 'after Nehru, who?', was steadfast to the end: *he resisted all pressures to name a successor to ensure the continuity of his policies*. There were several reasons. First was a genuine belief in the democratic ethic. Second, and closely linked, was his profound faith in the ability of India's political system to meet the test of an orderly succession. Not only was it not his task to arrange continuity, the attempt to do so might cause irreparable harm to the fabric of constitutional democracy, and this was a cherished value in his vision of India. And third, as he declared just a month before his death, to nominate someone would be the surest way of his not becoming Prime Minister, for it would arouse jealousy and envy. Events justified Nehru's assessment and his calculated risk.

He probably had the temptation of a father to see his daughter in a prominent position of responsibility. But he had a strong aversion to the idea of a dynasty which, he knew, in any case, would have been widely resented. Nehru's role in the 1964 succession contest, self-perceived and possibly consciously performed as well, was to ease the transition and tranquilize the process by casting symbolic approval on the choice, by bringing Shastri back into the Cabinet soon after he became incapacitated: it was not enough to foreclose the political game but sufficient to shape its character. In perspective, Shastri was the partial recipient of Nehru's mantle.

When, 19 months later, Shastri died in office, the Congress leaders chose Indira Gandhi, Nehru's daughter, as his successor because of a well-considered political calculus. Against her shortcomings—administrative inexperience, access to the Left, haughtiness, youth, the appearance of frailty, and independence—her assets were impressive: wide popular appeal, enhanced by the Nehru connection, the best possible public image of the Congress in the forthcoming general election, heightened by her association with Uttar Pradesh, the largest state in India. Unlike her father, once in power, Mrs. Gandhi consciously sought to create a dynasty, at first through her younger son, Sanjay, and, when an air crash intervened, via Rajiv, who succeeded her in 1984. In sum, the party chose Shastri to succeed Nehru, and Mrs. Gandhi to succeed Shastri, while she ensured her son's succession.[7]

An *independent judiciary*, too, was fostered by Nehru. And the basic freedoms of a modern democratic society—of speech, faith, assembly, organization, and so on—were, in large measure, protected by the Indian courts, except in the days of the 'Emergency' (1975–77). Certainly they had a high value in the Nehru era, though even then the implementation of individual rights was not without blemish. There was, too, frequent resort to 'President's Rule' by the Center over a State, sometimes for reasons other than good government; and this occurred under Nehru, as well as under his successors.

Overall, the record of parliamentary democracy in India since 1947 has been impressive, except for the brief lapse of the 'Emergency', when Nehru's daughter betrayed his trust by trampling on one of his highest values. (Even in the darkest days of India's China debacle in November 1962, Nehru did not undermine the authority of Parliament; on the contrary, he used it to mobilize national resistance when India's territorial integrity was in peril.)

It is true that the political institutions of the Republic of India had deep roots in the British *Raj*, certainly since the Reforms of 1919. But that legacy was near-universal among British colonies, from neighboring Pakistan to distant Guyana, from nearby Burma to far-off Rhodesia. And in most of the new states which emerged from British rule, democracy faltered or languished—or was replaced for lengthy periods by an authoritarian regime, military or civilian. India was the great exception, certainly the *most notable case of almost unbroken, genuine democracy in the post-colonial Third World.*[8]

While many factors help to explain this achievement, *Nehru's commitment* to *free elections, parliamentary control over the executive, an independent judiciary, and individual rights* was crucial to the flourishing of democracy, despite periodic crises and wars, economic dislocations, and ethnic, religious, regional, and caste strife during the Nehru era and after. Not that he was unaware of an authoritarian strain in his personality:

'Men like Jawaharlal ... are unsafe in a democracy,' he wrote about himself anonymously in 1937, as noted above. 'He calls himself a democrat and a socialist, and no doubt he does so in all earnestness ... but a little twist and he might turn into a dictator...he has all the makings of a dictator in him — vast strong will, allergy, pride ... and with all his love of the crowd, an intolerance of others and a certain contempt for the weak and inefficient. His overwhelming desire to get things done ... will hardly brook for long the slow processes of democracy.'[9]

Perhaps because of this self-insight or a belief that others so perceived him, perhaps because he sensed that democracy was a delicate plant that needed to be nourished, he did so throughout his tenure as Prime Minister. Even after the deterioration in his health, from 1961 onward, and especially after 1963, he displayed his unswerving respect for Parliament by being actively present at least for the Question Hour whenever possible. And, despite the comfortable Congress majority in both Houses at that time, he listened to the views expressed by Opposition MPs: it was a conscious attempt to make the legislative process by elected members and the institution of Parliament sacrosanct. Although no political system is invulnerable, the judgment from the perspective of the half century since his passing must be that Nehru's efforts to enshrine parliamentary democracy in India were exceptionally successful.

In the domain of *economic development*, Nehru's legacy was no less enduring. It was he who shaped the model for industry, science, and technology, on the basis of India's reality at the time of independence—mass poverty, underdevelopment, and military weakness, along with India's potential for great power status. The goals were, therefore, higher living standards and rapid industrialization. As Nayar observed: 'Quite dramatically in contrast to Gandhi, Nehru stood for an industrial society, a strong central government, economic planning and socialism, with an accompanying distrust of private business, aversion to capitalism and abhorrence of the profit motive together with emphatic support for an expanding public sector. For Nehru, socialism encompassed all that was good and desirable.'[10] Moreover, he was acutely conscious of the link between economic strategy, especially the creation of a heavy industry base, and the ensuring of political independence. Time and time again he declared: '[I]t is essential for our strength, for our military strength ... to have an industrial base. I say you cannot even remain free in India without an industrial base.'[11]

The entire thrust of economic planning in India must be credited to Nehru, for he presided over and infused the first three Five-Year Plans from 1951 to 1965. While Indian planning changed direction and its centrality significantly declined under his successors, the Nehru-instilled idea of planning as essential to economic growth and economic independence remained a permanent feature of India's public policy during the first 25 years after his death.[12] And the achievement of the decade of planning under Nehru was impressive—an annual growth rate in industrial production of 7% during the Second Plan, 42% from 1956 to 1960, and almost 8% annually in the Third Plan.

Closely related was Nehru's successful infusion of the *scientific spirit* into the consciousness of India's élites. His own belief in the importance of science dates back to his Cambridge student period. And from the mid-1930s onward, he urged his Congress colleagues and others to recognize the central role of science in modernization. In this he was assisted, during the early years of independence, by a trio of distinguished Indian scientists: S.S. Bhatnagar, a chemist; H.J. Bhabha, a nuclear physicist; and P.C. Mahalonobis, a statistician. From their combined efforts, India was to develop one of the largest reservoirs of qualified scientists and engineers in the world, a critical component in the continuing surge to economic development.[13]

There were *serious shortcomings in the socio-economic domain*: despite his logical and emotional commitment to egalitarianism, basic land reform, and communal harmony, performance did not always measure up to aspiration. The first was a chimera, far beyond the capacity of any democratic leader in the short time allotted to a Prime Minister of India confronting the cumulative legacy and hard shell of structural inequality in Indian society. Moreover, Nehru's failure to achieve the goal of a transformation in agrarian relations is not surprising: this was foredoomed by his higher commitment to non-violent, democratic means to achieve social and economic change. Nothing short of drastic, sustained authoritarian methods, including mass arrests, executions, and exile, as practiced by Stalin in the 1930s and Mao in the 1950s, could have attained Nehru's goals in this domain—and *he placed a higher value on consensual means than on revolutionary ends*. Thus his persistent verbal assault on an encrusted, antiquated, entrenched system of land relations, with tens of millions of landless laborers, did not lead to substantive land reform in the Nehru era, a fate shared by Egyptian peasants in Nasser's Egypt in the 1950s and 1960s and, indeed, in most Third World states after independence. A revolutionary leader might have accomplished this in India, as Stalin and Mao did in the Soviet Union and China—but at an enormous price in terms of curtailed, in fact, extinguished individual freedom and civil rights. *Nehru was not prepared to pay that price: Gandhi's admonition on means and ends held sway. Nehru was a reformer, not a revolutionary leader.*[14]

In terms of the long-term Nehru legacy, this failure was even more glaring because none of his successors—Shastri, Indira Gandhi, Morarji Desai, Rajiv Gandhi—placed land reform or the broader social goal of egalitarianism high on their political agenda, though Nehru's daughter paid lip service to these ideals, in her populist election slogan, 'remove poverty, remove unemployment'; and her son, Rajiv, revived the slogan in 1988. Thus, India's system of agrarian relations was no more progressive 25 years after Nehru's death than it was in 1964 and very little more so than in the days of the British *Raj*.

There were *political shortcomings*, too, with a continuing legacy to the present: Nehru's failure to solve the persistent Punjab problem at the time of states reorganization in the mid-1950s and beyond, in order to satisfy Sikh aspirations without undermining the territorial integrity of India; the inability to meet the demands of tribal minorities on India's peripheries, in Nagaland, Tripura, and elsewhere; and a compromise over the national language issue which satisfied neither Hindi nor non-Hindi advocates. However, this negative legacy was hardly of the order of the positive Nehru legacy in the political domain—national unity amid regional fissures, political stability, and sustained economic growth.

Nehru's achievements in foreign policy were more dramatic but less enduring. As noted, he was a founding father of the Non-Aligned Movement, through his pivotal role at the Delhi conferences in the late 1940s and Bandung in 1955. Acting through Krishna Menon, he was a visible and successful mediator in the Korean War and the first Vietnam War. He was the role model for many leaders of new states in Asia and Africa. He was a voice of reason in support of arms control and non-violent conflict resolution throughout the Cold War, though his credibility in this respect was diminished by his use of force to expel the Portuguese from Goa in 1961 and, in the view of some, by a willingness to use force in order to assert India's claims in the territorial dispute with China. Nehru was also the catalyst to the transformation of the British Empire into a club of formal equals by his magnanimous decision to retain India's association with the former colonial power, even with the British monarch as symbolic Head of the Commonwealth. And he was able to forge and sustain a profitable national interest relationship with the Soviet Union, reflected in long-term military and economic assistance and, where necessary, as in the Kashmir dispute and, to a lesser extent, in the conflict with China, valuable diplomatic support. Indeed, Indo-Soviet friendship was probably the most substantive enduring legacy of Nehru's foreign policy.

Much of the halo surrounding Nehru's role in world politics vanished with the 1962 China debacle. (*Inter alia*, this shattered the *Panch Sheel*, the Five Principles of Peaceful Coexistence, which Nehru considered his most important contribution to world order.) It would have declined steadily in any event as the superpowers moved from Cold War confrontation to détente following the Cuban Missile Crisis; that is, the changing structure of world politics—from tight bipolarity to bipolycentrism—made India's non-alignment and Nehru's mediation role less relevant to East-West and US-Soviet relations. As that change became more visible in the post-Nehru era, non-alignment became superfluous, as the decline of the influence of the Non-Aligned Movement in the 1970s and 1980s amply demonstrated. In these respects, then, the Nehru foreign policy legacy did not endure.[15]

Much more damaging to Nehru's record in foreign affairs than this system-generated decline in India's stature and role in world politics was Nehru's failure to solve major territorial conflicts with India's most important neighbor. The Kashmir dispute, trigger to three Indo/Pakistani wars (1947–48, 1965–66, and 1999), was a thorn for Nehru throughout his 17 years in power and caused more harsh criticism of his behavior in foreign policy from friend and foe than any other single issue. His intense effort to find a solution to this conflict, in the final months of his life, suggest that he too was unhappily aware of this negative legacy to his successors, none of whom, parenthetically, has moved the dispute closer to a settlement. Nehru alone was not responsible for the Kashmir impasse. Pakistani leaders, military and civilian, and Indian leaders since 1964 share the blame and demonstrate that the Kashmir dispute is not easily resolved. Nevertheless, great leaders are expected to rise above parochial interests and find a way through the morass; Nehru did not.[16]

The persisting India/China conflict over territory is even more complex. China's leadership, as well as Nehru's senior colleagues, *Pandit Pant* and *Morarji Desai*, imposed severe restraints on his freedom of action at the Delhi summit in April 1960 and after. Some scholars have claimed to find evidence that Nehru failed the test of leadership in this case by misperceiving China's intentions and capabilities, as well as its objectives in that conflict.[17] Others have been more generous in their interpretation of Indian leaders' perceptions and behavior.[18] Whichever view is correct, there appears to have been a basis for compromise at the Nehru-Zhou Enlai summit in 1960: if accepted in principle, India and Nehru would have been spared a humiliating defeat on the battlefield in 1962, and Nehru's successors would have been freed from the danger of a hostile China ever-ready to take advantage of India's external problems, as it tried to do in the India/Pakistan wars of 1965–66 (over Kashmir) and 1971 (over Bangladesh). Nehru's inability to initiate or accept a compromise settlement of the border dispute with China profoundly undermined his image in India and the world, then and since his death. Ironically, given Nehru's seeming preoccupation with foreign policy, his legacy in that domain is less enduring than in the struggle for independence and nation-building.

Encounters with Krishna Menon (1964–67)

Rationale for the Menon Project

An inquiry into the worldview of Nehru's closest adviser on foreign policy for all but the last two years of his pre-eminence as India's Prime

Minister and Foreign Minister, 1947–64, can be traced to *reading* and *reflections on foreign policy analysis* in the 1950s, a continuation of my IR studies at Yale in the mid to late 1940s. These were enriched by intense exchanges with graduate students in a McGill seminar in the 1960s, which suggested a *very close link between élite perceptions and foreign policy decisions* by states. More pointedly, they reinforced the idea that foreign policy decision-makers' choices derive primarily from their *psychological environment*, more specifically, from their *perceptions* of reality, threats, and opportunities confronting their state, that is, their *operational environment*. It followed from this intense intellectual activity that the master key to understanding the concept, *Foreign Policy System*, is the worldview of political leaders and trusted advisers within each state who make foreign policy decisions.

During my South Asia phase, it seemed natural and potentially valuable for both IR scholars and policy makers to test the idea in depth of a causal link between foreign policy perceptions and behavior on Nehru's principal adviser on foreign policy for all but the last two years of Nehru's tenure as Prime Minister and Foreign Minister, Krishna Menon (1947–62). The result was a three-year project designed to test the idea that the *perceptions* held by senior foreign policy decision-makers are, in fact, the master key to their *foreign policy decisions*, that is, whether or not images of their *operational environment*, both *threats from potential adversaries* and *opportunities to achieve their objectives* constitute the crucial *causal link to their behavior* on issues of war and peace and, more generally, to their foreign policy decisions.

The project took the form of *three paths to knowledge*, in accord with the conception of many *paths to knowledge*, presented in the Introduction to this book. The *first* path comprised the *oral recollections* of Krishna Menon, the most influential decision-maker in India's foreign policy during the Nehru era, apart from Nehru himself, and a controversial figure in world politics, from 1947 to 1962. (Menon's career—he was Defense Minister of India from 1957 to 1962—ended abruptly, a casualty of India's humiliating defeat in the war with China in October–November 1962. Nehru, too, was bruised by the military debacle, politically and emotionally, though his position as Prime Minister and Foreign Minister was not in jeopardy).

The *second* path attempted to break fresh ground in IR by providing a systematic analysis of Krishna Menon's View of the World and its impact on India's foreign policy. It focused on one of six components of a Foreign

Policy System—élite images—and was designed to test the postulated link between decision-makers' perceptions and policy choices. The essence of Menon's view of the world will be presented below.

The *third* path took the form of a Content Analysis of Menon's View of the World, prepared by Janice Gross Stein, then a colleague at McGill University and later a University Professor and Founding Director of the Munk School of Global Affairs at the University of Toronto. This path revealed the value of the quantitative method of foreign policy analysis. Moreover, the two principal methods of IR analysis, qualitative and quantitative, proved to be complementary: their conclusions were remarkably similar, though derived differently.

Background and Personality

V.K. Krishna Menon was born in 1896 in Calicut, Kerala. Much of his pre-India public service was spent in London—from 1924 to 1952. He received a BA from the LSE in 1927, at the age of 31, after two years at LSE. His revered mentor and the most profound influence on his political ideology and behavior was Professor Harold Laski, a political theorist of socialist persuasion, then at the peak of his academic fame. Thereafter, for two decades, Menon served the cause of India's freedom as the increasingly prominent, later the dominant, figure in the Indian nationalist movement's informal lobby in the UK, the India League. From 1947 to 1952, he was independent India's first, highly visible and vocal High Commissioner (ambassador) to the British Government.

Krishna Menon was the most controversial figure in India's foreign policy élite during the first 15 years of independence (1947–62). He was also the most Western, the most intellectually sophisticated, and, arguably, the most influential member of Nehru's foreign policy inner circle. Menon was abrasive, often acerbic, with unconcealed disdain for many of his colleagues in the Indian National Congress and many statesmen at the UN and elsewhere. He was also brilliant, charming, handsome, and exceptionally articulate. Indeed he was a compelling, though highly controversial advocate for India in public forums, as well as during intense negotiations over vital Indian interests.

More than five decades have passed since our encounters—they began in 1964. I have a vivid recollection of a fascinating, complex, moody, at times tempestuous intellectual in politics. The encounter took the form of an extended dialogue over *several years*—after Menon's ouster from the Cabinet and the key post of Defense Minister, following the debacle resulting from the China/India border war in the autumn of 1962.

Content of the Interviews

The dialogue began as one informal interview on the origins, rationale, and assessment of Non-Alignment (see below). It developed into 17 hours of taped, extemporaneous interviews covering 21 themes or events, most of them in world politics since India's independence (1947).

The interviews covered the following *topics*:

1. Non-Alignment
2. India's Decision to Remain in the Commonwealth, 1947–49
3. Korean War and After, 1950–54
4. Geneva Conference on Indo-China, 1954
5. Afro-Asian Bandung Conference, 1955
6. Suez War, 1956
7. Israel, the Arabs, and India
8. Hungarian Uprising, 1956
9. Congo, 1960
10. UN
11. Annexation of Goa, 1961
12. China, 1949–62, including the Border War
13. Indian Foreign Policy and World Politics: A Potpourri
14. Partition, Pakistan, Kashmir, and Indo-Pakistan Relations
15. Succession to Nehru
16. Policy in the Shastri Transition, Notably the Atomic Bomb
17. Indian Cabinet at Work
18. Pressure Groups, Parliament, and Foreign Policy
19. Economic Development
20. Education and Language
21. Nehru

The first series was held in Menon's home in New Delhi almost every morning for three weeks in November–December 1964. A second round of interviews was conducted in May 1965 in order to fill gaps that became apparent from my transcript of our initial discussions. The completed draft of the dialogue was edited by Menon early in 1966, during my return to India to observe and analyze the second succession contest, after Shastri's death in January. It was further edited by me in the autumn of that year, special care being taken not to alter the content or meaning of Menon's articulated images. My analysis of his View of the World was prepared during 1967 and was based on his edited version of the dialogue, that is, on his reconsidered thoughts about the topics under investigation. The upshot was my volume, entitled *India and World Politics: Krishna Menon's View of the World*, published in 1968.

Selections from only one of the topics covered in our discussions will be presented *verbatim*: Non-Alignment, the foundation of India's foreign policy during most of the Nehru era and beyond. Almost all of the other topics will be included in my analysis of Menon's view of the world below.

Interview on Non-Alignment

MB I would like to begin, Mr. Menon, with some questions on non-alignment. Who conceived the policy? What was your role in this? What was Mr. Nehru's role? In short, could you go back to the origins of non-alignment and its foundations?

Menon Even if nobody conceived it, non-alignment was more or less a residue of historical circumstances. In 1945, immediately before India got her independence, it was all 'one world'; but by 1947 it was 'two worlds', and we, for the first time, had to make up our minds on the issue, how we would function and what we would do. We would not go back to the West with its colonialism; and there was no question of our going the Soviet way; we did not even know them much. And with the attaining of our independence we desired not to get involved in foreign entanglements. All these things entered into it. But it is not as though we sat around the table deciding how we should non-align ourselves! There were two blocs. Both the Prime Minister [Nehru] and I exclaimed or thought aloud *simultaneously*, 'why should we be with anybody?'

MB But the word, 'non-alignment', itself: who conceived this and when?

Menon That, I used much later—spontaneously. I think it was at the United Nations but I couldn't say for certain. We were being ridiculed about being 'neutral'. I said then, 'We are not neutral; we are non-aligned. We are not aligned to either side, we are non-aligned.' In fact, the Prime

Minister didn't approve very much of the word at the beginning, but it had quickly gained currency.

MB It was, then, at some meeting in 1950?

Menon No, No. It was later than that. I don't think you will see the word 'non-aligned' used that early—to the best of my recollection. I think it was probably used some time in '53–'54; that is my recollection, but you had better check up on that. But the word 'non-alignment' was first used at the United Nations.
   What is non-alignment? It is merely independence in external affairs. What are external affairs? They are only a projection of internal or national policy in the field of International Relations. It is a logical extension of nationalism, yes, and of the conflict between nationalism and military blocs, the fact that we had little in common with the *raison d'être* of the blocs; with the West, because to us the West meant Empire.

MB Is it not true that non-alignment was thought of as the most efficient path to economic development?

Menon I don't think anyone thought about it that way at the time, because the question of foreign aid and things of that kind, which are so prominent today [1964], did not figure in our minds very much. We didn't think back from economics to politics.

MB So there was no direct material factor in the origins of nonalignment. This was to come much later?

Menon Much later.

MB Did you, in the early stage, think of it as something that could make a genuine contribution to international peace?

Menon I did, but to what extent the Prime Minister did, I don't know. I had an idea of what you might call the theory of it, but his mind didn't work like that.

MB How precisely did his mind work on these questions?

Menon He would pick up something which by intuition appealed to him and make use of it. What is more, if I said something and he adopted and repeated it—that is all that the world would know about it. We were the only one to be non-aligned. Burma came soon afterwards and then all the other countries that emerged from colonialism. This proves my thesis: it is part of historical circumstances.

MB How would you contrast non-alignment as it operated in the Indian case with what Nasser and Nkrumah called 'positive neutralism'?

Menon That was a different phraseology. Nkrumah, particularly, didn't want to use 'non-alignment'; we had used it. He was fighting for something called 'positive neutralism'. I am afraid I ridiculed it with banter. Then, in Belgrade [the 1961 first Non-Aligned Conference], 'non-alignment' became established.

MB Was there no difference in the way that Egypt and Ghana looked at their role in the world?

Menon I imagine so, but not in their relation to the power blocs. They probably did not see non-alignment in the beginning as a moral force or as an instrument of world peace. Now, I think, they know better. Nasser understands it more, and well, I think. He is far more intelligent, far more honest, and a much bigger man than some people think. I have a great regard for him and faith in his integrity. We said from the very beginning that there must be something, an 'area of peace', I called it, not territorially, but politically, diplomatically, morally, etc.

MB So an 'area of peace' is to be distinguished from what came to be called a Third Bloc?

Menon Third Bloc, never! The Third Bloc is a foolish idea. How can there be a Third Bloc?

My understanding of non-alignment is that it cannot be a Third Bloc, for a bloc means power and a Third Bloc to be effective must have at least two and a half times the power of one bloc! That will never happen and if it did it would be a super bloc dangerous to mankind. Secondly, Third Bloc also means superior economic power. This [an area of peace] is a policy of independence and peace; that is, materially speaking, a weak man's policy. In a sense, now that I think about it, it is like Gandhi's non-co-operation. In his weakness he invented an *instrument* which was stronger than anything else.

Panditji [Pandit Nehru], even more than I, was anxious to keep away from their [bloc] conflict. 'Why should we get involved?' That was, in general, his reaction. But India acquired that degree of influence for several reasons, not only because we were non-aligned.

People trusted us. We established a degree of respect with them because they believed we had integrity. *We never hesitated to vote against one side or the other.* Also, there was the fact that *we were not frightened of the American strength at the UN.* Nehru allowed me—in effect, he put me on—to draw their fire.

MB Was *mediation* a necessary, integral part of non-alignment? Did it grow logically?

Menon It grew, and I found that somehow or other I fitted into it. It came with Korea. There was the Korean War and a deadlock, so we started on this. I started on Korea when I was High Commissioner in London [1947–52].

Mediation came about for these reasons: (1) the two blocs talked themselves into a deadlock; (2) nobody wanted to destroy the UN's prestige—some may have wanted to, but not at the cost of war; (3) there wasn't anybody able to feel a way out. For example, when the French walked out [of the General Assembly], nobody could bring them back; we did so.

MB Would you argue that a non-aligned state would have to engage in mediation or, alternatively, that only a non-aligned state could be a mediator?

Menon I think it was very much the latter.

MB Is it not true that, in the Suez case [1956], it was Canada, an aligned state that was a mediator?

Menon No; that is what Pearson [Canada's External Affairs Minister at the time] tells everybody. I had the greatest difficulty in getting the Egyptians (I telephoned Cairo from New York and so on) to accept Canadian units in the U.N. [Emergency] Force; they did not want British helmets there; they said, 'they are British'.

MB But are you also saying that mediation is a role that can be played only by a non-aligned state?

Menon No. It depends on circumstances, on who you are mediating with.

MB But if two great powers are involved, if the two blocs are involved, is it only a non-aligned state that can mediate?

Menon It is history, isn't it?

MB I am asking you.

Menon But how else can it be?

MB What do you regard, Mr. Menon, as the main accomplishments of non-alignment as a foreign policy for India? Was it prestige?

Menon No, it established India, not as a major power but as an important quantity in world affairs. Secondly, it prevented us from becoming a satellite state. Even today the Americans are trying to rope us into their orbit. Thirdly, I should say it has on several occasions put a brake on war, though the Indochina problem is still in a bad state, [1964] largely thanks to the United States. It also showed a way for the newly independent countries. Otherwise, they would all have been pushed around this way and that way, and the balance of power would have played a very much more important part in new Africa. Fourthly, I think non-alignment enabled us to strengthen ourselves, too. It gave us a considerable degree of self-confidence, inner strength, things of that kind. It has been built up into a philosophy. I believe it also enabled us to establish relations with China, whatever may have happened afterwards. It prevented, in my opinion, deterioration in regard to our relations with the Soviet Union. It certainly did not give us 'leadership' over non-aligned people.

I say that a non-aligned nation must be non-aligned with the non-aligned, if you can put it that way! Otherwise, where is independence? It may be that a common view about Suez [1956] or a common view about the Congo [1960 ff.] or about other things may all lead us into one lobby, but we don't by definition go there; affinity may take us there. That is the essence of nonalignment.

MB Then, in terms of the principles of non-alignment, the attitude of many African and Asian States toward the India/China border dispute makes perfect sense?

Menon Of course it does, even if not to us, but given the fact that these states are independent, it does.

MB Does that mean that once the conflict between the two blocs recedes, non-alignment ceases to have any kind of operational meaning?

Menon No, I don't mean that, but other conditions come about. A newer situation arises. But the basic position of independence need not change. In my opinion, apart from the national excitement, disappointment, and anger in India, the China clash, if anything, only reinforces non-alignment.

The other parts of a lengthy dialogue with Krishna Menon were no less insightful. Further discussion of the wide range of topics covered in this verbal exchange of ideas will be found in the following pages.

Analysis of Menon's View of the World

There were several points of concentration in Krishna Menon's perception of world politics. One was the *struggle between the two power blocs*, the US-led West and the USSR-led East. Another was the notion of *'area of peace'*. A third was the *UN*. There were also lesser themes in his image of the setting in which India's foreign policy had to be made. All these points emerged during the lengthy dialogue from 1964 to 1966.

On the Superpowers and the Bloc Struggle

Like most participant–observers, from 1945 to 1989 Menon viewed world politics as dominated by *two power blocs* led by the USA and the Soviet Union, in sharp and continuous conflict with each other. The Western bloc was, for him, invariably the greater culprit: this part of his image can be traced to his acceptance of the Leninist theory of imperialism as a phenomenon of expansion linked to the stage of 'Monopoly Capitalism'. The term 'Imperialism' was a favorite in his lexicon, frequently recurring in speeches at the UN and in India's parliament, as well as other public forums, and in extemporaneous reflections, as evident in this Dialogue. Whether or not explicitly identified, 'Imperialism', for Menon, referred to the Western bloc, more specifically to those states that control or controlled territories overseas; it was the policy designed to enlarge, perpetuate, or prevent the dissolution of colonial empires—and 'colonial' was, by definition, restricted to *overseas* lands and peoples.

The twin epithets, 'Imperialist' and 'Colonialist', were never used by him with reference to the Soviet Union or China: these designations were inconceivable to Menon, for the two Communist powers did not possess colonial, that is, overseas, empires. Thus, even in a mood of regret and sadness over China's 'betrayal' of India's trust and friendship, through its 'incursion' of 1962, Menon found solace in his discovery that China had always been 'expansionist', a lesser order of iniquity than 'imperialism' or 'colonialism'. The harsher epithets, imperialist and colonialist, were reserved for Western empires.

The central place in Menon's verbal assault on imperialism was given to the USA, despite its modest record as a colonial power. But Menon was never an unqualified adherent of Marxist ideology: it was, rather, Harold Laski's neo-Marxism—as noted, he was a student of Professor Laski at LSE in 1925–27—that shaped this part of his image. And like all radical socialists of the contemporary era, Menon did not regard formal colonial rule as necessary to the policy of 'Imperialism' or 'Colonialism'. The characteristics of 'Capitalism' and 'Interventionism', whether overt or covert, direct or indirect, political, economic, cultural, or military, justified, in Menon's eyes, the designation 'Imperialist' for the USA.

The tone and breadth of Menon's derisive comments on 'American Imperialism' indicate an intense emotional antipathy, as well as intellectual disdain. A passionate *j'accuse* was rarely absent from his interview reflections, as he moved from one problem or issue of international politics to another. He began with moderation: among the reasons for India's choice of *Non-Alignment*, '[W]e would not go back to the West because to us the West meant empire' (Topic 1). In recalling the *decision to remain in the Commonwealth*, '[I]t was probably a way of keeping out intruders. Looking back, I didn't think about it at the time; at least at that period American infiltration into India was less' (Topic 2). He blamed American intransigence for the delay in ending the *Korean War* (1950–53) on the basis of his proposals, especially regarding prisoners of war (Topic 3). This too was evident in his discussion of the 1954 *Geneva Conference on Indo-*

China (Topic 4). In explaining the founding non-aligned conference at *Bandung* in 1955, he remarked: 'The Americans were against the idea; they tried to kill it – until it emerged and succeeded. Then they simulated enthusiasm about it. (Using a well-worn British expression), they "came to scoff and remained to pray", the same as with the Korea Resolution' (Topic 5). Apropos of the Korean War, Menon castigated US Secretary of State Dulles and President Eisenhower: 'They didn't care too much about those American prisoners in China. I cared more for them than they did. They were quite prepared to make them a kind of bond in the political game' (Topic 13).

In recalling the *Suez War* of October–November 1956, Menon shifted his attack to the lesser 'Imperialist' powers, Britain and France. The Soviet role in terminating the invasion of Egypt by the UK, France, and Israel—through its threat to bomb London, Paris, and Tel Aviv—received high praise, while the US contribution was treated as innocuous (Topic 6). In a passionate defense of his attitude to, and his voting on, the *Hungarian Uprising* the same months, at the UN, Menon displayed bitterness at what he termed the US exploitation of this unhappy episode for Cold War purposes and American indifference to the human aspects of the problem (Topic 8). On the Congo, too, he was harsh, particularly when referring to the landing of Western troops in *Stanleyville* in December 1964: 'I don't believe for one moment this sob-story about saving every white man or woman; it does not wash.' And on the 1960 *Congo crisis-war* generally, '[T]he Western group are basically responsible' (Topic 9). On India's 1961 annexation of *Goa*, Menon's criticism of American behavior was severe; and the roles of US Ambassador to India, John Kenneth Galbraith, and its UN Representative, Adlai Stevenson, were the objects of a searing attack (Topic 11).

The long discourse on *China* (1949–62) [Topic 12], to be elaborated below, was characterized by Menon's mood of sadness about Beijing's strange and painful actions. Much of the blame was attributed to the uncompromising attitude of Indian 'reactionary circles'. Once more, America was brought into the picture—for claiming to have come to the aid of India: Menon emphatically denied this. Indeed, he suggested that the USA urged India to take a forceful initiative regarding China; had Delhi yielded to this advice, '[W]e might have been...bombed'. As for American pledges to aid India, he declared emphatically that a nuclear umbrella was a myth; the USA would never resort to nuclear war merely to defend India against aggression (Topic 16).

Menon's image of the two superpowers and the inter-bloc conflict was also illuminated in his discourse on *Partition, Pakistan, Kashmir, and Indo/Pakistan Relations* (Topic 14): 'You take the world since the [Second World] war. Who has created all the wars? What is the difference between this and the situation in 1917 or 1918 except that...the imperialists attacked the infant revolutionary Russia on twenty-two fronts? Now, basically, what is the difference between now and then?' In the same stream of words, '[L]et us hope...that (in the near future the world will be) in a fitter state to reject Western imperialism. Otherwise they will say that Krishna Menon has it on the brain, they will say that he wants somebody to hate.' On *Kashmir,* '[T]he villain in all this is and always has been Britain ably assisted later, not initially, by the United States.' And, on the possibility of an Indo/Pakistani settlement, '[T]here will be no peace on this continent unless the United States retires from the Far East. It's a withdrawal of a state of mind, that is to say, the withdrawal of the assumption that they are born to police the world.'

The evidence is overwhelming: Krishna Menon equated the USA and the Soviet Union in the global power hierarchy; they were the two superpowers; but he distinguished very sharply their responsibility for the world's ills. 'American Imperialism' was unquestionably the pre-eminent evil force. In fact, his criticism of the Soviets was rare and invariably mild. There was acknowledgment that Moscow, in the last years of the Stalin era, *aggravated* the tension but not the slightest intimation of blame for the conflict. The contrast between derision, disdain, accusation, and denunciation of the US role, and rare, mild regret with reference to Soviet actions, reveals an enormous bias in Menon's image of this crucial component of world politics. It was deep-rooted and pervasive, an extension of his political philosophy and his emotional propensities—bitterness toward 'the West', a compound of colonialism, imperialism, and racism, with a specially intense hostility to the USA's 'state of mind', and a predisposition to approve, explain away, forgive, and forget the Soviets and their bloc.

On the Concept, 'Area of Peace'
Menon's image of world politics was not confined to the two power blocs, though he acknowledged their dominant role in shaping events. There was a Third World, a vast and amorphous community of states which cross the boundaries of geography, race, and culture. Like Nehru, he called this an '*area of peace*', to distinguish it from the arena of bloc politics which was, by inference, an 'area of war'.

'Area of peace' was a value-charged concept. It had a superficially positive aura, but the basic criterion of membership was negative—non-association or non-alignment with a power bloc. Most, but not all, of its constituent units were new states, the former European colonies or trust territories in Asia and Africa which acquired independence since WWII. Beyond these precise negative categories, however, the concept was riddled with anomalies which permitted, indeed facilitated, highly subjective judgment. Thus, one European state that eschewed bloc affiliation after 1948, Tito's Yugoslavia, was an honored member, while four others more unattached—Austria, Sweden, Switzerland, and Finland—did not qualify, this despite the fact that the first and third had been neutralized by international agreement and the second pursued a policy of non-alignment for two centuries! More pointed were the exclusion of neutralized Austria and the inclusion of neutralized Laos in the 'area of peace'.

There were other inconsistencies. China, which had a network of treaty arrangements with the Soviet bloc since 1949, participated in conferences of non-aligned states. With similar illogic, Cuba entered the non-aligned group and the 'area of peace' after it disaffiliated from the US-led American security system and became attached to the Soviet bloc, at least to the extent of accepting Soviet military protection. And in Menon's eyes, some Latin American states, like Mexico and Brazil, were quasi-non-aligned and, therefore, potential recruits to the 'area of peace', while others were not; yet all were bloc-affiliated through the military and related networks of the Organization of American States (OAS). In short, one is confronted with a maze of conflicting criteria, some of which were determined by emotion or whim.

Thus, in the context of Non-Alignment, Menon remarked: '[T]here must be something, an "area of peace", I called it, not territorially, but politically, diplomatically, morally, etc.' He reacted sharply to a question about the possible affinity of 'area of peace' to 'third bloc': 'Third Bloc, never! The Third Bloc is a foolish idea. My understanding of non-alignment is it cannot be a Third Bloc, for a bloc means power. Non-alignment is a policy of independence and peace, that is, materially speaking, a weak man's policy. In a sense, now that I think of it, it is like Gandhi's non-co-operation.'

Despite its brevity, this passage is revealing. It reveals the fuzziness of Menon's concept, 'area of peace'. It reveals, too, his emotional antagonism to the term, 'bloc', and its connotation of power. There was, as well, a curious equation of non-alignment and independence, with the implication that participation in a military alliance results in the loss of independent statehood. Yet he later rebutted the charge that Hungary, a member of the Warsaw Pact, was a 'colony' of the Soviet Union—because it was a full-fledged member of the UN. Canada, by contrast, an active member of the UN from its creation, was described as a colony of the USA. Most important, though perhaps unwittingly, Menon shattered the myth, fostered and sustained by proponents of non-alignment, Indian, and other, that this is a policy of superior morality; rather, as he declared with candor, it is 'a weak man's policy'. And finally, there was a facile interchangeability of non-alignment and 'area of peace', yet these are not really synonymous. The former is a policy, while the latter a loose metaphysical communion of those states which remain aloof from inter-bloc conflict.

From these and other remarks by Menon, its most articulate advocate, it is possible to delineate the *indicators of an 'area of peace'*. Most of them are negative: non-affiliation with a bloc-sponsored or bloc-led military alliance; the withholding of consistent support for a bloc's policies in the UN and other forums; non-dependence on either bloc for economic and military assistance; aid from both, which is not only beneficial but also strengthens the claim to non-alignment, hence membership in the 'area of peace'; military weakness and, especially, the absolute repudiation of nuclear weapons; and opposition to the 'Cold War'. There is only one positive feature—active, purposeful pursuit of a foreign policy of 'peace', that is, non-alignment.

Menon never systematically clarified the metaphysical concept, 'area of peace', its meaning, and content. He made high claims for non-alignment as a policy—'it established India as an important quantity in world affairs; it prevented us from becoming a satellite state; it has on several occasions put a brake on war; it also showed a way for the newly-independent countries'—but he did not bother to elucidate the meaning of 'area of peace'. It is 'one of those things that the world requires' as a counterpoise to the bloc struggle. And there was a strong emotive connotation to his terms. An 'area of peace' is inherently good, just as 'Imperialism' and, to a lesser extent, the 'blocs', whose goals and values they reject, are evil.

On the UN
The third major component in Menon's image of world politics was the UN. His view was favorable but not without reservations. Indeed, one discerns ambivalence to the institution and the men who directed its affairs

(Topic 10). The most important contribution of the UN was 'that it survives'; and this is crucial 'because things get debated; it's better to talk at each other than to shoot at each other; in that sense the U.N. has been a good safety valve and often delays crises'. He praised it as the central vehicle of decolonization and as a cushion against 'a head-on collision between the superpowers', as well as a stimulus to aid for economic development. At the same time, he termed peace-keeping 'a dismal failure, except for U.N.E.F. It can be a reality only when the world is disarmed and by disarmament I mean real disarmament'.

He criticized all innovations designed to enlarge the ambit of UN activities, seeing them as an intrusion into the sacrosanct realm of sovereignty. In the same way, he opposed all suggestions for a standing UN Peace Force and all efforts at UN-directed plebiscite tests of popular opinion—in Hungary, Kashmir, and elsewhere. His rationale, repeated frequently in speeches to the General Assembly or one of its committees, was that, until the establishment of World Government and the effective rule of International Law, about which he was surprisingly optimistic, the core principle of the UN as presently constituted, sovereignty, must not be violated or undermined. An expansion of UN powers in the political and military spheres would merely facilitate 'Imperialist' intervention in the affairs of weaker states.

On Britain

The UK and the British were spared by Menon, with few exceptions; their decolonization policy was the recipient of one of Menon's rare encomiums to the West. His special regard for British decolonization must be set in the context of Menon's *ambivalence to the UK*. His long lean years of struggle against British rule in India had bred an intense hostility to the ideology and the substance of colonialism. Yet the India League phase of Menon's life, 1929–47, was not without compensation: a higher education at the LSE, then at its peak of intellectual vitality; friendships with men who helped shape the climate of opinion for what Menon would consider Britain's 'finest hour'—withdrawal from Empire; a special attachment to Harold Laski, *guru* of the Left and inspiration for a whole generation of students from Asia and Africa; and a feeling of freedom, political and personal, so different from his earlier life in India.

In sum, Krishna Menon went through the indelible process of political socialization in England. Along with an intellectual commitment to Laski's neo-Marxism, he acquired an admiration for some of the values and traits of the 'British way of life': the liberal values of free speech, free press, and free assembly; respect for the individual; tolerance of opposition; safeguards for minority opinion and rights; decision by consent and conciliation; the central place of Law; and the system of parliamentary government with all its ramifications—theory, institutions, conventions, and pragmatic spirit.

The impact of these *two strands of 'the British connection' in Menon's life*—the *struggle for independence* and the *attraction to liberal values in the British 'way of life'*—was evident everywhere, in deed and word. He felt strongly about India's continued membership in the Commonwealth and acted accordingly; in fact, he played a crucial role in devising the formula to 'square the circle' (Topic 2). Moreover, the essence of his diplomatic technique, as displayed in the Korean War, the Indo/China conflict, Bandung, and other areas of disagreement, namely, the patient application of conciliation, may be traced to his familiarity with British party politics. A notable lapse, as in the Suez crisis, was almost certainly due to his instinctive, reflex-like antagonism to what he perceived as the colonialist–racialist syndrome, combined with an ideological blind spot on the question of Israel (Topics 6 and 7). Similarly, in many debates at meetings of the UN Trusteeship Council, he paid tribute to the magnanimous manner of Britain's dismantling of its empire. It was, perhaps, his personal experience with the British form of colonialism and the relative ease of the transfer of power in India that induced his partisan attitude.

On Nuclear Weapons
The Dialogue on nuclear weapons (Topic 16) reveals Menon at his intellectually most brittle and irrational. It also points up an important *admixture in his personality and outlook—militancy and pacifism or non-violence*. The first was inherent in Menon the man; the second derived partly from the prevalent attitudes of the British Left in the 1930s and partly from Gandhi's creed and practice. On the Bomb, however, Menon was very emotional, and his image of nuclear weapons in the global environment was fuzzy.

Irrationality is evident not only in his categorical refusal to *debate* the issue or even in his attempt to elevate this to a First Principle of statecraft: 'Why should I debate mass suicide? The fundamental national interest of this country is not to talk of the use of nuclear power for destructive purposes.' In no circumstances should India build or acquire nuclear weapons. Nor should India seek or accept a nuclear umbrella from one or more nuclear powers, for this would undermine non-alignment; and, in any event, he was certain that such protection would never be offered or provided. Apart from a passionate distaste for nuclear war, a feeling not unique to Krishna Menon, there would seem to be an unstated belief that no state would use nuclear weapons against India. There is little evidence to support this optimism. And since Menon's image of China's intentions toward India proved to be so tragically wrong in the past, a rigid posture on the nuclear question would seem to be at least a doubtful basis for India's security. (In fact, it was to become a nuclear weapons state in 1998.)

On Pakistan

Krishna Menon's image of India's most important neighbors, Pakistan and China, was no less pronounced than his view of the world. For Pakistan there was *an unconcealed passion akin to his aversion to the USA*: the two were frequently coupled and served as Menon's *bêtes noires*. (His very different image of China is presented below.)

Menon's view of *Pakistan* (Topic 14) derived from an ideology acquired in the 1920s and 1930s: both remained constant over the decades. The point of departure was his commitment to the secular ideal and a rejection of the idea of religion as the legitimate basis of nationalism. Seen through this lens, Pakistan was a throwback, in a modern guise, to the retrogressive notion of a theocratic state. There was, however, a complex web of ideological, political, and emotional strands that underpinned this anti-theocratic image. Taken together, they explain why Menon always regarded Pakistan as the principal threat to India's security, values, and institutions.

For Menon, *Pakistan was the handiwork of Britain. Once created, its function 'is like Northern Ireland*, a remnant of imperialism. It's the British classic solution of empire and they rely on the fact that they don't have to fight us any more than they need to fight in Ireland. The six counties [of Northern Ireland] wage their fight against the rest of the Irish. More or less, it's the same position as Pakistan'.

Closely related to this perception was a contemptuous view of Pakistani nationalism as hollow and its nationalist movement as artificial. A corollary was the provocative judgment that Pakistan was the recipient of independence by proxy: '[I]t really was not the result of a nationalist struggle of Pakistani leaders, but the result of the Indian struggle led by the Congress.' In short, Menon hurled a formidable ideological indictment at Pakistan: it was theocratic and authoritarian; it was created by one dying imperialism and was sustained by another, on the basis of a retrogressive and illegitimate principle of nationalism.

In Menon's eyes, Pakistan committed grave political sins as well. By accepting US military aid from 1953 onward, it weakened the 'area of peace', brought the Cold War to the subcontinent, and opened the gates to the 'return of empire'. All this was compounded by its hostile behavior during India's time of troubles, its collusion with China, and the consequent accentuation of a massive burden on India's resources for defense and economic development. These and other acts created for Menon—and many other Indians—a profound mistrust of Pakistan's intentions, as evident in his assessment during this interview:

> 'My belief is that Pakistan's leaders looked upon Pakistan as a first installment, "take what you can and fight for more", the English doctrine. They never seem to have accepted Partition as final, as we did. Their main approach to the problem was that India was theirs. India was a Muslim country historically. The British had taken it away from them. Now the British had gone away, and it should be handed over to them. We professed—and I think we did and do so honestly with the exception of some communalists—that, good or bad, we agreed to Partition, and we don't want any of their territory. We have no *arrière pensée* about it. It's not because we are virtuous; it's because we know why we did it.'

It is only in this context, Menon insisted, that the Kashmir issue can be properly assessed. Referring to the 'original Pakistan doctrine', he asked, 'What haven't they got? They have not got half of Punjab, Kashmir, half of Bengal, and Hyderabad. So when we talk about Kashmir, this is only part of that map, and [once more the core image] there is of course the larger map, which could place almost all of India in Pakistan.'

In a rare expression of doubt and modesty, Menon added: 'It may be said that this is a far-fetched or fanatical or unrealistic or academic doctrine. I don't say that this is right; it is my analysis of it.' The crucial fact is that he believed it to be so, that he saw Pakistan in this untrustworthy and aggressive light, and that his behavior flowed logically, indeed inevitably, from this image. The policy choice for Menon was clear, and he adhered to it consistently: India must stand fast on Kashmir and not yield an inch. There was no display of revisionism, as with some right-wing Indian nationalists.

On China

Menon's image of China (Topic 12) differed from all other components of his view of the world, in two respects: it revealed the impact of China's unanticipated behavior in 1962 on his thought and attitudes; and it lacked the rigidity displayed in his perception of global politics, notably of 'American Imperialism', and of Pakistan's behavior toward India during the two decades since the 1947 Partition. There are, indeed, constant and variable elements in his outlook on China, the breakpoint being the trauma of 1962: toward China he exhibited respect and a feeling of Asian and anti-colonial kinship tempered, after 1962, by a sense of betrayal.

From the outset of the People's Republic of China (PRC) (1949), Menon viewed the 'New China' as a progressive state, secular, socialist, and modern. It was a revolutionary movement in the best sense, pursuing with vigor the noble ends of economic development and social change. As such, it was worthy of encouragement. However, like Nehru, Menon never praised the ruthless totalitarian means employed by Beijing; nor did he criticize Communist China, for this would be unwarranted interference in the internal affairs of another state. In fact, he remained a steadfast adherent of democratic planning.

Menon was drawn to the 'New China' for other reasons, which lie in the realm of spiritual kinship. He perceived a natural affinity to India—two great civilizations that asserted their national independence after a century or more of foreign rule. They shared as well a secular outlook and a commitment to anti-colonialism. Their paths were different, but their ends were the same: hence the foundations for cooperation between the two peoples and regimes. There was, too, great respect for China's historic role as a great power, rightfully restored after an era of humiliation by Western Imperialism. It was that interplay of China and the West, paralleling India's subordination to Britain, which added an emotional dimension to Menon's empathy for China. And as so often, in UN speeches and elsewhere, the Dialogue on China began with a lengthy discourse on history, with its stress on imperialist perfidy.

The combined thrust of Menon's images of China was to create a positive perception of Communist China, unqualified until 1962 and retained in its essentials thereafter. The outcome, in policy terms, was remarkable consistency. He never wavered in his conviction that Beijing had the inherent right to represent China at the UN. Nor did he ever doubt its claim to Taiwan as an integral part of China's territory. He defended China's intervention in the Korean War, applauded Zhou Enlai's role at the 1954

Conference on Indo-China, and found no fault with China's behavior in the Vietnam War. He steadfastly declared that Tibet is part of China. He did not seem to be disturbed by China's acquisition of a nuclear capability, apparently content with Beijing's assertion that China would not be the first to use these weapons of mass destruction. And on the prolonged US/China conflict, his sympathies remained clearly with the latter.

Menon's basic orientation to China, as to Pakistan, had a strong emotional flavor rooted in his experience and ideology of the 1930s. This emerges frequently in a long, discursive, defensive, and painful dialogue on China in 1964–65. One example will suffice: 'Our idea about China—this is quite true—is that she never invaded us in the past. I myself was one of the active people in the China Campaign Committee in London in the 1930s; and that had its roots in our hostility to Western intrusion into China, extra-territorially. The emotional base was there. Equally now they [our emotions] are affected and are bound to be by the betrayal of our friendship and good faith.' That indeed was the cause, for Menon and for Nehru, of a reluctant redefinition of China after 1962.

The pervasive tone of Menon's revised image of China was regret, not anger, as displayed in his comments on Pakistan and 'American Imperialism'. It was, rather, a feeling of hurt, a sense of dismay, even of surprise, a mood of disenchantment. India had championed Beijing's claims at the UN, had introduced it to Asia at the Bandung Conference, and had defended its interests in Korea, Vietnam, and elsewhere—and now the reward was betrayal.

Speaking of Nehru's reaction to the events of 1962 [China's invasion], 'I think it affected him deeply; it had a very bad effect on him. It demoralized him very much. Everything that he had built was threatened; India was to have a militarist outlook which he did not like.' On the theme of personal betrayal: 'I think that is a wrong way of looking at it—he was far too big for that. He felt that the Chinese action betrayed the world, betrayed, in the sense that it broke faith, the cause of Afro-Asian solidarity, etc.' In defense of Nehru (and perhaps himself as well), he added, '[B]ut it was not as though he [Nehru] was mesmerized by the Chinese before the invasion; he was too realistic for that.'

There were several elements in Menon's post-1962 image of China. First, India had befriended its northern neighbor, and Beijing had simulated reciprocity—but had then betrayed Delhi's trust and friendship. No less important, China had shattered Asian solidarity and had undermined the non-aligned 'area of peace'. The result was to strengthen the forces of imperialism in world politics and the forces of reaction within India. Menon recalled the descent into conflict in 1959: 'That is what I told Zhou Enlai [then, Premier of the PRC] when he came here [1960]: "you may hurt us but you hurt yourselves more; you have hurt the world even more; you have strengthened every reactionary element in this country and the forces of tension in the world."'

A third element of change in Menon's perception of China was his sad reflection that a victim of imperialism had itself penetrated into the territory of other states—Burma, India, Nepal, and, in intent, the Soviet Union. Along with this was his 'discovery' that China had always been expansionist: '[B]asically they are expansionists—they have always been—and you have to put this side by side with their expansionism in the Soviet Union.' This belated recognition dated back to the Chinese incursion into India's North East Frontier Agency [NEFA] in the autumn of 1959.

The China segment of Menon's reflections was full of contradictions, indicating that both strands were present in his image. On the one hand, China was 'basically expansionist', and this had 'certainly become pointed' in 1959. Yet, in a later reference, '[A]t that time we certainly had no idea that the Chinese were going to wage war on us'. This disbelief in China's hostile intent appeared side by side with the view that it was inherently expansionist, though the epithet 'imperialist' was avoided. He also exhibited ambivalence on responsibility for the 'tragic conflict', which could have been avoided: 'If the Prime Minister [Nehru] had been able to leave himself alone, without unmodern [Indian] minds and China's own mistakes, it would have probably been different. We could have got, not a settlement, a kind of Korea business, a kind of no-war situation.'

All these verbal gyrations reflected the feeling of anguish that China had betrayed India. The gap between image and reality was too great for someone as sensitive as Menon to ignore. And so he revised his view of India's most powerful neighbor but only reluctantly and in part. The will to believe that this was atypical Chinese behavior, aggravated by America's presence in Asia, prevented a transformation of Menon's deep-rooted image of China.

In sum, Menon's image (shared by Nehru) was widely at variance with Beijing's real posture toward India. The gap continued until it was too late (October 1962). And the perception of China as a good neighbor with peaceful intent, indebted to India for championing its cause at the UN and elsewhere, and as co-cqual leader of the Asian political renascence, led to a policy of unrestrained friendship, 'do-nothing' on the quiescent but unsettled frontier question, and indifference to security along the vast 2500-mile border with China. There was also a surprising touch of *naiveté* about how decisions were made in Maoist China: 'It is very difficult for me to believe that a man who appeared so sensitive to argument [Zhou Enlai] would be the Prime Minister of a country that invaded India.'

This analysis of the Dialogue with Krishna Menon in 1964–66 was based on *the thesis that élite images constitute the master key to understanding and predicting probable choices in foreign policy*. An exploration in depth of Menon's perceptions of many of the major topics in world politics during the two decades after WWII seemed to illuminate many of the choices which he as a member of the Indian foreign policy élite selected over the years. As noted earlier, this *qualitative* analysis was accompanied by an independently conducted *quantitative, content analysis* of frequencies, attitudes, and factors evident in Menon's myriad speeches on India's foreign policy at the UN and elsewhere. The most striking discovery from the *qualitative and content analyses* was the *remarkably similar findings about the basic features of Menon's view of the world*. This strongly pointed, five decades ago, to *the value of combining the two approaches* to image analysis as a reliable means of testing the accuracy of conclusions derived from both. Subsequent *research on conflict, crisis, and war* in the ICB project since 1975 (to be reported in a later volume), *using both quantitative and qualitative methods of analysis, reinforced this finding and strengthened our ability to predict probable foreign policy behavior.*

[The complete text of the 17 hours of interviews with Menon, along with the systematic *qualitative* and *quantitative content* analyses of Menon's world view, were reported in my *India and World Politics: Krishna Menon's View of the World* (1968).]

The last research project in my South Asia phase was a study of the voting behavior of India's political, academic, and media élites in the 1967 fourth general election, when the near-monopoly of the Indian National Congress at the all-India level since independence was undermined, opening the door to an embryonic multi-party system. This book, *Political Leadership in India: An Analysis of Élite Attitudes* (1969), sought to uncover élite images and opinions about various facets of India's political system, notably the causes of the changes in the pattern of voting and the underlying attitudes of these groups. This took the form of intensive interviews of Congress and other party leaders at the all-India, State, and constituency levels, as well as of a large number of journalists and academics, using a structured questionnaire to generate comparable data for this inquiry.

Their views were analyzed on the *causes and results of the Congress Party setback in the 1967 elections*, the *impact of the Congress's (second) succession contest in 1966*, the *role of economic factors in electoral behavior*, the *desire for change*; and the *effects of internal party cleavages*. The results of these interviews were reported in 52 tables and their analysis, on *four broad themes*: *causes of the Congress setback* in the 1967 elections, the *effects of the election results*, an assessment of the *leadership qualities* or lack thereof among *Congress candidates*, and the *effect of the 1966 succession contest*.

INTELLECTUAL LEGACY OF THE SOUTH ASIA PHASE (1951–1989)

The lengthy period of research on *political leaders* and *international conflict* in South Asia generated several *benefits*. One was the *first book* by a Western scholar on the core issue of the still-unresolved India/Pakistan protracted conflict (PC), *The Struggle for Kashmir* (1953). The *second benefit* was an awareness of the *methodological value of in-depth case studies* in a quest for knowledge about world politics. Specifically, it became apparent in that early stage of a Political Science-International Relations research program that the task of unraveling the India/Pakistan conflict over Kashmir (or, later, any interstate PC) required area specialization and *in-depth research*, that is, *vertical or qualitative* inquiry and analysis. The *third benefit* was a discovery of *two closely related concepts* and an initial exploration of what became a long-term research program on *international systems* and *subsystems*.

This, in turn, made necessary immersion in the politics, economics, history, and IR of South Asia, a research program that lasted almost two decades. A second methodological strand was added in 1975, *horizontal* or *in-breadth* or quantitative (aggregate) research and analysis. The result was a commitment to a two-track research strategy, a combination of methods that found its most enduring expression in the *ICB project*, launched in 1975 and continuing four decades later. (An updated report on this project will be presented in a later volume on Intellectual Odyssey III.)

At the conceptual level, close observation of South Asia's international politics during the 1950s and 1960s triggered an interest in the concept of *subordinate system*, primarily geographic in scope, with three or more actors engaged in intense interaction, conflictual and/or cooperative, and deeply penetrated by major powers from the dominant system (the central subsystem) of global politics. This concept and the regional focus were combined in 'International Relations and Asian Studies: The Subordinate State System of Southern Asia', *World Politics*, January 1963.

During the decade after its initial formulation, this concept was applied to a second region, the Middle East, with the findings communicated in a paper on 'The Middle East Subordinate System and Its Impact on Israel's Policy' (*International Studies Quarterly*, June 1969). Moreover, a closely related broader concept of *foreign policy system* became the organizing device for a large-scale project on *Israel's foreign policy as a system of action* (*The Foreign Policy System of Israel* [1972] and *Decisions in Israel's Foreign Policy* [1974]).

The following year, the concept of system served as one of the two levels of analysis in the ICB Project, a continuing quest for knowledge about crises and interstate PCs in the 20th and early 21st centuries. In that context, the macro-level systemic concept, *international system*, was redefined in 'System and Crisis in International Politics', *Review of International Studies*, 1985.

Another intellectual legacy of the long encounter with South Asia was the concept of PC. This concept, too, was triggered by the reality of India/Pakistan relations from the carnage that attended the partition of the subcontinent in 1947, through four wars, frequent crises, and disputes that penetrated their economic, social, political, and religious domains for the last 69 years, most recently highlighted by a nuclear weapons non-violent crisis in 1998, their mini-war over Kargil in northern Kashmir in 1999, and another high-risk crisis in 2001. Taken together, these crises, and others dating back to 1947, reflected the reality of an interstate PC. Later, in the 1970s, 1980s, and 1990s, the significance of another PC as an influence on world and regional politics, the Arab/Israel PC, became a continuing focus of two paths to knowledge—qualitative (in-depth case studies) and quantitative (aggregate data analysis).

Long-term field research in South Asia also generated another conceptual legacy, noted in the Introduction to this book—the realization that world politics is not synonymous with relations between the major powers. While the centrality of the two superpowers, the USA and the USSR, was a necessary starting point, it was not the totality of world politics from 1945 to 1990. There was another domain of conflict and cooperation: although on the periphery of the dominant system of international politics, in terms of geography, military power, and economic development, the domain of lesser powers' conflicts (and cooperative acts) is an essential component of world politics. With the beginning of a dispersion of *decisional centers* in world politics from the early 1960s onward, *polycentrism* merits recognition in a restructuring of the international relations/world politics (IR/WP) paradigm. In sum, the core concepts of a research agenda for IR from the 1960s onward—subordinate system, international system, foreign policy system, crisis, and PC—emerged from theory-building and systematic empirical research.

Other Research-Related Activities in the South Asia Phase

The New States of Asia (1963)
Between the two stages of the *NEHRU* project—the *political biography* (1955–59) and the sequel, *Nehru's Mantle* (1966), which analyzed the two successions to Nehru and Shastri (1964–66)—the research focus broadened beyond the Indo-Pakistani subcontinent to Asia as a whole. The result was the third book in this Phase. *The New States of Asia* comprised a group of six essays written in 1961 and 1962, which combined geographic breadth—a region extending from Pakistan to Indonesia—with political analysis in depth. One essay focused on *Colonialism and the Coming of Independence*. Another analyzed *The Search for Political Stability* in this region, both the record and the causes of instability. A third presented a novel framework for the analysis of the IR of Southern Asia, *A New Subordinate State System*. A fourth essay applied this framework to *The New States in World Politics*. A fifth essay presented an analysis of the concept of *Neutralism*, and its foreign policy derivative for many new states, non-alignment. The final essay extended the geographic domain of analysis to Asia and Africa, with a focus on Israel's relationship with the new states of these two regions, *Israel and Afro-Asia*.

By then the re-emergence of Asia as an important element in world politics and the world economy had become increasingly likely. This led to an evaluation of *Asia's current and future roles*, viewed from the perspective of 1961–62, when these essays were written:

'It is difficult to see the future clearly but nothing has occurred to alter this writer's view that the new states, and especially the non-aligned among them, perform functions necessary to general inter-state stability. At times they can mediate between the blocs. On other occasions they can provide the small contingents of troops for the United Nations' peace-keeping function. At all times, in the foreseeable future, they offer an enormous area for genuine peaceful competition between the blocs to the advantage of all concerned.' (191)

This conviction about Asia's emerging significance in world politics was also expressed in my dedication of this book to our children: 'To Leora, Diana and Seegla, whose generation must not be indifferent to the fate of Asia and her peoples'. The resurgence of China and India during the last two decades of the 20th century, accentuated in the early years of the 21st century as high-growth economies, with China an increasingly visible rising power in world politics, seemed to vindicate this expectation in 1962.

University Of Chicago (1963)
The South Asia phase also included a sojourn at another major academic center of IR and South Asia studies. The most stimulating members of the Department of Political Science at the University of Chicago were three pioneers of IR: *Quincy Wright*, whose *A Study of War* (1942) had opened the mind of readers to the challenge and the promise of unraveling the continuing mystery of war—through its awesome exploration of this pervasive malaise in world politics during the preceding half millennium; *Hans J. Morgenthau*, whose trenchant essay on *Scientific Man and Power Politics* (1946) reaffirmed the primacy of Realism as the IR paradigm, and whose celebrated treatise on *Politics Among Nations* (1948) transformed the field of International Studies, until then dominated by International Law and Diplomatic History, into a discipline of International Politics; and a much younger scholar, *Morton Kaplan*, whose creative foray into *System and Process in International Politics* (1957), a complex and difficult work for colleagues and students, set a very high standard for theory in IR, which few have matched over the decades. One was *Kenneth Waltz*'s *Man, the State and War* (1959) and *Theory of International Politics* (1979). Another was *Robert Keohane* and *Joseph Nye*'s *Power and Interdependence* (1977). All of these were pathbreaking works. During my early years at McGill, Morgenthau's treatise served as an ideal text for undergraduate students of a hitherto neglected discipline.

Wright was the most open-minded of the three, a scholar whose book, *The Study of International Relations* (1955), provided a wide-ranging map of an emerging discipline and its burgeoning literature. Moreover, Wright's emphasis on international law and organization provided a corrective to the theoretical work of Kaplan. Morgenthau and Kaplan were, intellectually, polar opposites. Like Wright, Morgenthau was trained in law and displayed a profound respect for history in his treatise on IR. By contrast, Kaplan was, in his *magnum opus*, as close to a pure theorist as anyone in the past 70 years of IR scholarship.

Kaplan was remote and then absolutely convinced of the validity and originality of his work on system and process—it was only six years since his book was published in 1957. Only 25 years later, in a fragment of an intellectual autobiography, did he offer a candid acknowledgment of shortcomings: 'It is not that I am entirely satisfied with the understanding of theory in *System and Process*, for I have modified some of my positions subsequently. When I teach a course on the book, I call attention to the methodological confusions or insupportable statements in the book' (in Kruzel and Rosenau, 1989, p. 48). It was a very different intellectual disposition from Kaplan in 1963. However, *System and Process* was a stimulating and sophisticated book, regrettably treated with marginal interest over the decades.

Morgenthau, too, was not free from arrogance. The most disquieting evidence emerged during a discussion about the state of IR as a discipline. Although I had long admired his work, I gently suggested that it would be a great service to the IR field if he took the time to write a considered response to his critics. He rejected all dissent from the 'truth', as conveyed in his treatise on world politics, *Politics among Nations*, then in its widely used third edition. In a tone that seemed a reflex of Germanic authority, he declared: 'There is nothing I have read among the criticisms of my work which is worth replying to'—end of discussion! And Morgenthau never deigned to defend the method, theory, or substance of his IR treatise.

A year after the encounter with the University of Chicago, there were two opportunities to deepen my research on political leaders and India's political system. The first occasion, as noted above, was the struggle for the succession to Nehru, who died in May 1964, a process that I observed and analyzed 'at first hand' by exploring the process of decision-making which led to the orderly succession to Nehru, an issue that had long generated widespread concern and uncertainty about 'After Nehru Who and What'.

The second unanticipated experience, as noted, was the lengthy set of interviews, almost daily for three weeks, in November–December 1964, supplemented by further interviews in May 1965, with V.K. Krishna Menon, India's political and diplomatic voice at the UN and throughout the world, and India's most controversial public figure from 1947 to 1962, Nehru's confidant in the shaping of India's foreign policy during most of his tenure as Prime Minister and Foreign Minister. The third experience was the founding of the Shastri Indo-Canadian Institute (SICI) in 1965.

Creation of the Shastri Indo-Canadian Institute (1965)
The SICI is a flourishing educational and cultural bridge between Canada and India. It has generated programs of India studies at more than 25 Canadian universities and programs of Canadian studies at a large number of Indian universities. As such, it is one of the most successful bilateral higher educational institutions in the Commonwealth and in the world at large. Where did the idea originate? And how did it come into existence, in 1965, formally in 1968?

The idea of such an institute arose in the spring of 1965. Until then there were no relations between the academic communities in both states, a virtual mutual non-awareness of the two societies, except for a flourishing diplomatic relationship between them, along with Canada's participation in a Commonwealth aid program for South Asia, the Colombo Plan. During the mid-1950s, there was intense diplomatic interaction, inspired largely by the enthusiasm, energy, and vision of Canada's High Commissioner [Ambassador to India] at the time, *Escott Reid*. Earlier, in the difficult task of finding a formula to enable India to remain in the Commonwealth—as a republic—Canada, through the diplomatic skill and empathy of Lester Pearson, then Secretary of State for External Affairs, played an important role in 'squaring the circle'. Yet these were episodes of cooperative activity in an otherwise passive relationship. Economic ties between Canada and India were minimal. Cultural relations were non-existent. The Indian ethnic presence in Canada was confined to the large Sikh community in British Columbia. There were a handful of Canadian university courses on India. And few Canadian scholars engaged in research on India. In short, Canadians knew little about India, and Indians little about Canada.

It would not be an exaggeration to designate the early years as a period of the 'Two Solitudes'. I recall vividly this atmosphere during my first visit to the subcontinent in 1951–52, as a graduate student eager to understand the complexities of the India/Pakistan conflict in its most persistent expression, the unresolved struggle for Kashmir. It was disquieting, too, that Canadian scholars interested in India usually had to rely on non-Canadian sources for funding: In my own case, the Oxford-based Nuffield Foundation funded one extended visit (1955–56), and the New York-based Guggenheim Foundation supported another (1964–65). Moreover, the inadequacy of library materials on India in Canada was glaring. This was the context in which the idea of an institute to forge a scholarly link between Canada and India came to mind.

The key to a solution for both of these problems was clearly the Government of India: its approval and support were essential to the attainment of the twin goals of encouraging research on India by Canadians and sending documentary materials to Canadian institutions of higher learning. Moreover, a precedent existed, namely, the American Institute of Indian Studies, founded by Prof. Norman Brown, a well-known American Indianist of the University of Pennsylvania and the autonomous but related Library of Congress and the American Libraries Book Procurement Center (ALBPC). And there were ample financial resources—hundreds of millions of counterpart rupee funds, that is, rupees that had accumulated in a Government of India account to permit the repayment by India to Canada for Canada's flow of dollar aid to India. Surely a Commonwealth member, perceived generally as friendly to India, merited equal treatment.

Convinced that the idea was plausible, though perhaps not promising, I phoned for an appointment with India's Finance Minister, T.T. Krishnamachari, in mid-May 1965. I had met the urbane, sophisticated TTK a decade earlier during interviews related to my political biography of Nehru. He responded immediately and invited me to his home the following evening.

My brief was as follows: first, Canada and Canadians knew little about the wonder that was India, its history and civilization, its mosaic of languages and cultures, its struggle for independence, its achievements in the political, economic, and social arenas, and the enormous tasks that lay ahead. Second, Canada and India were senior members of the evolving post-colonial Commonwealth and were middle powers with a shared interest in ensuring change amid stability in world politics. Third, each country could benefit from the dissemination of knowledge, personal contact, and the awareness of challenges and aspirations of both nations, despite their many differences. Finally, given India's sensitivity to foreign aid, *per se*, the creation of an institute to serve as an educational and cultural bridge and funded by counterpart rupee funds to match Canada's dollar aid was an opportunity for India to reciprocate Canada's friendship.

'Splendid idea,' he said. 'Who should be the initial members?' I replied—McGill, Toronto, and the University of British Columbia (UBC), along with the National Library of Canada. I explained that the University of Toronto and UBC offered courses on Indian languages and literature as part of their East Asian and Asian Studies Departments, respectively, while McGill concentrated on Indian politics and economics, through its Department of Economics and Political Science and its Center for Developing Area Studies, and Indian Islam, through its Institute of Islamic Studies. I made it clear, however, that this membership was designed as the first stage of what was anticipated would become an all-Canada organization, with as many university members as wished to participate and were prepared to allocate staff and resources to promote Indian studies, formally or informally.

Very quickly, my hopes were realized. The Institute was formally created in 1968, with my recommended four members. By 1969, seven other universities, Brock, Carleton, Manitoba, McMaster, Queen's, Sir George Williams (later Concordia), and Windsor, became Associate Members, and they were admitted to full membership in 1972, with considerable access to library materials from India. The University of Alberta and Calgary followed in 1977, and Regina and Ottawa joined the Institute before its 15th anniversary. By 1986, another seven universities became members (Athabasca, Dalhousie, Memorial, St. Mary's, Simon Fraser, Waterloo, and Western Ontario), making a total of 21 universities and the National Library of Canada. Several others joined in the next two decades.

In my discussion with the Finance Minister that evening, TTK asked where I thought the Head Office of the Institute should be located. It seemed only natural for me to suggest my own university, McGill. Regarding the amount needed from counterpart funds, I mentioned one million rupees per year, a not insignificant sum at that time. On the no less vital question of how should these funds be allocated, my formula was crystal clear—half for research fellowships and half for the acquisition of library materials from India. That decision was taken in principle during the first discussion in New Delhi in May 1965. It was formalized by the Board of Directors soon after the Institute began its operations in 1968.

My first meeting with TTK lasted barely an hour. My proposal was accepted—indeed, warmly welcomed. So too were the issues of founding membership, location of the Head Office, the size of the first rupee grant, and the principle of equal division of funds for research fellowships and library materials. At the close of our meeting, the Finance Minister suggested that the High Commissioner of Canada and I meet him the next day at his office to formalize our agreement.

I informed Mr. Roland Michener, then High Commissioner, later, Governor-General of Canada, the following morning. His response was spontaneously positive. Within an hour, we found ourselves in the Finance Minister's office putting the terms of agreement into quasi-official form. At no time was there ever hesitation on the part of TTK or Mr. Michener.

It was our and the Institute's good fortune that Prime Minister Shastri was preparing to leave for Canada where, *inter alia*, he was to receive an honorary degree at McGill's spring convocation. During the morning discussion at TTK's office, the idea suddenly emerged: would it not be appropriate to have the Prime Minister announce in his commencement address at McGill the Government of India's support for the establishment of the Institute? Naturally, Mr. Michener and I concurred. An official of the Finance Ministry, who was present throughout the meeting, was asked by TTK to contact the Ministry of External Affairs about the matter. Within minutes the idea was approved, with the suggestion that I draft a paragraph for the Prime Minister's speech at McGill announcing the Government of India's commitment to fund the Institute.

A few days later, it was duly read to an unsuspecting McGill audience, including a surprised Principal and Dean. It remains to clarify how the Institute's name emerged? The original name, as proposed by me to TTK and Mr. Michener, and announced by Prime Minister Shastri at McGill, was the Canadian Institute of Indian Studies. The name was changed to honor the Prime Minister who died in January 1966, immediately after the USSR-brokered Tashkent Conference between India and Pakistan to formalize the end of their second war.

The Institute was, in its conception, first and foremost, a Canadian institution to study India, as specified in its charter of incorporation: '[T]o support and promote the advancement of knowledge and understanding of India through studies in the fields of the humanities and social sciences.' No one on the Indian side of this negotiation questioned the appropriateness of this focus—at that time. Once progress toward the initial goal was attained, the reciprocal flow of Indian scholars to Canada and Canadian library materials to India was set in motion. From its inception, the Institute concentrated on academic research and university teaching: these were its core dual mission. Over time its scope expanded, to include: the awarding of fellowships to senior and junior Canadian scholars and students, and Canadian artists and musicians, to visit India; an ambitious library program; summer programs for Canadian students in Canada and India; invitations to Indian scholars to lecture at Canadian universities; fellowships for Indian scholars, artists, and musicians, to visit Canada; and a Canadian Studies program at member-universities in India.

I served as President for two years, 1969 and 1970, but became inactive thereafter, for I was on an extended leave from McGill in Jerusalem until 1974. With the creation of the SICI (1965–68) and the publication of my *Succession in India/Nehru's Mantle* book in 1966, the *Krishna Menon* book in 1968, and the *Élite Attitudes* book in 1969, the India phase of my intellectual odyssey was drawing to a close, to be succeeded by a new phase, Israel's foreign policy and the Arab/Israel Conflict.

Notes

1. Written on the occasion of a conference marking Nehru's centenary in November 1989, 'Nehru's Place in History'; published in Milton Israel (ed.), *Nehru and the Twentieth Century*, Toronto, ON: University of Toronto South Asian Studies Center, 1991, pp. 23–52.
2. Some—but not Nehru—may have thought that I was too harsh. Taya Zinkin, then correspondent in India for the *Economist* and the *Manchester Guardian*, reported on Nehru's reaction to the book, as expressed during an interview: 'He realizes that Dr. Brecher's criticisms are devastating, the more devastating because he is such a friendly and admiring critic; yet he feels that every criticism is justified.' 'The Lonely Man' (a review of *Nehru: A Political Biography*), *The Economic Weekly*, Bombay, 24 October 1959, p. 1464. An elaboration of Nehru's reaction is contained in Zinkin, *Reporting India*, London, 1962, pp. 216, 217, 219.
3. The most thoughtful, but unconvincing, expression of concern about the future of Indian politics and democracy was S.S. Harrison's *India: The Most Dangerous Decades*, Princeton, NJ, 1966.
4. *Nehru's Mantle: The Politics of Succession in India*, New York, Praeger, 1966.
5. See, for example, S. Gopal, *Jawaharlal Nehru: A Biography, Vol. I: 1889–1947,* Cambridge, MA, 1976; S. Sarkar, *Modern India 1885–1947*, Madras, 1983; R. Suntharalingam, *Indian Nationalism: An Historical Analysis*, New Delhi, 1983; and J.M. Brown, *Modern India: The Origins of an Asian Democracy*, Delhi, 1984; and *Nehru: A Political Life*, New Haven, CT, 2003.

6. See M. Weiner, *Party Building in a New Nation: The Indian National Congress*, Chicago, IL, 1967, and S.A. Kochanek, *The Congress Party of India: The Dynamics of One-Party Democracy*, Princeton, NJ, 1968.
7. Brecher, *Nehru's Mantle, op. cit., passim*.
8. Morris-Jones, reflecting on the political domain, offered a no less positive assessment: '[T]here can be no doubt that in the first half of the 40-year period [corresponding largely to the Nehru era], a massive political thrust of modern institution-building issued from the innovative apex and pressed downwards, with variable but always perceptible effect, through the layers of the whole society. This drive had essentially five prongs: the federal..., the representative..., the administrative..., the judicial..., and, above all, perhaps, the prong of party. By any standards... these were surely years of enormous achievement.' 'India 40 Years On', *South Asia*, X, 2, December 1987, p. 78. See also W.H. Morris-Jones, *The Government and Politics of India*, London, 1964; R. Kothari, *Politics in India*, Boston, 1970; and R.L. Hardgrave, Jr., *India: Government and Politics in a Developing Nation*, 3rd ed., New York, 1980.
9. Chanakya, "The Rashtrapati," *The Modern Review*, Calcutta, 62, November 1937, pp. 546–547.
10. Baldev Raj Nayar, *India's Quest for Technological Independence*, Vol. I, New Delhi, 1981, p. 149. See also his *The Modernization Imperative*, Delhi, 1972.
11. *Lok Sabha Debates*, Third Series, Vol. 19 (22 August 1963).
12. See A.H. Hanson, *The Process of Planning*, London, 1966, esp., p. 48: 'What emerges with the greatest clarity ... is the decisive role played by one man: Jawaharlal Nehru. This inspiration and leadership continued throughout the 1950s and into the 1960s, up to the very end of Nehru's life.' Nehru's centrality in India's economic planning is analyzed sympathetically in Nayar, *India's Mixed Economy: The Role of Ideology and Interest in Its Development*, Bombay, 1989, Chaps. III, IV.
13. See Nayar, *India's Quest for Technological Independence, op. cit.*, Chap. 4, for an instructive discussion of 'Science Policy in the Nehru Era'.
14. For critical assessments of the economic record, see F.R. Frankel, *India's Political Economy, 1947–1977: The Gradual Revolution*, Princeton, NJ, 1978, and L.I. Rudolph and S.H. Rudolph, *In Pursuit of Lakshmi: The Political Economy of the Indian State*, Chicago, IL, 1987.

15. A more positive assessment was presented by a group of Indian scholars and civil servants in B.R. Nanda (ed.), *Indian Foreign Policy: The Nehru Years*, Delhi, 1976.
16. See M. Brecher, *The Struggle for Kashmir*, Toronto, ON, 1953; J. Korbel, *Danger in Kashmir*, Princeton, NJ, 1954; Lord Birdwood, *Two Nations and Kashmir*, London, 1956; S. Gupta, *Kashmir: A Study in India-Pakistan Relations*, Delhi, 1966; A. Lamb, *Crisis in Kashmir 1947–1966*, London, 1966; R. Brines, *The Indo-Pakistani Conflict*, London, 1968; Gopal, *Jawaharlal Nehru: A Biography*, Vol. II, Cambridge, MA, 1975, pp. 18–23, 57–59, 113–133, 181–186; Vol. III, Cambridge, MA, 1984, pp. 43–52, 83–88, 91–93, 214–217, 255–264, 274–275.
17. N. Maxwell, *India's China War*, London, 1970; and Y. Vertzberger, *Misperceptions in Foreign Policymaking: The Sino-Indian Conflict, 1959–1962*, Boulder, CO, 1984.
18. K. Subrahmanyam, 'Nehru and the India-China Conflict of 1962', in Nanda, *op. cit.*, pp. 102–130; S. Gopal, *Jawaharlal Nehru: A Biography, Vol. III*, Cambridge, MA, 1984, Chaps. 4, 6, 10; and S. Hoffman, *India and the China Crisis*, Berkeley, CA, 1990.

CHAPTER 4

First-Generation Israeli Leaders (1948–77)

DAVID BEN-GURION AND MOSHE SHARETT

David BEN-GURION Chairman of the Jewish Agency for Palestine, the crucial decision-making body of the pre-state Jewish community in Palestine, 1935–48; Israel's first Prime Minister and Defense Minister, 1948–53, 1955–63). [MB Interviews 1966 and 1971]

Moshe SHARETT Head of the Political Department and a member of the Executive of the Jewish Agency for Palestine, 1933–48; Israel's first Foreign Minister, 1948–56, and Prime Minister, 1953–55. [MB Interviews 1960]

My encounters with the two commanding figures during the first phase of Israel's independence took the form of several lengthy and insightful interviews: four with *Sharett* at his home in Jerusalem in July 1960, lasting eight hours; and three with *Ben-Gurion* at his home in Sde Boker, a Negev settlement, in June and July 1966 and May 1971, lasting 12 hours. [At my request, both checked my summaries of their extensive remarks and, with very minor changes, affirmed their accuracy, with permission to use them in future publications.] I had met Sharett in 1950 but did not have a serious discussion with him until a decade later. I did not meet Ben-Gurion until 1966, three years after he had left the positions of Prime Minister and Defense Minister, but he was still actively involved in Israel's politics.

Contrasting Personalities: 'Courage versus Caution'

Ben-Gurion and Sharett differed in personality, character, and worldview. 'There has been a temperamental incompatibility throughout', said Sharett with refreshing candor in the first of my 1960 interviews. (Except where otherwise indicated, all quotations are from the interviews with both men). 'I am quiet, reserved, and careful; Ben-Gurion is impulsive, impetuous, and acts on intuition. My capital C is CAUTION, Ben-Gurion's is COURAGE'. There was indeed a clash of personalities. Ben-Gurion was decisive, Sharett was hesitant. Ben-Gurion could not bear Sharett's procrastination but respected his technical skills. Sharett admired Ben-Gurion's daring but could not tolerate his indifference to external criticism, which was summed up in the latter's frequent aphorism, 'it is not important what the *Goyim* (nations other than Israel, non-Jews) *think*, rather, what the *Jews do*'.

Ben-Gurion was here expressing his profound belief that the Jewish national renascence could be realized only through rebellion. Sharett, like Chaim Weizmann, the long-time pre-State moderate leader of the World Zionist Organization and a rival of Ben-Gurion for decades, saw this revival as a natural flow of modern history: the problem was how to harmonize its coming with the international community. This difference went deeper. Ben-Gurion aspired to be what he conceived as a totally free Jew, contemptuous of *Galut* (exile, Diaspora) mentality, and the traditional feeling of dependence. Sharett was much more a product of the Middle East than was Ben-Gurion but he was always overwhelmed by the external factor—'what will the *Goyim* think'.

Ben-Gurion's indifference to 'what will the *Goyim* think' occasionally created a major international political crisis for Israel from which he could not easily extricate himself. One such storm occurred in the immediate aftermath of the Suez-Sinai War. On 7 November 1956, in a mood of exhilaration created by Israel's swift and decisive military victory, he delivered what came to be known as his 'victory speech' in the *Knesset* (Israel's parliament). Throwing caution to the winds, he declared: 'The Armistice Agreement with Egypt [dating to 1949, after the first Arab/Israel War] is dead and buried, and cannot be restored to life.... [Moreover] On no account will Israel agree to the stationing of a foreign force, no matter how called, in her territory or in any of the areas occupied by her.' Western leaders were aghast and made known their chagrin. What to do?

As noted later in these recollections of encounters with political leaders, it was Abba Eban, the consummate Israeli diplomat and advocate, then Israel's Representative to the UN and Ambassador to the USA, who saved the day, rescuing Ben-Gurion from a political abyss. For me, however, the most illuminating aspect of Ben-Gurion's speech was its display of the sometimes emotional behavior of decision-makers, either under stress or, in this instance, in an intoxicating atmosphere of military triumph.

During my June 1966 interview with Ben-Gurion, I asked how he could have made such a provocative speech to a tense and expectant world; surely, I added, he must have known that his words would create a backlash. He did not demur from this provocative remark. Rather, he acknowledged: 'I made a few mistakes in that speech.... I went too far; and it was against the views I had expressed in the Government (Cabinet) [on 28 October 1956], that they [the world] would not let us stay in Sinai'. And then, after a thoughtful pause, as if debating with himself about the wisdom of making such an admission, he leaned forward in his chair, looking straight at an excited interviewer, and made a candid and human admission: '*But you see, Mr. Brecher, the victory was too quick. I was too drunk with victory*'.

Both Ben-Gurion and Sharett came to Palestine in 1906, Ben-Gurion at the age of almost 20, Sharett at 12, Ben-Gurion alone, with a passionate commitment to Labor Zionism, Sharett with his family (his father had been among the earliest Jewish pioneers from Eastern Europe, the *Biluim*, in the 1880s); Ben-Gurion came from the Pale of Poland, Sharett from the Ukraine, the heartland of Russian Jewry. In his manner of speech, his accent, and other superficial traits, Ben-Gurion remained 'the man from Plonsk'. But in his undisguised activism, toughness, and ruthless determination he heralded the coming of the free Jew in the historic Land of Israel, prepared to fight for what he considered Jewish national rights. Sharett's Hebrew was a model for a whole generation of Israelis. But in his temperament and character, he displayed a greater affinity to the Diaspora Jew—hesitancy, subservience, a reliance on diplomacy, a tendency to compromise, and a preoccupation with Gentile attitudes to Jewish behavior.

Ben-Gurion spent his early Palestine years on the land, at Sejera. In 1910, he moved to Jerusalem as editor and party official for *Po'alei Tzyon* (Workers of Zion). The Sharetts lived for two years in an Arab village, a formative influence on Moshe's later outlook. He then attended the Herzliya

Gymnasia in Tel Aviv and stood first in the first graduating class in the first Hebrew secondary school in the country. Both men were studying law in Constantinople at the outset of the WWI. Sharett served most of the war years in the Turkish Army; Ben-Gurion was active in the organization of the pro-Allied Jewish Legion, in North America as well as in Palestine.

Soon after the war, Ben-Gurion played a major role in two significant political and economic developments within the burgeoning *Yishuv* (the Jewish community in pre-independent Israel), the formation of *Ahdut Ha'avoda*, the Unity of Labor Party, in 1919, and the *Histadrut* (literally, organization; The General Federation of Jewish Labor in the Land of Israel), the following year.

Sharett was a member of the party's executive from 1920 to 1925. In that year, he began his studies at the LSE, another formative influence on his view of the world. He returned in 1929 and became Assistant Editor of *Davar* ('Word'), the daily newspaper of the *Histadrut*. He entered the *Yishuv*'s diplomatic service as Secretary of the Jewish Agency's Political Department. He succeeded the assassinated Haim Arlosoroff as Head of that key department in 1933 and remained in this post until Israel's independence in 1948. It was regarded as natural that he should become Israel's first Foreign Minister just as Ben-Gurion was the certain choice for Prime Minister. Throughout this period, Ben-Gurion strengthened his political primacy in the Labor Zionist Movement—succeeding Arlosoroff as the leader of *Mapai* from 1933 onwards—and in the *Yishuv* as a whole; he was Chairman of the Jewish Agency Executive in Jerusalem—Palestine Jewry's 'shadow government'—from 1935 to 1948.

Ben-Gurion and Sharett were colleagues for 35 years. And for more than two decades, until the rupture of 1956, when Ben-Gurion ousted Sharett from the Cabinet and Foreign Ministry, they worked intimately together in the Jewish Agency and then as Prime Minister-Defense Minister and Foreign Minister of the new state, in its formation and its time of greatest trial. Yet they were not friends, for in Sharett's view, shared by most, Ben-Gurion was 'a solitary figure preoccupied with himself, his thoughts, deeds, and emotions' (MB Interview June 1960).

Ben-Gurion's estimate of Sharett was no less ambivalent. He was capable of an effusive tribute, as on the occasion of the conferment of the 'Freedom of the City of Jerusalem' on Sharett in August 1964, when Sharett was gravely ill: 'One of the greatest personalities of our generation…, the architect of the policy of the sovereign State of Israel for many years…. one of the few exemplary spirits of our generation…', and so on.

(*Jerusalem Post*, 8 July 1965). Yet one year later, Ben-Gurion absented himself from Sharett's funeral.

During my June 1966 interview with Ben-Gurion, he was more critical though not hostile: 'He [Sharett] knew more about the details of foreign affairs than I did; but when it came to an important problem he didn't know how to distinguish words from deeds.' Further, 'he was the greatest Foreign Minister of our day in peacetime but not in time of war'. And of Sharett's personal qualities, 'he was honest – and there was great nobility about him'.

No one, friend or foe, and Sharett had few of the latter, would disagree with Ben-Gurion's last remark. Indeed these qualities were stressed when he died. Eban, who later became Foreign Minister, in 1966, referred to 'Moshe [Sharett] incarnating the public conscience.... He knew that no man in Israel commanded a similar affection' (*Jerusalem Post*, 8 July 1965). And world Zionist leader *Nahum Goldmann* praised him as 'the greatest moral figure in Jewish life' and a man who 'became (in his later years) a kind of moral conscience of this country' (*Jerusalem Post*, 24 June 1966).

Sharett recognized Ben-Gurion's political greatness, a further measure of his honesty. And Ben-Gurion assumed this higher status without hesitation. As *Shimon Peres*, a Ben-Gurion devotee, remarked 50 years ago, 'Ben-Gurion respected the personal qualities of Sharett, his precision and thoroughness; he thought of him as a brilliant technician; but he felt that Sharett lived in an artificial world where gestures, words, were given great importance' (MB Interview, Tel Aviv, June 1966). In short, the two men combined respect for each other with disdain for some of the other's traits, a not uncommon ambivalence among comrades in public life.

Contrasting Worldviews

Ben-Gurion's actions were always dominated by a single-minded purpose—the rebirth and survival of a Jewish state. It is not surprising, therefore, that his worldview changed little over the decades.

Sharett was no less inspired by the Zionist ideal. But his personality and life pattern were different, with the result that other concerns affected his worldview. There were in fact three basic threads in his image. One was an outlook rooted in the Old Testament as the sourcebook of Jewish nationhood, acquired in his father's home. Another was a feeling of awe about how the world looked at Jews, the product of his LSE years. And close contact with Arabs from adolescence onward created a fascination for the Canaanite idea—that the Hebrews (Jews in Palestine) were primarily another Middle East nation. Sharett wavered between his sense of the universal Jewish People and Canaanism.

There were other differences in *perception* and *attitude*. For Ben-Gurion, Diaspora Jewry had a legitimate, important function, even an obligation—to assist Israel achieve its foreign policy goals. For Sharett, Israel and Diaspora Jewry each had to take the other's interests into account in their public behavior. Sharett was concerned about the impact of Israel's acts on world opinion; Ben-Gurion was not. Ben-Gurion had little use for diplomacy; Sharett understood its role better but exaggerated its importance.

There were also contrary views about the possibility of peace with the Arab states from the early 1950s onward [to be discussed in my *Dynamics of the Arab/Israel Conflict: Intellectual Odyssey II* (forthcoming, 2017)]. Stated more generally, their worldview differed along virtually the whole spectrum: of Israel's recent past, that is, of the forces that led to independence; of the global system, notably the UN; of the Middle East system and the Arab mind, polity, and society; of Israel's proper place in the world and region; and of the time and proportionate role for diplomacy and force as techniques of Israeli statecraft. Thus, their choices of policy, style, and specific decisions differed markedly.

Two Views of the Road to Statehood

Insight into the mind-set of Ben-Gurion and Sharett was provided by their contrasting views of the road to statehood, conveyed in their writings and during these interviews. For Ben-Gurion, 'the state was the result of our daring'. The Ben-Gurion image has an attractive simplicity. The Ben-Gurion view granted the role of, and even the need for, vision, as articulated by Herzl, the founder of the world Zionist movement, and others, as well as the fact of the age-old Jewish emotional attachment to Zion. However, the turning point in the modern history of the Jews, for Ben-Gurion, was the *aliya* [immigration] of the late nineteenth century and beyond. For him, it was the presence of Jews in the Land of Israel that constituted the true beginning of the rebirth of a Jewish commonwealth. Everything preceding this in time or parallel to it, such as political agitation, diplomatic battles, and the raising of funds, was distinctly secondary to the creation of a living *Yishuv*.

The conclusions for Ben-Gurion were inescapable. The entire epoch of the longing for Zion in the millennia of Dispersion does not form a part of the road to statehood. At most, it was a preface in time to the cardinal fact of Jewish settlement, of physical presence. The path to independence begins in time and substance with the *Biluim* and the early villages of Mikve Israel, Petah Tikva, and so on. Moreover, to Ben-Gurion (BG), the state 'was the result of our daring'. Thus the diplomatic struggle, especially at the UN, was peripheral. In its most extreme form the BG interpretation, communicated in these interviews and elsewhere, asserted that, regardless of the outcome at the UN in 1947–48, the state would have or could have survived—provided that courage and will and daring were present in the *Yishuv*. Conversely, no UN resolution could have created the state if that determination were lacking.

Was this paramount stress on the role of the *Yishuv*—where Ben-Gurion dominated—a mere coincidence? Sharett termed this virtually exclusive emphasis on the role of the *Yishuv* a further expression of Ben-Gurion's egocentrism: 'Only that is important to which he [Ben-Gurion] himself contributed, and the diplomatic battle was outside his sphere of action. Deep in his heart', remarked Sharett during my first 1960 interview, 'Ben-Gurion knows the vital role of the diplomatic battle at the United Nations but he cannot bring himself to admit this in public'. Others perceived Ben-Gurion's indifference to diplomacy as a function of his activist philosophy and its necessity for morale within Israel.

Whatever the Ben-Gurion motivation, the *single-factor* image of the road to statehood—the presence of Jews in the Land of Israel—has long been shared by many Israelis. Moreover, this image had profound operational significance. His disdain for the UN role in making history, especially in the creation of Israel, carried over into the post-1948 period of Israel's high policy: his contempt for the UN, his reliance on the *Yishuv* and, particularly, on the Israel Defense Forces, is a logical, inevitable extension of his image of the events of 1947–48. 'The United Nations counted for little then in the Middle East, it counts for nothing now'—this has long been the essence of Ben-Gurion's view, with far-reaching consequences for Israeli foreign policy from 1948 onwards.

To assert that Israel's security in the 1950s and 1960s depended upon its own armed strength, even if correct, does not prove that this was so in 1948 when Israel was much weaker, relatively and absolutely. It is more plausible to argue that the UN was crucial in 1948, when Israel needed international sanction, but not later when it was firmly established.

The Sharett image of the path to independence was set within a different frame of reference. [The following exposition is my reconstruction of the first of four interviews with Sharett in July 1960, confirmed by him as accurate.] The Jewish presence in the Land of Israel was, of course, important but it was not primary in time or substance. To take the *aliya* of the 1880s as *the* turning point was to distort history and to abstract one concrete phenomenon from the broad and complex movement of the Return to Zion. For Sharett, the novel and decisive event in modern Jewish history was the *reawakening of a national will* among various sections of the Jewish People and the capacity to translate that will into action. The reawakened national will, he declared, was the product of faith and vision, not of the Jewish presence. On the contrary, it was that faith, with the added impetus of the Russian *pogroms,* (massacres, usually referring to periodic raiding, looting, and the massacre of Jews in Eastern Europe) which generated *aliya*. But not only did vision operate through this channel: it was a factor in itself with influence on the Return, both by its impact on Jews to migrate and on world chancelleries to support Zionism. Finally, the reawakened national will was not confined to those who settled in Israel. It affected the whole Jewish People, and their awakening led them to contribute to the Return in different ways.

Sharett proceeded with a dialectical reading of the Return. It was the continued presence of a small Jewish community in Palestine during the preceding two millennia and the unbroken spiritual attachment of Jewry to Zion which persuaded Gentile statesmen to accept the claim of a Right to Return. These, along with diplomacy, secured the Balfour Declaration (1917) and the League of Nations British Mandate (1922). They, in turn, created the possibility for the Third *Aliya* [migration of Jews to Palestine] and a more rapid building of the National Home in the 1920s. Further, the strengthening of the *Yishuv* [Jewish community in the Land of Israel] gave greater weight to the diplomatic and political struggles of the 1940s. Together this interplay of forces, practical (the *Yishuv),* and political (diplomatic), created the state.

Sharett argued vigorously, in that interview, that the road to statehood could not be torn from its international and political context, for the Return was an *international* phenomenon—in the composition of *aliyot* (plural of *aliya,* immigration), in the catalytic force of the Holocaust, and in the struggle for world support. On the relative importance of internal and external forces, he was emphatic in giving primacy to the diplomatic battle. His reasoning was as follows: it required courage to proclaim independence on 14–15 May 1948 (Ben-Gurion's act), but that act was possible only in a political vacuum—and that vacuum was created by the termination of the League of Nations UK Mandate and the physical withdrawal of the British, their army, police, and administration. The termination of the Mandate was achieved by diplomacy at the UN and elsewhere, not in Israel. Moreover, [British] Foreign Secretary Bevin sought UN support for the *continuation* of the Mandate, after which he would seek economic and other sanctions. 'This could easily have brought us to our knees. We might have gone down fighting, but the objective was to win through to victory. Thus the great achievement at the United Nations was to terminate the Mandate and secure the British withdrawal, thereby creating the indispensable condition for independence.'

In Sharett's view, the struggle both at home—in Palestine—and abroad contributed to independence. The difference with Ben-Gurion, then, was not one of emphasis. Ben-Gurion virtually ignored the external factor— 'the state is the result of our daring'. Sharett admitted both dimensions but was driven to an extreme view: 'I am not ashamed to say it—we owe our state to the United Nations.' He ridiculed the Ben-Gurion contention that UN assistance in 1948 was insufficient because it did not include an international army: 'This was a political impossibility at the time, for the United States would not agree to Russian troops in the Middle East, and the Russians could veto any other international force; the UN did what it could, and that was vital.'

The contrast in their perception of the past is basic. How much was due to conviction and how much to the imperatives of one's place in history is difficult to discern. One aspect is clear, however: as with Ben-Gurion, the impact of Sharett's image on his foreign policy decisions was pervasive. For one thing, his image of a crucial U.N. role in 1947–48 led him to a reliance on the world organization, at least to the maximum avoidance of acts which might alienate the UN. Second, his pride in the accomplishments of diplomacy in 1947–48 and his faith in the UN strengthened his personality predisposition to a policy of caution, antipathy to violence, and opposition to border raids; that is, it was diametrically opposed to the Ben-Gurion hard line toward the Arabs. Indeed, 'the basic specific question over which we clashed was the question of [military] retaliation [against the Arabs]', Sharett reaffirmed in the interviews. It was over this issue that Sharett was forced by Ben-Gurion to resign in June 1956

(Caplan 2016), a few months before Israel launched the Sinai Campaign-Suez War.

On that momentous Ben-Gurion's decision Sharett demurred. 'It was unnecessary', he said in 1960. When pressed by me, he acknowledged that by 1956, perhaps, there was no way of avoiding the clash—but the tension built up between 1953 and 1956 could have been drastically reduced by another policy. 'Every Arab act on the border was magnified and led to Israeli retaliation; this in turn led to continuous aggravation and escalation of the conflict.' The alternative path was implicit in this comment.

Ben-Gurion's View of World Politics

David Ben-Gurion never concealed his World View. Indeed, he used his pen assiduously over the decades as part of the struggles for a 'Restored State of Israel'. The result has been a dozen volumes of essays—many of them polemical—speeches, interviews, letters, and memoirs. They are not equally important nor of uniform quality, but they are rich in insight into BG's 'public philosophy'. For Ben-Gurion's view of world politics, the most valuable and accessible sources are four essays which he contributed to the *Government Year-Book* during his tenure as Prime Minister: 'Israel Among the Nations' (1952–53); 'Israel's Security and Her International Position before and after the Sinai Campaign' (1959–60); 'Towards a New World' (1960–61); and 'Achievements and Tasks of our Generation' (1961–62). According to his closest political aides at the time, the first and second are the most authoritative expression of the images underlying Ben-Gurion's basic foreign policy decisions (MB Interviews in 1966 with *Shimon Peres*, Director-General of the Defense Ministry and then Deputy Minister of Defense during Ben-Gurion's tenure as Prime Minister and Defense Minister, and *Yitzhak Navon*, Ben-Gurion's Political Secretary from 1952 to 1963, and later, the sixth president of Israel).

The Contemporary Era
'Towards a New World' contains little that is new or original, but there are very few, and only marginal, errors in a sweeping historical survey. There is evidence of wide reading, a thorough grasp of essentials, an ability to place the modern world in historical perspective, an understanding of the main forces at work in contemporary world politics, and, as in much of his writings, a striking arrogance. Ben-Gurion notes at the outset that we live in a new and unprecedented era in human history, with two interrelated devel-

opments—the coming of freedom to all peoples and the growing dependence of all nations on each other. There is also a dual set of psychological forces—the rising expectations of the underprivileged and the increasing acceptance of responsibility by the developed states. Asians and Africans are not innately inferior to Westerners, he observed, as the Japanese victory over Russia in 1905 revealed dramatically. Further, 'the peoples of Europe were not always in the van of culture', and the Afro-Asians are destined to exert a powerful influence on the future of mankind. These were his conclusions from a detailed and accurate survey of European expansion overseas and the reasons for its success ('Towards a New World', in State of Israel, *Government Year-Book 5721*, 1960/1, Jerusalem, 11–33).

Set against the sweep of history, Ben-Gurion's image of the contemporary era began—and ended—with the place of Jewry: no epoch had been more appalling and heartening, more tragic and heroic, with greater suffering and havoc, yet with more hope and salvation; nor was there any parallel to Jewish tribulations and endurance. Over and over again, there is reference to the uniqueness and mission of Jewry which, unlike other nations, never succumbed to other faiths. But while Jewish history is unique it does not develop in a vacuum, it is part of world history.

Ben-Gurion perceived an era of: global wars; totalitarian regimes—with 'no parallel among the tyrannies hitherto chronicled; they exist, they spread, they may spread further'; a revolution in transport, communications, and technology; continued disunity among the nations, but with narrowing gaps and falling barriers; the liberation of peoples and continents—'the mightiest and most revolutionary development in history'; the glaring chasm between rich and poor—'a grave and painful problem, perhaps no less so than the dominion of man over fellow-man'; Cold War, and a necessary but weak UN. He emphasized the revolution in science, noting that scientists are, legitimately, involved in everything, for pure and applied science are necessarily integrated, yet science must also be related to morality. He was proud of the notable role of Jewry in the scientific revolution, from Spinoza to Einstein and including Marx and Freud, but their Jewish identity, he regretted, was masked—until 1948. He then closed the circle of Jewish consciousness by extolling the renascence of the Jewish state—an extraordinary phenomenon, particularly when viewed against the absolute negation posed by the Holocaust to Jewish creativity and, indeed, survival ('Achievements and Tasks of Our Generation', in State of Israel, *Government Yearbook 5722*, 1961/2, Jerusalem, vii–lxxx). Elsewhere he elaborated on the accomplishments of Israel restored (this was done at length in *Medinat Yisrael Ha-mehudeshet*, vol. 2, and in *Ben-Gurion Looks Back*, 171 ff.).

'Israel Among the Nations' (1952)
The outlines of Ben-Gurion's early post-Independence image were friendliness and aid by the two superpowers, international sanction by the UN and a natural community of Arab-Jewish interests. These were the perceptual foundations of the 'five principles' of foreign policy enunciated by Israel's first elected Government in March 1949. But it was not until four years after independence that BG provided a substantive exposition of his View of the World in his essay 'Israel Among the Nations'. The pre-eminence of security is already apparent, but this pivotal concept was fully expounded only after the Sinai Campaign.

Few countries enjoy a security based upon geography, observed Ben-Gurion at the outset, and even those which did so, like Britain and the USA, are no longer immune to assault—from the air. Yet in comparison with history, 'geography varies little or not at all'. Certainly, this is true of Israel: 'Its geographico-physical definition is practically unaltered, although vast and vital changes have taken place in its geopolitical surroundings.' He cautioned that 'no historical situation is like the next' and that 'experience is likely to turn into a canker and a moral risk if we pursue it blindfolded'. In that context, he noted that Israel's two ancient epochs were alike in three respects: 'the centre of gravity of the world in which the Jewish people lived...was the Mediterranean region'; Israel was surrounded by different peoples, whose quarrels could be exploited for its security; and the Jews 'entered the Land from the East'.

None of these conditions exists in the age of the third Jewish commonwealth. Indeed, 'only two exceptional portents of our times need be mentioned here', he wrote in his 1959–60 essay. 'First, the waning hegemony of Europe and the rise of Asia, [whose three principal nations, India, China and Japan] are pregnant with a destiny no less great and fruitful than Europe once knew. The second portent is the struggle for leadership of the world between two mighty powers, the United States of America and the Soviet Union.' Yet the global system was not rigidly bipolar, in Ben-Gurion's early image.

Within that non-Communist world, Ben-Gurion perceived various types of actors: 'primitive states still existing under a theocratic-monarchical régime'; feudal or semi-feudal societies; capitalist-democratic countries; dictatorships; and 'progressive, socialistic' nations. A notable omission in this perceptive image of global politics is the UN; by 1952, perhaps earlier, BG had dismissed the world body as of no consequence.

There is a conspicuously softer tone in the emotive words which Ben-Gurion used to describe the West. He distinguished three kinds of states encountered by Israel: those which refuse any links, those which permit relations with their Governments only, and those which allow contact with their people as well. 'The difference between the third and the second group', he wrote, 'is hardly less important than that between the second and the first'.

Ben-Gurion's image of global politics was only partly rooted in the reality of Jewish dispersion. It also derived from the *raison d'être* of Zionism. 'The State sees itself as the creation of the Jewish people and as designed for its redemption. It sees Jews throughout the world as one nation, not only in the past but in the present and future as well.' Still another conscious source was his perceived affinity of Israel's values and those of the West. 'Israel is not indifferent to the ideological conflict', wrote BG. 'Its devotion to the values of human freedom, freedom of thought and spirit, freedom of choice and criticism ... is ingrained in its character.' And finally, Ben-Gurion's socialism was of the democratic type, formed in the spirit and at the time of the first (1905) Russian Revolution; he never abandoned that commitment. In short, interests and ideology—perhaps temperament as well—created an image of the superpowers favorable to the USA; and experience molded his view of the UN.

In the most general terms, he expounded 'five paramount missions of Israel'; these include three impinging on external policy—immigrant absorption, military and political security, and the safeguarding of sovereignty. '[I]ts wishes and its capacity are not a negligible quantity.... In international politics, too, there are imponderable forces, and there is no doubt that, in a fair degree, Israel is one of them. Israel stood up by its own strength and will stand firm only if it trusts first and foremost in itself as a power of growing greatness' (the above analysis and quoted extracts are taken from 'Israel Among the Nations', State of Israel, *Government Year-Book 5713*, 1952/3, Jerusalem, 1–47).

'Israel's Security and Her International Position' (1960)
The behavior of the super powers and the UN during the Sinai Campaign only strengthened Ben-Gurion's image of world politics—and of the path to independence. The Soviet Union's relentless hostility, which reached its peak in the dire Bulganin threats of direct intervention and air assault

in the early days of November 1956, and continued with the attempts to impose UN sanctions against Israel, appeared to BG and others as total confirmation of his image. The USA was also opposed to the Sinai Campaign. Yet, in the prolonged diplomatic crisis over Israeli rights in the Tiran Straits, during the early months of 1957, the USA showed much sympathy. Thus the image of the USA as a friend, though critical of some aspects of Israeli policy, was solidified by its perceived behavior.

Ben-Gurion's suspicion about Secretary General Hammarskjöld's 'objectivity' was also fortified. So too was his disdain for the UN role: the UN was unable to secure peace or to assist Israel to defend herself and passed pro-Arab resolutions. Yet Ben-Gurion had a marked ambivalence toward the United Nations. 'It has not the power, the authority or the will to put its principles into practice', he wrote on another occasion. 'The State of Israel felt that weakness the very day it was born.... All the same... some kind of supreme authority for mankind is taking shape.... The UN may yet do great things in drawing the peoples closer and building peace in the world' ('Achievements and Tasks of Our Generation', ix, x).

On Ben-Gurion's denigration of the UN role in the Arab/Israel conflict, Abba Eban, then one of the four *younger* Israeli leaders explored in this book, below, echoed the Sharett view: 'Ben-Gurion has a monistic view of history; his perspective does not encompass a plurality of factors influencing the course of events. More than de Gaulle or Churchill he identifies the nation's history with himself; whatever does not involve him he simply ignores; and since he played no role in the U.N. theatre he dismisses it as of no consequence' (MB Interview in Rehovot, December 1965).

Much of 'Israel's Security and Her International Position' deals with a landmark in Israeli foreign and security policy, the Sinai Campaign—its complex background, the decision, the ensuing political struggle, and the consequences of that 'second round'. But this essay also provides insight into other aspects of Ben-Gurion's image, especially concerning Israel's proper role in the global system. To begin with, BG offers a precise and comprehensive definition of 'security' (op. cit, 22–4):

> just as the problem of Israel's security is different from that of other countries, so too the scope of our defense is wider than that of any other country, and does not depend on our army alone.
>
> Israel can have no security without immigration.

Security means the settlement and peopling of the empty areas in north and south; the dispersal of the population and the establishment of industries throughout the country; the development of agriculture in all suitable areas; and the building of an expanding (Self-sufficient) economy.

Security means the conquest of the sea and the air, and the transformation of Israel into an important maritime power.

Security means economic independence.

Security means the fostering of research and scientific skill on the highest level in all branches of [science and] technology.

Security means vocational training of a high standard for our youth.

And, finally, security means a voluntary effort by the youth and the people in general for difficult and dangerous tasks in settlement, security, and the integration of the immigrants.

But Israel can have no security without her Defence Forces, and...we must meet their needs in equipment of the finest quality.

Ben-Gurion had no illusions about the impact of the 1956 Sinai Campaign. It produced respect and admiration among many Asian and African peoples, he claimed, as well as tranquility on the borders, 'inner confidence of the nation', and 'faith in its army'. It also led to freedom of navigation in the Tiran Strait and the Gulf of Aqaba. At the same time, *'there is one illusion... born of the Campaign that must be destroyed without compunction.... namely that the Sinai Campaign has completely solved the problem of our security.... Basically... the problem has not been solved.... It is doubtful'*, he added philosophically, *'whether war can solve historical problems at all'; but he hastened to add, 'although there are unavoidable wars that have to be fought'*. (Government Year-Book 5720, Jerusalem, 1960, 22–24, emphasis added)

Ben-Gurion referred to the two different spheres in which Israel must function, the 'small' sphere or the Middle East, and the 'large' sphere or the global system. The importance of the latter he attributed to three factors: first, the dispersion of the majority of the Jewish People, 'from which we draw manpower, material and cultural resources, and moral and political support'; second, 'the forces at work in the wider sphere [who] will not lightly accept all the decisions secured by the Israel forces, *if these decisions are in opposition to their true or imagined interests*'; and, thirdly, the continued dependence of Israel's armed forces *'on the good will of those who manufacture the arms'*; and, he added, only a few are prepared to make them available (*Ibid*, 57–58).

Yet BG was not unaware of the impact of the new states on the global system: 'The adhesion of new countries to the United Nations has considerably altered the relationships between world forces, and to some extent has mitigated the domination of the great powers, the United States and the Soviet Union.' And 'there is no doubt', he declared, 'that Israel's international standing has improved thanks to ... ties with the new countries' (replies to questions by Joel Marcus, in *Davar* (Tel Aviv), 27 April 1961).

In what sphere does Israel belong? It is not only Middle Eastern, asserted Ben-Gurion, but a Mediterranean nation as well. Further, 'in effect Israel is neither ... but *a world people* .... It is the attachment to the scattered Jewish people that is decisive for Israel'. In a later essay he extended Israel's regional links to 'the Red Sea region and, through it, to the Indian Ocean' ('Achievements and Tasks of Our Generation', lv).

In that context, he specified two basic foreign policy goals: (1) the maintenance of an effective military deterrent—'deterrence and the prevention of war are more important and desirable than military victory'; and (2) friendly relations with the maximum number of states, for this might 'weaken the Arab wall of hatred and finally pave the way for a pact of peace'.

The most authoritative statement of Ben-Gurion's image of global politics and his view of Israel's proper role in that 'sphere' is 'Israel's Security and Her International Position' (1960). There were no substantive changes for the rest of his tenure as Prime Minister and Defence Minister, or even after 1963. Ben-Gurion was, *par excellence*, an adherent of the Realist or 'national interest' approach to foreign policy.

"The Arabs": Ben-Gurion's Perception

Ben-Gurion was a 'Ben-Gurionist' during most of his tenure in office. Yet Ben-Gurion did not always perceive 'the Arabs' in suspicious, hard-line terms. On the eve of independence and during the early years of statehood he (publicly) perceived a natural harmony of interests, which was temporarily blurred by fanaticism and hate, and he advocated 'a Jewish-Arab alliance'. This is evident in three brief extracts (as quoted in 'On Peace and Negotiations', *New Outlook* [Tel Aviv], vol. 6, no. 1 [50], Jan. 1963, 41–2):

(1) The historical interests and aspirations of the Jews and Arabs are ... complementary and inter-connected.... Cooperation between Jews and

Arabs will prove the truest blessing for both peoples. Such cooperation can rest only upon equality ... [upon a] Jewish-Arab alliance.
(4 July 1947 to UNSCOP)
(2) We extend the hand of peace and good neighbourliness to all the neighbouring states and their peoples and invite their cooperation.
(Declaration of Independence, 14 May 1948)
(3) Israel wishes to see Egypt free, independent, progressing. ... We have no enmity against Egypt. ... We have never sought to exploit Egypt's political difficulties with a Great Power [England].
(To the *Knesset*, 18 August 1952)

In 1948, too, as he recalled, he welcomed the idea of a customs union with Jordan; further, 'we can also participate in a federation, but only as a fully independent state' (*Medinat Yisrael Ha-mehudeshet*, vol. 1, 218). By 1954, however, a deep suspicion had taken root in Ben-Gurion's image.

From his reading of the Nasser-led revolution in Egypt and the failure of various sub-rosa efforts at negotiation—'I personally was involved in four attempts at mediation with Nasser'—he became committed to a 'realistic' view. (Ben-Gurion elaborated on this 'secret' at an informal meeting of the Israel Institute of International Affairs in June 1965.) Two of these attempts, he said, were initiated by Americans, one an emissary of President Eisenhower and the other 'a very high State Department official'. The third attempt was by an English journalist who had interviewed Nasser. The fourth, which Ben-Gurion related to this writer in detail at Sde Boker in July 1966, was through an Israeli friend of Tito who tried to establish contact when Nasser was in Yugoslavia [in July 1956]. Nothing came of these efforts, added Ben-Gurion (as reported by Mark Segal in the *Jerusalem Post*, 29 June 1965). Shortly after Nasser's death in September 1970, Ben-Gurion revealed further details concerning some of these contacts, notably in 1956 via Robert Anderson, a former US Secretary of Defense. And he divulged details of an abortive expression of interest by Nasser in meeting him in 1963. Indeed, added BG, eight days before his death Nasser told someone he wanted to meet him as soon as possible (Interview in *L'Actualité* [Paris], reproduced in *Ha'aretz* [Tel Aviv], 12 Oct. 1970). Its essence is that Israel lives in an inherently hostile Arab world, that the best one can work for is acceptance of Israel, and that the only way to achieve this is to hammer away at the Arab states whenever possible—a policy of strength, for this is all the Arabs respect. A soft line, the argument proceeds, would weaken Israeli security by giving hope to those Arab groups who look for signs of weakness and an opportunity to destroy Israel. In short, one cannot buy security with concessions. Thus, Israel must persist with a strong line until 'the Arabs' become reconciled to its existence.

The long-term goal, as with the 'Weizmannist' approach, is positive coexistence after 20 years or more of hostile acquiescence. The 'Ben-Gurionists' assert, however, that no alternative to a hard line exists, for the Arabs do not have a compelling motive for peace. The absence of an incentive for a settlement is attributed to three factors: *self-delusion*—'the Arabs' are victims of their own propaganda about Israel's survival potential; *idealism*—'the Arabs' genuinely feel the obliteration of the Palestine Arab community and the alienness of Israel, which they would like to eliminate; and *self-interest* in the perpetuation of the conflict—Israel provides an excellent focus for Arab unity. Nasser can always negotiate with Israel—why now, the question was posed before the 1967 War. If Israel were to offer to repatriate one hundred thousand refugees, why should Nasser accept this as sufficient for peace? He could take this as a starting point and wait for more, so too with territorial adjustments. Moreover, he could hope that Soviet arms and a shift in American strategic policy would enable him to destroy Israel. If not, he could always meet the Israelis at a later date. In short, as long as there is no Arab *need* for peace there will be no peace. This 'Ben-Gurionist' image and its policy consequence—firmness as the key to acceptance—commanded widespread support in Israel. The perception that there were no compelling Arab motives for immediate peace was plausible *until the Six-Day War of 1967*. The critical question is whether this view was valid after 'the third round'. Most Israelis appeared to think so in 1970; BG himself did not, since that War.

Ben-Gurion expressed these views frequently from 1955 onwards with varying points of emphasis. A few illustrations of this image may be cited (the last two of the following extracts were made available by the Government Press Office in Jerusalem):

(1) Peace and co-operation with the Arabs ... must always be our major objective. ... But I have no illusions about peace with the Arabs. ... I doubt if we shall get it until there are thoroughly stable governments in the Arab States instead of cliques.
(Interview with correspondent of *The Times*, London, as reported in the *Jerusalem Post*, 29 August 1955)

(2) Peace cannot be achieved until the Arabs, or rather the Arab leaders, will be persuaded they cannot destroy Israel either by economic boycott

or by political pressures or by military offensives. ... And no foreign Government can compel the Arabs to make peace.
(Interview with Golda Zimmerman, 25 March 1958)
(3) The hope of peace depends on three factors: whether democracy will grow in the Arab countries, whether our neighbours will realize that it will not be easy to destroy Israel, and whether world tension will be less than it is now.
(To foreign correspondents, 2 February 1959)

Yet his early call to Israel's neighbors to forge a co-operative relationship was reaffirmed from time to time. Thus in 1965, soon after Tunisia's President Bourguiba urged a new Arab look at Israel, Ben-Gurion told the *Knesset*: 'We should not also ignore the isolated voices that emerge here and there among some of the Arab peoples, from those who adopt a sober and realistic view of Israel-Arab relations...those Arabs who aspire for peace' (*Jerusalem Post*, 23 Nov. 1965). And in March 1967 he predicted that, when peace came, Israel would be able to find its place 'even in some loose form of Middle Eastern Federation' (*The Israel Digest*, Jerusalem, vol. x, no. 7, 7 April 1967). Paradoxically, BG had subjected the same idea to sharp criticism when it was mooted by Nahum Goldmann during the 1961 Israel election campaign: then Ben-Gurion had lashed out at 'the important visitor from New York', ridiculed the idea of integrating with the Arab world, and accused Goldmann of 'knowingly misleading the public'.

The main thrust of Ben-Gurion's image of 'the Arabs' and his related policy lay in the realm of toughness and no compromise. Only after the Six-Day War did he perceive a compelling Arab need for peace—and the logical derivative, a policy of concessions. Not by accident did he advocate a virtual return to the 4 June borders, apart from Jerusalem and the Golan Heights—in exchange for a genuine peace settlement (in various statements and interviews during June–August 1967 and reiterated frequently thereafter). (He continued to advocate this in 1970: 'We should evacuate all territories conquered in June 1967, except Jerusalem and the Golan Heights. There is enough room in Israel, as it was before the Six-Day War, to receive all future Jewish immigrants, and that is all that matters' [interview with *Le Nouvel Observateur*, 15 November 1970, as reported in the *Jerusalem Post*, 16 November 1970]).

In the language of image analysis, Ben-Gurion revealed an 'inherently bad faith' perception of 'the Arabs'. The commanding figure of

Ben-Gurion in foreign and security policy had few parallels—Adenauer, de Gaulle, Mao, Nehru, Stalin, and during WWII, Churchill and Roosevelt. Yet his perception of 'the Arabs' bears the most striking resemblance to the John Foster Dulles image of 'the enemy'. The influence of the US Secretary of State on American foreign policy from 1953 to 1959 is generally regarded as massive. Ben-Gurion's influence on Israeli foreign policy was even greater—and for a longer period. There were some common factors—an elaborate conception of their role, frequent crises, widespread support from their publics, intellectual arrogance, and a deep-rooted, carefully rationalized image of 'the enemy'. Ben-Gurion had, however, an even wider latitude, by virtue of his role as 'father of the nation', and for many years an almost universally trusted Head of Government and Defence Minister.

Sharett's View of World Politics

While Ben-Gurion's four essays in the Government Year-Book were the major source for his view of world politics, the primary source for this exposition of Sharett's articulated image was a cluster of key speeches at the UN (11 May 1949, 27 September and 4 October 1950, and 15 November 1951), along with speeches before the *Knesset*, Israel's parliament (4 July 1950 and 23 January 1951) and in the USA (19 June 1952 and 21 November 1955). Sharett also kept a massive Personal Diary, which was published in a seven-volume Hebrew version. [An English abridged version in three volumes is currently in process, edited by Sharett's son, Yaacov (Kovi) Sharett, and Neil Caplan, containing a multitude of detailed recollections on his tortured relations with Ben-Gurion.]

Like Ben-Gurion, Sharett was reluctant to take a stand on the increasingly hostile bipolar character of global politics—until the escalation of the Korean War in December 1950. One reason was Israel's interest in continued support by the two superpowers, a prospect which, in the first two years of independence (1948–50), was realistic. Another was an ideological presupposition—and hope—that the gulf between the two blocs could be bridged. A third, tangible interest, was the wish to maintain access to the then-two largest Jewish communities in the world, in the USA and the Soviet Union. These considerations led both men to what seemed a logical advocacy for Israel in world politics—non-alignment with the contending blocs or, in the Israeli term, *ee-hizdahut (non-identification)*.

Sharett seemed to have been more committed to the doctrine and the policy of non-identification. For Ben-Gurion, Israeli interests narrowly conceived were the compelling motive, with Sharett, the ideological dimension and the vision of a link between the two contending global forces also loomed large. For both, however, the trauma of the Korean War, in particular, President Truman's blunt demand that friends of the USA 'stand up and be counted', necessitated a reappraisal of Israel's then-basic posture in global politics. Before the year 1950 was over a pro-Western orientation was already apparent—in word and deed.

Sharett's image of the Soviet bloc never matched Ben-Gurion's harsh perception, however: a difference in tone was evident all through the ensuing years of Soviet hostility to Israel, Zionism, and Jewry. Moreover, Sharett was much more sensitive to the Third World: it was he who prepared many of the intellectual and policy guidelines for Israel's far-reaching presence in Africa in the late 1950s and 1960s that Golda Meir, his successor as Foreign Minister, was to transform into a major foreign policy initiative from 1958 onwards.

The differences in the images of global politics held by Ben-Gurion and Sharett, while fewer than the points of affinity, had immense policy significance. The UN and correct policy to the world body, as noted, stood at the core of this contrast. A closely related difference in global system perception pertained to *legitimacy*. For Ben-Gurion, Israel achieved that status when it proclaimed its independence and established its *de facto* conditions: control over a defined territory, a stable government, the habitual obedience of its people, and so on; that is, self-rule, internally induced. For Sharett, statehood was legitimated when Israel was formally accepted by the international community and was admitted into the UN, in March 1949.

On the preferred path to achieving national security, too, they differed. As one of Ben-Gurion's admirers acknowledged, 'certainly Sharett was sensitive to the security factor in foreign policy; but he believed his methods were better; he attached great importance to world opinion and the attitudes of other states' (MB Interview with Yitzhak Navon, in Tel Aviv, May 1966).

There was another contrast in outlook—Sharett's greater awareness of the economic dimension of foreign policy. Ben-Gurion, like one of the few foreign statesmen whom he admired, de Gaulle, displayed an Olympian indifference to economic problems. Sharett had a more balanced image of the instruments of statecraft, with an awareness of the interplay of military, political, and economic components. Ben-Gurion emphasized the first and ignored the third.

The state of siege experienced by Israel, especially in the early years, superimposed on the pervasive Jewish prism, gave rise to the most distinctive element in Ben-Gurion's image of the global system—the 'two-camp thesis'. Israel and world Jewry constituted one camp, the rest of the world, the other. The only *completely reliable ally* of Israel for Ben-Gurion was the Jewish People, as demonstrated in 1948, 1956, and 1967, and on innumerable less dramatic occasions during the years of independence. The two segments of world Jewry are inevitably and inextricably interlocked, members of one family who are bound together by a thousand ties of history, religion, culture, sentiment, and experience (MB Interview with BG, July 1966). Sharett, too, valued the support of Jewry, but never subscribed to the extreme bifurcation of global politics symbolized by the notion of two camps, Jewish and non-Jewish.

In sum, there were *more* shared themes in the *global system perceptions* of Ben-Gurion and Sharett, but the points of divergence were *more serious*. Yet even in their shared themes, there were *differences* in *tone, emphasis,* and *nuance*. And their basic difference in outlook—the place of the UN in global politics and, particularly, in the Middle East conflict, as well as in Israeli foreign policy—overshadowed all the points of convergence. For the implications of this disagreement extended to diplomacy versus force, the attitude to external factors in Israeli policy, the issue of legitimacy, and so on. The single-mindedness of Ben-Gurion also led to indifference to the economic aspect of policy and to the pivotal 'two-camp thesis'.

Their *images of the Arabs* were even more sharply at variance. The crux was the contrary interpretations of Arab character—'the only language the Arabs understand is force' (Ben-Gurion) versus 'the Arabs are proud and sensitive; they are people, not just enemies' (Sharett). In policy terms, this was expressed as *retaliation* versus '*creating an atmosphere conducive to peace*'. Not by accident, there were no major acts of retaliation during Ben-Gurion's retirement to Sde Boker, from January 1954 to February 1955, when Sharett, as prime minister, was in formal control of policy toward Israel's principal adversary. It was their contrasting images of the Arabs which gave rise to this basic policy disagreement. And that, in turn, led to the irrevocable split between Ben-Gurion and Sharett in June 1956 (Caplan 2016). The two men represented, then and later, *alternative approaches to the cardinal issue in Israel's foreign policy—relations with neighboring Arab states and with the Palestinians in the West Bank and Gaza*. A successful formula eluded them and almost all of their successors (to be elaborated in a later book on *Dynamics of the Arab/Israel Conflict*) [forthcoming, 2017].

As noted at the beginning of this comparative analysis, Ben-Gurion was the pre-eminent public figure in the shaping of Israel's and pre-State *yishuv* policy—throughout their period of collaboration and competition in Israel's government, 1948–56, and during the preceding 13 years in the Jewish Agency for Palestine, Israel's government-in-the-making. Ben-Gurion's dominance extended to foreign policy, as well as domestic policy. This is evident from his pivotal role in all the crucial decisions during his tenure in office, including all those issues that impinged upon foreign policy: the *proclamation of independence* in mid-May 1948; the *declaration of Jerusalem as the seat of Israel's government*, in December 1949; the *decisions to negotiate with West Germany and to accept German Reparations*, in 1952; the *decisions to accept the Johnston Plan on the distribution of the Jordan Waters*, in 1953–55—even though Ben-Gurion was then 'in retirement', in the Negev; he was consulted on all key aspects of the negotiations, and his approval was necessary for Israel's acceptance of the Plan; and the *decisions to form a military alliance with France and the UK, albeit secret, and to launch the Sinai Campaign against Egypt, in September-October 1956*.

To conclude this comparison of Israel's two foremost political leaders in the first decade of independence: all agreed, including Ben-Gurion, that Sharett was endowed with nobility; but Ben-Gurion was a greater political leader. Sharett possessed impressive knowledge about politics but less insight. He was enamored of the art of persuasion but he had little understanding of the mechanics of power in domestic politics. Ben-Gurion was preoccupied with power and had this understanding in abundance, along with an intuitive grasp of political forces and a vision of history. And his achievements were of a much higher order—in independence and nation-building.

Ben-Gurion's vision was two-fold: the transformation of part of world Jewry into a normal people through 'ingathering of the exiles' into the Land of Israel, and the centrality of social democracy in the new society. He established his primacy through two formidable institutions— the *Mapai* Party, the social–democratic Israel Workers Party (formed by a merger of several parties in 1929–30, the largest and most influential Israel political party until 1977), and the *Histadrut*, as noted, a nationwide organization for Jewish workers. At the time of independence and in the early years of statehood he successfully met three tests to his power: a war imposed by Israel's Arab neighbors on its Independence Day, 15 May 1948; challenges to a unified Israel army from right- and left-wing militias dating to the pre-state era; and the doubling of Israel's population from 1948 to 1951, through Jewish immigration from 60 countries, without undermining the administrative structures or essential unity of the state. In short, Ben-Gurion built a state and effected the social transformation of millions of immigrant Jews.

The achievements of Ben-Gurion, as of Nehru, the two *pre-eminent political leaders* that I encountered, were of an exceptionally high order; [my encounter with a third major political leader, Trudeau, occurred in his pre-political, early years]. However, the Israel case was fundamentally different from India—and from all other new states in Asia and Africa: Ben-Gurion was faced with the task of creating a new state and society from an old, dispersed people, Nehru, with the modernization of a traditional, economically underdeveloped society after two centuries of British colonial rule and the schism of partition.

Levi ESHKOL

Levi ESHKOL **Director-General of the Defense Ministry, 1948–49; Director of the Settlement Department, Jewish Agency for Israel, 1949–63; Minister of Agriculture, 1951–52; Minister of Finance, 1952–63; Prime Minister, 1963–69; and Defense Minister, 1963–67. [MB Interviews, 1966]**

Road to Aliya *and Early Years*

Eshkol, along with Golda Meir (see below), the third and fourth Israeli prime ministers, can be described as among the 'last of the first': the term refers to the generation of founding figures that shaped the character of modern Israel. His background was typical of the Second *Aliya*, the second wave of Jewish immigration to the Land of Israel (1904–14). He was born in 1895 and spent his formative years in a little town or *shtetl*, Oratowa, in the Kiev district of the Ukraine. A traditional *heder* (literally, room, religious primary school) education was followed by preparation for the Russian *Gymnasia* (high school); but he had to complete his formal studies (1911–13) in then-distant Vilna, Lithuania, because of the *numerus clausus* that was imposed on Jews in Russia proper and the Ukraine. It was not without compensation, for that historic center of Jewish learning was then in ferment with new ideas—of revolution, socialism, and Zionism.

Among the reasons for his *aliya* was the pervasive anti-Semitism of the Tsarist realm, especially the Russian variant of race-religious hatred and physical persecution, the *pogrom*. Many years later, Eshkol recalled that the atmosphere of *pogroms* 'hung over our heads all the time, although the storm passed our district by [in one assault, during 1905]. For weeks we sat at home with doors barred and boards nailed over the windows, expecting an attack that never came' (Cited in T. Prittie, *Eshkol of Israel*, 1969, 4). He was not often brought face-to-face with the more brutal forms of persecution experienced by some of his colleagues. And yet, Eshkol recalled: 'It was the beginning of the century—riots, pogroms. I myself received not once a severe blow with a wagon tongue' (Eshkol obituary, *New York Times*, 27 February 1969, 32). Moreover, his father was killed in that town in 1917 by followers of Petlura, the Ukraine's most notorious anti-Semite of the day. Yet *pogroms* alone did not lead Eshkol to the historic Land of Israel.

Levi Shkolnick, as he was known until after Israel's independence, set out for Palestine early in 1914. This important personal decision was marked by *caution* and *multiple influences*, the twin characteristics of Eshkol's decisions throughout his public life. He began to think about *aliya* at the age of 13 or 14; he acted five years later. Perhaps the normal hesitations were accentuated by the pull of an affluent home: in this aspect of his background, Eshkol was not typical of his contemporaries.

One of the positive influences on the young Eshkol was socialism, notably the humanist strand as espoused by a unique association of Jewish workers in Poland, Lithuania, and Russia, the *Bund*. As he was to demonstrate over the decades in the socialist movement of the *Yishuv* and of Israel, Eshkol was attracted to its values and ideals, not to its theory and ideology. His view of socialism was derived from the *Ha-po'el Ha-tza'ir* (Young Worker) leaders, 'who were my guides and mentors, and who developed important elements in the ideology of the Jewish workers—the principle of labor, labor settlement, Hebrew culture, a working nation, and a new society' (Prittie, 52). Marxism and the class struggle were anathema to him.

A closely related influence, with a direct thrust to Zion, was the philosophy of A.D. Gordon, a mentor to Jewish workers in Palestine: 'We wanted to build Israel with our own hands', remarked Eshkol some months before his death in 1969. 'Our whole philosophy was contained in the phrase, "back to the soil"' (Prittie, 14). The ghetto—in his case, the *shtetl*, a small Jewish town or village in Eastern Europe—provided a full Jewish life. And

'*Yiddishkeit*' (Jewishness) was embedded in Eshkol's character and personality. The Vilna experience was important, too, in directing him to the Land of Israel: there, he joined the *Tza'ir Tzyon* (Young Zion) youth group, an affiliate of *Ha-po'el Ha-tza'ir* (The Young Worker, a Zionist-Socialist, non-Marxist party, founded in 1905, which merged with *Ahdut Ha'avoda* [Unity of Labor Party] in 1929–30 to form the mainstream *Mapai* (Labor Party of the Land of Israel).

The Zionist vision was another powerful inducement for Eshkol: 'In Jaffa [where he set foot in Palestine],' he told his biographer, 'I was born a second time'. However, unlike Ben-Gurion and others who had received the call at an early age and could not be deflected, Eshkol admitted, with typical honesty: 'To tell the truth, I thought that after a year I would return to Russia.' (*New York Times* obituary) Like most men of the Second *Aliya*, he was also inspired by 'the light of the vision of the Prophets', the belief in social equality before God. Among individuals, 'a tremendous impression was made on me by Jabotinsky [founder of the Revisionist strand of Zionism, a celebrated orator and intellectual]; what temperament, what speech, what Russian' (*ibid.*).

During Israel's pre-independence period Eshkol did not attain the first rank of *Yishuv* leaders, men like: *Haim Arlosoroff*, one of the most brilliant Labor Zionist leaders, Secretary-General of *Mapai* and the first Head of the Jewish Agency for Palestine's Political Department, the precursor of Israel's Foreign Ministry, who was assassinated on the Tel Aviv beach in 1933; *Ben-Gurion* who, as noted, was Chair of the Jewish Agency from 1935 to 1948 and the first Prime Minister-Defense Minister of Israel; *Sharett*, who succeeded Arlosoroff as Head of the Jewish Agency's Political Department and, as noted, was Israel's first Foreign Minister and Israel's second Prime Minister; and *Eliezer Kaplan*, the financial head of the Jewish Agency and, later, Israel's first Finance Minister. Yet Eshkol was active in many fields; and he revealed himself to be a hard-working, persistent, patient, and modest man of organizing ability. Throughout this 35-year gestation period, Eshkol displayed an abiding interest in the twin problems of *water and agriculture*.

His happiest and most productive role after Israel's independence was that of Head of the Jewish Agency for Israel's Land Settlement Department from 1949 to 1963 (and simultaneously, in 1951–52, Minister of Agriculture): in that dual capacity, he directed the massive absorption of immigrants, almost 700,000, many of them to the land. From 1952 to 1963, he also held the key Government of Israel portfolio of Finance and exercised ultimate authority over the economy as a whole: Prime Minister Ben-Gurion gave him—almost—a free hand.

Jordan Waters Negotiations (1953–55)

It was during his lengthy tenure as Israel's most influential minister in the economic and financial domain that Eshkol was actively involved in high-policy decision-making on an issue with potential far-reaching foreign policy implications—the prolonged indirect negotiations with representatives of Arab states, via President Eisenhower's Personal Representative, Eric Johnston, on the *Jordan Waters* issue, 1953–55.

According to the long-time Secretary to the Government [of Israel] at that time, 'very little was said about Jordan Waters in meetings of the Government [Cabinet]; certainly it was not discussed in detail' (MB Interview with Zeev Sharef, 1971). Ben-Gurion, Sharett, and Eshkol were the decision-makers at the policy level (MB Interview with *Yaacov Herzog*, Director-General, Prime Minister's Office, 1966). Ben-Gurion was in 'retirement' at Sde Boker in the Negev during the second and third Johnston tours but 'he was kept informed and participated in all major decisions, even when he was out of the Government' (MB Interview with Aharon Wiener, an engineering expert on the Israel delegation to the Johnston-led talks on the Jordan Waters issue, 1971). Sharett, who was then-Prime Minister and Foreign Minister, carried the issue through the Cabinet and the *Knesset*. And Eshkol was the central figure in the negotiations, especially as Head of Israel's delegation during the decisive third round.

Both engineering experts on the delegation termed Eshkol's influence decisive. One of them, *Simha Blass*, explained it thus: 'The founder of *Mekorot* [Water Planning for Israel, a public corporation] and a man of the settlements, he [Eshkol] was considered knowledgeable in the matter' (MB Interview, 1971). The other, *Aharon Wiener*, noted the interaction among the decision-makers and the intangible negative veto: 'Had Eshkol taken a negative stand, [Prime Minister] Sharett would have accepted it, for Eshkol was respected as having a special feel and knowledge about the water problem. At the same time Eshkol was close to Ben-Gurion then. If *he* had taken a hard line it might have been decisive. They sought Ben-Gurion's confirming support for a course of action already selected' (MB Interview with Wiener, 1971).

Ben-Gurion rarely spoke in public about Jordan Waters; and when he did it was related to the constant core of his worldview—security. As he acknowledged a decade after the Jordan Waters negotiations, 'The things I thought about most concerned security. I didn't take a special interest in economic matters. I left these to Eshkol and Kaplan [Eshkol's predecessor as Finance Minister]' (MB Interview with Ben-Gurion, June 1966). This preoccupation with national security and broader political implications is evident in Ben-Gurion's reported reaction to the proposed water quota for Israel in February 1955: 'we shouldn't forget we are discussing a possible breakthrough with the Arabs.' More precisely: 'the quantity was close enough to what Israel would accept; a dialogue with the Arabs was important in itself; and it was preferable to work on the basis of an agreed distribution of water because the Jordan is an international river' (MB Interview with Wiener, 1971). As another member of Israel's delegation to the water talks recalled, the Ben-Gurion view was: 'sacrifice a certain amount of water, if that is necessary to get an agreement—but keep the U.N. out of any central function' (MB Interview with Yaacov Herzog, Eshkol's principal aide at the time, 1966).

Eshkol approached the Jordan Waters issue in more down-to-earth economic terms. He had always been close to the land, by experience and conviction: he was *a kibbutz* member for almost 50 years and an active rural laborer for 15; he admired A.D. Gordon's call for national redemption through a return to the soil, and by predisposition he was an *'eesh meshek'*, that is, a practical man concerned with the day-to-day problems of increasing productivity. As he recalled to his biographer in 1968: 'No one had been keener than I was on getting back to the land. I loved the land, and it was central to my philosophy of life' (Prittie 1969, p. 181). This theme emerges also from his only remark to the *Knesset* on the Jordan Waters issue: 'Certainly when [the U.S. President's adviser], Johnston was here, we argued for our rights and for the quantity of water....We are arguing over the area and the quantity per dunam.'

In terms of the *decision-making process* on Jordan Waters, Eshkol, who was Head of Israel's delegation during the crucial third round, assured Johnston: 'If you bring the Arabs' agreement to the Revised Plan, we will go along with it' (MB Interview with Herzog, 1966). When *Blass* objected to this 'improvisation', without consulting the delegation, the Finance Minister replied brusquely: 'This is how I understand it and we must finish it.'

Eshkol's attitude was undoubtedly strengthened by the concurrence of the other two persons in Israel's decision-making triumvirate on this issue. Sharett, from the outset, had emphasized the larger political dimensions of a Jordan Waters agreement. Ben-Gurion was much more 'water-minded', but he was no less aware of the political implications. Then in the final days of his 'retirement' at Sde Boker (1953–55), his advice was sought by a Government delegation—Eshkol, Sapir, and Wiener. Ben-Gurion decided on 17 February 1955 to return to the Government as Minister of Defense; he took the oath of office in Jerusalem on the 21st, the day of the crucial last negotiating session with Johnston during the third round. 'Ben-Gurion's point was that we were discussing a difference of a few per cent [the 15 mcm]; was this enough to torpedo an agreement? He felt we should make the sacrifice and advised acceptance of the Revised Plan.' Wiener added: 'Johnston returned to Israel with a set of figures and related conditions close to what we considered acceptable. All of us except Blass felt that we should see this in the larger terms of an accommodation with the Arabs.'

The conditional acceptance of Johnston's Revised Plan was Israel's strategic decision on Jordan Waters: it shaped all subsequent Israeli behavior on that issue. On the basis of Johnston's assurances in February 1955, the Israeli delegation recommended acceptance. The confirming support of Ben-Gurion was sought—and received.

In the interplay of personal views, Eshkol played the *crucial role*. The final *decision*, however, must be ascribed to the Sde Boker meeting with Ben-Gurion. The delegation's prior acceptance decision was tentative. Further, Eshkol by temperament never regarded decisions as final. And he held Ben-Gurion at that time in awesome respect. Thus, if 'the Old Man' had opposed the Revised Johnson Plan, Eshkol would almost certainly have changed his stance, so too would Sharett.

Eshkol responded to a skeptical question, 'Why did Israel not officially and unconditionally accept the Revised Plan? We *did* accept but did not say so in writing, officially, because we were afraid that, if we did so, the Arabs would bargain for more, as is the Oriental mentality in these matters.' Later [July 1955] 'we put our acceptance of the Johnston Plan in writing' (MB Interview with Eshkol, 1966). Ben-Gurion was even more emphatic: 'The fact is that *we* accepted' (MB Interview, 1966).

Comparison with Ben-Gurion and Sharett

Not without reason did many Israelis feel—Ben-Gurion among them at the outset—that Eshkol was well prepared by experience to succeed him as Prime Minister and Defense Minister in 1963. Yet in character and personality, Eshkol was very different from Ben-Gurion and Sharett. He was much closer to the latter along the Courage–Caution spectrum. He possessed neither the intellectual talent nor the pretensions of his two predecessors as Prime Minister. He wrote very little, at any rate for publication. He never articulated a vision of Israel's past and of the forces that led to independence. His interests were more mundane and practical. He was in fact more at home in Yiddish than in Hebrew and was well known for his fund of Yiddish jokes and aphorisms, his sense of humor being a quality that neither Ben-Gurion nor Sharett shared.

Eshkol was totally lacking in Ben-Gurion's charisma and Sharett's diplomatic finesse. Rather he was a born committee man, a careful determined planner with a special gift for getting on with people. Pragmatic and adaptable, he genuinely loved the soil and believed in the value of manual labor but he did not venerate Spartan ideals for their own sake. His calm demeanor verged on the phlegmatic. Tireless in discussion, he won over his colleagues by solid and patient persuasion not by force of personality or brilliant advocacy. He was a tough taskmaster, according to subordinates, but he worked as hard as they did and displayed tremendous energy and durability in all spheres. He was a well-liked *haver* (comrade, friend, colleague), down-to-earth, kind, and tolerant. He had a common touch and never talked down to people. Moderate in outlook, he was known for his skill at bargaining and conciliation.

Israel's formative, heroic phase (1948–63) was followed by one of consolidation in nation-building. As the successor to Ben-Gurion in 1963, Eshkol adhered to type: he was, in Israel's political evolution, the Shastri who followed Nehru, the Erhard after Adenauer and, in a different context, the Attlee after Churchill, or the Pompidou after de Gaulle. And like some of these men his skills were not unimpressive. He was a better administrator and political manager than either Ben-Gurion or Sharett. He had an open mind, a proven ability to improvise, and a capacity to choose able men.

The fundamental difference in approach between Eshkol and Ben-Gurion—*pragmatism* versus *dogma*—pervaded the gamut of foreign policy images. Underpinning this was a psychological pattern which may be termed 'BG contrariness': consciously or otherwise, Eshkol was aware that Ben-Gurion's shadow hung over him, and some of his decisions seemed in part to be a reaction to this status.

Views on the USA, the USSR, World Jewry, and Germany

At one level, it may seem contrived to attribute a coherent worldview to Eshkol: there is no evidence that he thought carefully about Israel's external problems and goals before becoming Prime Minister-Defense Minister. And unlike Ben-Gurion and Sharett, he depended on his technocratic aides for the drafting of speeches on foreign and security policy, notably Yaacov Herzog, one of the most talented members of the Foreign Ministry, who served as Director-General of the Prime Minister's Office under Eshkol (and earlier, in 1961, acquitted himself with distinction in a celebrated debate with famed British historian Arnold Toynbee on the Arab/Israel conflict, at McGill University). Herzog remarked after Eshkol's death that he never understood foreign policy: 'this was the greatest frustration of his public life' (MB Interview, 1969). Moreover, Eshkol was not an accomplished public speaker, unlike Sharett, the master of logical persuasion, and Ben-Gurion, who was endowed with an inspirational rhetoric.

Like all Israeli leaders, Eshkol perceived the reality and significance of superpower and East–West bloc conflict, and the *friendship of the USA for Israel*. Unlike the later-frequent visits by Israeli prime ministers to Washington for consultation, Eshkol was the first in 13 years to make the pilgrimage to the USA, in 1964; Ben-Gurion had visited Washington in 1951 and achieved an important breakthrough, the launching, in the USA, of the State of Israel Bonds, which has raised billions of dollars for the new state. Eshkol, who was invited by President Johnson to his Texas ranch, an important symbolic gesture, also did not return home empty-handed; rather, he received an assurance of a major increase in arms aid by the USA.

Whereas Ben-Gurion viewed Moscow as rigidly hostile to Israel and Soviet Jewry—and was temperamentally incapable of a new approach—Eshkol perceived the need to re-examine policy periodically. Thus, during his 1964 visit to the USA he adopted a *conciliatory line towards the Soviet Union*: 'My impression of Mr. Khrushchev's visit to Cairo is that he spoke about Israel in a much milder tone than before. I am inclined to believe that the Soviet Union is not interested in molesting Israel' (*New Outlook* [Tel Aviv], July–August 1964, 57). Sharett was capable of such tolerance and pragmatism; Ben-Gurion was not.

In the context of Israel's pervasive sense of national insecurity, Eshkol, like Ben-Gurion and Sharett, *attached special importance to world Jewry*. However, he was a strong advocate of 'Israel centricity of Jewish peoplehood today' and rejected the 'Israel and Babylon' analogy of two parallel centers of Jewry, with US Jewry playing the Babylon role. At the same time, 'Israel cannot carry the burden unaided.... All the resources of our people [Jews everywhere] are needed [for] Israel...as the heart of Jewry' (*Government Year-Book* 5725, 1964–65, 12).

He shared the deeply rooted Jewish distrust of *Goyim* (non-Jews) and the feeling of total trust in his fellow Jews. He rejected the Ben-Gurion view that 'everything depends on us', though he acknowledged that, in the last analysis, self-reliance was crucial. And he attached much more importance to diplomacy than did Ben-Gurion. Yet in the aftermath of the June 1967 Six-Day War, he came close to formal acceptance of the latter's 'two-camp thesis', discussed above, Jewry and the rest of the world.

In his perception of *Germany*, the most agonizing issue in Israel's foreign policy during the first two decades of independence, Eshkol differed considerably from Ben-Gurion: to the latter, Germany had changed; to Eshkol, Germany was in the process of changing. Thus, Ben-Gurion declared as early as 1959: 'I say that Germany of today, the Germany of Adenauer and the Social Democrats, is not the Germany of Hitler.' And in 1960, he made the historic gesture of reconciliation by meeting Adenauer in New York, paying tribute to the German Chancellor as a wise and great man.

'My view towards Germany', Ben-Gurion remarked during my lengthy interview in 1966, 'is based upon the words of two Prophets, Yermiyahu [Jeremiah] and Yehezkel [Ezekiel].' Their essence is, 'don't hold a father responsible for the acts of his son or the son for the acts of his father'. Yet for Ben-Gurion, the thrust to reconciliation lay in *realpolitik*: 'Germany', he continued, 'is definitely a rising power.... To us, it cannot be unimportant whether West Germany is for or against Israel.... A hostile Germany might endanger the friendship with Israel of other peoples of Western Europe, and could also have an undesirable influence on the United States. It is therefore doubly important for Israel to promote closer relations with Germany.' (MB Interview)

Eshkol, always reflecting more traditional Jewish attitudes, was not prepared to ease the German conscience with such finality. Even after diplomatic relations had been established in 1965, during his prime ministership, Eshkol declared that the process of change was incomplete and that Germany had not yet fully expiated its heinous crimes in the 1930s and 1940s. He made this point bluntly at a dinner for Adenauer in Jerusalem in 1966; the former Chancellor was perplexed and annoyed for he had become accustomed to Ben-Gurion's clean bill of forgiveness.

1967 Crisis-War: Nadir and Turning-Point Role

After a relatively tranquil period as prime minister (1963–early 1967), Eshkol's leadership suffered a serious setback as a result of a dramatic failure to cope effectively with the escalating stress of the May–June 1967 crisis-war. On 27 May 1967, five days after UN Secretary-General U. Thant acquiesced in Egypt President Nasser's demand to withdraw the UN Emergency Force (UNEF) in Sinai that had served for a decade as a peace-keeping force between Egypt and Israel, Israel's Cabinet was deadlocked (9-9) on the crucial issue, to launch an interceptive strike against the now-mobilized Egyptian forces in Sinai or, as urged by the US president, to avoid a pre-emptive war. Eshkol, in his inimitable manner, informed his Cabinet, 'Children, on a divided vote, we cannot go to war'. He suggested that his colleagues 'sleep it over' and reconvene the next afternoon. His method, as always, was to try to achieve a consensus on a grave issue. So far, he was coping well.

The next morning, a note arrived from US President Johnson, with an unmistakable warning to Eshkol and Israel's Cabinet: 'As your friend, I repeat even more strongly what I said yesterday to Mr. Eban [Israel's Foreign Minister, in Washington]: "Israel just must not take pre-emptive military action and thereby make itself responsible for the initiation of hostilities".' What Johnson said to Eban the previous day, as recalled in the President's memoir, was no less ominous: 'The central point, Mr. Prime Minister, is that your nation not be the one to bear the responsibility of any outbreak of war. Then I said very slowly and positively: Israel will not be alone unless it decides to go alone' (Lyndon Johnson, *The Vantage Point*, 1971, 293–294). The *aide-memoire* that Johnson gave Eban at the end of their meeting added the following sentence: 'We cannot imagine that Israel will make this decision' (Israel, Ministry for Foreign Affairs, [unpublished] *Cables and Communications*, 1967). (These words were corroborated by Israel Ambassador to the USA, A. Harman's record of the minutes of the meeting with the President, *ibid.*, and in a MB Interview, 3 March 1972, with E. Evron, Israel's minister to the US, [no. 2] in Washington, who was present at the meeting with Johnson). There were also cautionary notes of pressure from the UK and France governments to Eshkol.

The pressure was irresistible; and, at its resumed meeting on the afternoon of 28 May, Israel's Cabinet decided to further delay military action—for up to two weeks: the initial delay had occurred on 23 May. At that point in the crisis, too, Eshkol seemed to be coping well; and he resisted the growing demand from Israel's generals to launch an immediate interceptive attack.

Then Eshkol stumbled, in an incident that evening which undermined his leadership for the rest of the 1967 crisis-war and during his remaining time in office. The Cabinet decided to inform the nation and the world of its delay decision. While Eban and Yisrael Galili, a leader of the *Ahdut Ha'avoda*, a Left Zionist party within the governing coalition, drafted the speech, no one bothered to give Eshkol a clean copy! The result was unintelligible gibberish: 'Furthermore, lines of action were decided for the removal.' Then came a long pause. Eshkol's breathing could be heard, picked up by the sensitive mike, as well as his whisper, 'What's this?' The word, 'removal' did not please him. He changed it to 'movement' of military concentrations in the south. And so it went throughout an unintelligible authoritative statement to his insecure, frightened people and the world anxiously waiting to find out what the Government of Israel intended to do. The speech only reinforced a growing image of Eshkol's caution, hesitancy, and indecisiveness in the nation's hour of crisis, and a search for consensus before making controversial and consequential decisions.

Soon after the 'stammering' incident, Eshkol went to the Israel Defense Forces (IDF's) General Staff HQ to report on the Cabinet decision in favor of further delay. He was totally unprepared for the storm that erupted: the generals bluntly called for immediate military action against Egypt's barrage of threatening words and acts. Eban referred to it as Eshkol's 'tempestuous meeting with the generals' (MB Interview, 1968).

The 'stammering' incident had a disastrous effect on public morale and strengthened the hands of the political Opposition, as well as dissenters in Eshkol's own party, *Mapai*, and the disappointed generals following the renewed delay decision. The substantive comments in his report were forgotten. What remained etched in everyone's memory was its mode of delivery. The result of the 'stammering' incident was that, within days, 1 June, Eshkol was forced to yield the Defense portfolio to Ben-Gurion's protégé for decades, former IDF Chief of Staff *Moshe Dayan*, the first time in Israel's political history that an incumbent prime minister was stripped of the prize cabinet portfolio. That incident also bedeviled his prime ministership until his death in 1969. [It need not have happened if his aides had given him a clean text and had allowed him time to read it, at least once, before delivering his report to the nation and the world.]

Notwithstanding his dramatic gaffe during the 1967 crisis, Eshkol played a crucial role in one of the most significant military-strategic decisions in the history of the state, the decision in the last half of 1966 to choose the nuclear weapons option. Cautious and hesitant, as always, Eshkol resisted the escalating pressure of most of the generals to hold a nuclear test. Such a step would have ended the ambiguity surrounding Israel's nuclear intentions, which was feasible in 1966. Moreover, it would have violated a written commitment by Eshkol, as prime minister, to the USA, in a Memorandum of Understanding, in March 1965, not to be the first to introduce nuclear weapons into the Middle East. Eshkol was also convinced, and argued, that such a step would alienate the then-existing five-nuclear powers, especially the USA. He held his ground and won. At the same time, he gave his approval to proceeding with Israel's nuclear weapons program, quietly. According to the leading academic authority on Israel's nuclear program, Avner Cohen, *Israel and the Bomb*, 1999, Eshkol's role in this two-track decision—against a nuclear weapon test, in favor of pursuing the nuclear option, quietly—was central (Cohen, 'Going for the Nuclear Option', in *Ha'aretz* (Tel Aviv), 22 May 2007, B5).

My encounters with Israel's third Prime Minister during his week-long mission to Africa in May–June 1966—this was the period of Israel's high visibility in Africa as a welcome source of economic and military aid from a non-threatening, small 'Western' state—and on 4 August 1966 in a Jerusalem interview reinforced the images of Eshkol's caution, hesitancy and indecisiveness, along with pragmatism and humaneness, noted above. Eshkol was the first Israeli leader to convey Israel's friendship to new and old states in Africa, directly, since his successor as Prime Minister, Golda Meir's visit as Foreign Minister to Africa eight years earlier. During his brief interactions with six African Heads of Government and State, he exhibited some of the traits noted above: person-to-person friendly informality; the total absence of a 'white man's burden' attitude to newly independent African leaders; a commonality based upon a shared struggle for independence; the lack of pretentiousness; an emphasis on shared problems in the aftermath of independence, and down-to earth communication between leaders facing grave problems. In this respect, it was a highly successful mission to Africa, although Israel's prominent diplomatic, economic, and military relations with most African states suffered a severe, long-term setback in the aftermath of the 1967 War.

GOLDA MEIR

Golda MEIR **Minister to the USSR, 1948–49; Minister of Labor, 1949–56; Foreign Minister, 1956–66; Prime Minister, 1969–74. [MB Interview, 1968]**

Formally, Mrs. Meir was the 'last of the first' (generation) to attain the summit of political power in Israel. But the Second *Aliya* was more than a wave of immigration in the years before WWI. It was primarily a state of mind, a view of the world and a set of values that embraced most Jewish pioneers to the Land of Israel before the rise of Nazi Germany. This included Golda Meir, the only woman in Israel's high policy élite during the first 25 years of independence, and the only 'Anglo-Saxon', other than Abba Eban (see below): she came to Palestine from the USA in 1921 in the Third *Aliya*. Yet in all other respects, she was more akin to the founding fathers, Ben-Gurion, Sharett and the other political leaders of embryonic Israel.

Early Years and Road to Aliya

Golda Meir was three years younger than Eshkol and four years younger than Sharett: she was born in 1898, like them in the Ukraine (Kiev). When Golda Mahovitz was five, the family moved to Pinsk in the Pale of Settlement, and in 1906 they joined the exodus of Russian Jews to America. Her formative years, from the age of 8 to 23, were spent in Milwaukee.

Her East European phase provided Meir, as it did Eshkol, with a negative inducement to Zion—the reality and persistent threat of *pogroms*. The positive motivation for *aliya* came from the American milieu. Caught up in the ferment of ideas toward the end of WWI, she rejected all in favor of Jewish nationalism and became immersed in the socialist *Po'alei Tzyon* (Workers of Zion), the Jewish People's Relief for East European Jewry, the American Jewish Congress, and Yiddish-language folk schools. Her *aliya* in 1921 was a natural conclusion to this period of self-created *hakhshara* (preparation, prior to immigration and settlement in a *kibbutz*).

Golda Meir's life in Palestine was typical of the pioneering generation. The Myersons—she retained her married name until 1956—settled first in *Kibbutz* Merhavia in the Jezreel Valley, then briefly in Tel Aviv in 1923, and in Jerusalem a year later. She became Secretary of the *Mo'etzet Hapo'alot* (Council of Working Women) in 1928, was a founding member of *Mapai* (the Labor Party, which dominated Israel's politics from 1948 to 1977) in 1929, and served for two years (1932–34) as emissary of the *Mo'etzet* to its sister movement in America, the Pioneer Women. She joined the Executive Council of the *Histadrut* upon her return and its powerful Secretariat a year later. In 1936, she began to organize its mutual aid services, especially its sick fund, *Kupat Holim*. During the WWII years, she served on Palestine's War Economic Advisery Council. And in June 1946, when most of the Zionist leaders in Palestine were arrested by the British Mandate authorities on 'black Saturday', Meir became Acting Head of the Jewish Agency's Political Department. She negotiated with Jordan's King Abdullah twice, in November 1947 and early in May 1948, in a futile effort to persuade him not to join the Arab states' invasion of the new Jewish state. Between these quiet diplomatic missions, in January 1948, she raised $50 million for arms—a gargantuan sum at the time—in a triumphant personal appeal to American Jewry.

Résumé of Government Offices

During the first 26 years of Israel's independence (1948–74), Meir was at or near the center of influence. As Israel's first Minister to the Soviet Union, she provided the spark for Russian Jewry's massive demonstration of Jewish national consciousness, at Moscow's main synagogue on the High Holidays in 1948. She was a highly successful Minister of Labor from April 1949 to June 1956 and then succeeded Sharett as Foreign Minister for almost a decade. A brief respite in 1966 was followed by two years as Secretary-General of *Mapai;* and then, after another withdrawal from office in 1968, she succeeded Eshkol as Prime Minister, in March 1969. She was the obvious successor in an 'old guard'-dominated Israel Labor Party. Within a few months, she became the popular choice as well.

Personality, Character, Intuitive Approach to Decision-Making

Whereas Eshkol shared Sharett's penchant for caution, Meir was in the Ben-Gurion mold—quick, decisive, and a strong personality. In other traits, she was more akin to Eshkol—simplicity, modesty, lack of intellectual sophistication, and earthiness. She also possessed a 'fantastic intuitive sense', with a sure grasp of the essence of a policy issue. Perhaps the most poignant and consequential illustration was her two crucial decisions, regarding IDF mobilization and a pre-emptive strike against Egypt and Syria, made only minutes apart on the morning of 6 October 1973, the first day of the October Yom Kippur War.

After listening to the competing recommendations—in favor of full mobilization of the reserves (IDF Chief of Staff Elazar) versus the mobilization of only two divisions (Defense Minister Dayan, a former IDF Chief of Staff)—she exclaimed, 'My God, I have to decide which of them is right?' But decide she did, despite her total lack of military knowledge: she decided in favor of large-scale—not full or small-scale—mobilization because 'if there really was a war, then we had to be in the very best position possible'. On the related and even more fundamental issue, whether or not to launch a pre-emptive strike that day, 6 October, Meir decided against the long-established IDF strategic doctrine of interceptive war, enunciated by *Yigal Allon*, a military hero of the 1948 War of Independence (see below). She did so because 'there is always the possibility that we will need help, and if we strike first, we will get nothing from anyone' (Meir, *My Life*, 1975, 358, 359).

Her calculus on pre-emption was elaborated by *Mordekhai Gazit*, a senior Foreign Ministry official who had worked closely with Meir for many years in both the Foreign Ministry and as Director-General of her Prime Minister's Office:

> 'she was *afraid* that this time she could not count on U.S. support.... Secondly, Golda had great *confidence* in the IDF's ability to win.... [Thirdly], neither Dayan nor Dado [Elazar] showed any *apprehension* or made a recommendation for a pre-emptive strike as a necessity; why should she then order it.... [However], if Dayan and/or Dado would have said that a strike was essential, there is no doubt in my mind that Golda would have decided in favor of such a step' (MB Interview, 27 July 1974, emphasis added).

As evident, there was a strong intuitive element in her decision process. An emotional attitude, too, was reflected in some of her foreign policy postures, notably in her unbending refusal to be reconciled to the 'new' Germany: as Foreign Minister, she disagreed sharply with Ben-Gurion's Realism in this sphere. She was unhappy with his decision to accept reparations in 1952 and steadfastly refused to ride in a German-made automobile. She opposed the arms deals with Germany in 1957 and 1958, along with Ben-Gurion's advocacy of diplomatic relations. The widely publicized role of German scientists in Egypt in the early 1960s reinforced her negative attitude. In these matters, she was closer to the unforgiving Menachem Begin—leader of the Revisionist *Herut* (Freedom) Movement, formed in 1948 as the political successor to the Para-military *Irgun*, enlarged to *Gahal* (abbr. for *Gush Herut Liberali*, the *Herut*-Liberal Bloc), formed in 1965, and in 1973 the *Likud*, the center-right bloc engineered by a daring, controversial Israeli military leader, Ariel Sharon—than to Ben-Gurion, her mentor for a long time.

In more positive terms, she was drawn by emotion to the plight of Africans struggling for dignity, autonomy, and welfare. Mrs. Meir acted much more on intuition than on reason or evidence; and she did not conceal her contempt for the expertise of most professional diplomats. Like Eshkol, her speeches were written by one or more staff members. And she read only 'the most necessary papers'. She enjoyed her years in the Labor Ministry more than those in the Foreign Ministry 'because there you can get something done that people need and see the results'. For the same reason her most ambitious—and successful—foreign policy initiative was Israel's technical assistance program in Africa. Her encounter with Asia was less productive.

As a political leader and a diplomat, Meir's strength lay in the realm of human relations. She was at her best in extemporaneous remarks, especially with American Jews, to whom she spoke directly, from the heart, often bluntly but never with a patronizing air, and as one of them.

Her Jewish sense of humor, like that of Eshkol, was proverbial in Israel. Three illustrations were recorded by her long-time assistant, *Simha Dinitz*, who served as ambassador to the USA during the 1973 War. Once, after a furious pace of work for two years, he suggested that she take a vacation. 'Why', she asked. 'Do you think I'm tired?' 'No,' he replied, 'but I am.' 'So take a vacation', she said. Moreover, 'she is always telling people, "don't be so humble—you're not that great"'. And thirdly, in a remark that would resonate with many Israelis more than three decades later, in the aftermath of the *Hamas* electoral victory in Gaza in January 2006, 'she insists that Israel's problem is not territorial but rather that the enemy refuses to sit down and talk to us. "Suppose we want to return the territory we have taken. To whom", she would say. "We can't send it to Nasser by parcel post"' (*New York Times*, 18 March 1969). More than Eshkol, however, she was tough and determined—in spirit and action.

She was always immovable on basic convictions, notably the natural right of Jews to an independent state and the welfare of Jews everywhere.

As for Israel's security, she was as rigid and unyielding as Ben-Gurion: reportedly, he referred to her as 'the best man I have in the Cabinet'.

Views of the World, the UN, and Diaspora Jewry

Meir, like Eshkol, never attempted to conceptualize a view of the world. Yet she possessed more (common-sense) insight into the forces impinging on Israel's foreign policy than did Eshkol, perhaps no less than Ben-Gurion and Sharett. She had a feel for friend and foe, apart from the obvious enemy of Israel, and an ability to influence the uncertain among men and nations.

Concern with the *Soviet-American struggle* for world hegemony was rarely expressed in the Meir utterances. Nor did she place a high value on the *UN's role* in the search for a viable Middle East peace settlement. Moreover, her relations with Secretary-General Hammarskjöld, in the 1950s, were icy: she distrusted and disliked him. To her, he symbolized the UN's indifference to Israel. And when the UN, 20 years after Israel's independence, stood by helpless and seemingly little concerned during the grave crisis of May–June 1967, which she and most Israelis perceived as a direct threat to survival, she moved more and more toward Ben-Gurion's dismissal of the world body as irrelevant. Yet she never emulated his utter disdain for diplomacy.

Like Eshkol's speeches or writings, but not those of Ben-Gurion or Sharett, or Abba Eban (see below), there was little worth remembering in the formal addresses of Golda Meir. Only on one topic, *Africa*, did she approach eloquence, on occasion. She constantly sought to identify Israel with emergent Africa—their past colonial rule, their recent attainment of independence, and their future aspirations. She often referred to the gap between rich and poor states as 'the central problem of our generation'. Her genuine affection for Africans and empathy with their plight and demands was doubted by none. Yet Meir was no starry-eyed idealist about Africa: a positive Israeli presence there also meant 'jumping over the Arab fence'.

As for Israel's ties with *Diaspora Jewry*, Meir was much closer to Eshkol and Sharett than to Ben-Gurion. At the same time, she exhibited, like Ben-Gurion, a deep disdain for the Zionist organizations. To many in Israel and abroad she was the most effective ambassador to world Jewry. And she openly subscribed to the dual function view of Israeli diplomacy: the Israel ambassador to the USA, she told an Israel Bond rally in 1959, 'is not merely ambassador to Washington but also an ambassador to the Jewish people'. Through word and deed she attached supreme importance to the bonds between Israel and world Jewry, emphasizing the crucial role of Jewry for the benefit of Israel in all spheres of public policy—financial and economic aid, pressure on friendly (and not so friendly) governments, immigration, the sense of solidarity, and in the last analysis the willingness to make the supreme sacrifice so that Israel might survive.

CHAPTER 5

Second-Generation Israeli Leaders (1960–77)

OVERVIEW

It is doubtful that any new state since the end of WWII had a more talented second-generation leadership than *Yigal Allon, Moshe Dayan, Abba Eban,* and *Shimon Peres,* the four then younger men in the decision-making inner circle during the period 1948–77. There were many other talented persons in that generation, notably: *Menachem Begin,* the founder and long-time leader of *Herut,* the Revisionist-Zionist political party, who was in permanent opposition in the *Knesset* from 1949 to 1977, except for a brief period as a Minister without Portfolio in the National Unity Government, 1967–70, during and after the May–June 1967 Six-Day Crisis-War; *Yigael Yadin,* the second IDF Chief of Staff, later a noted archaeologist at the Hebrew University of Jerusalem, and still later a Centrist politician as founder and head of a short-lived party, *Dash* (the Democratic Movement for Change, 1977–80); several long-serving army officers, who later became political leaders, in particular, *Yitzhak Rabin,* IDF Chief of Staff during the June 1967 Six-Day War, who entered politics in 1974, after a five-year period as Ambassador to the USA, and served as Prime Minister from 1974 to 1977 and from 1992 until his assassination in 1995; and *Ezer Weizman,* one of the creators of Israel's Air Force, Deputy Chief of Staff of the IDF during the 1967 crisis-war, then a politician and a key peacemaker, along with Dayan, in the negotiations with Egypt, 1977–79, and finally, President of Israel, 1993–2000. However, none of these or other prominent second-generation Israelis played a key decision-making role in the *political inner circle* prior to 1974.

Four members of the second generation of Israeli leaders, whom I encountered, were selected for attention in the Political Leaders segment of this project:

Yigal Allon was the most acclaimed field commander in Israel's War of Independence, 1948–49, as commander of the *Palmah*, the shock troops of the *Hagana*, Israel's IDF–in-the-making, when he was 27–30; later, he was a long-time leader of the left-nationalist *Ahdut Ha'avoda* party, Labor Minister and Deputy Prime Minister in Israel's inner circle during the October Yom Kippur War, 1973, and Foreign Minister, 1974–77.

Moshe Dayan, less well known during Israel's War of Independence, later shared with China's Lin Piao and North Vietnam's Vo Nguyen Giap the halo of the most successful soldiers since WWII, largely because of Israel's and his triumph in the Suez/Sinai war, 1956, as Chief of Staff of the IDF, and his crucial role as Defense Minister in Israel's stunning victory in the June 1967 Six-Day War, a position he held in the October Yom Kippur War of 1973–74 as well; and, in 1977–79, he played a key role as Foreign Minister in the Egypt/Israel negotiations that culminated in their 1979 peace agreement.

There was no more eloquent orator and persuasive advocate in the world of diplomacy since WWII than *Abba Eban*, the voice of Israel at the UN from 1948, when he was 33, and in the USA from 1949, both until 1959, then Minister of Education and, from 1966 to 1974, Foreign Minister.

Shimon Peres, an outstanding Israeli technocrat in his early years: he created a formidable bureaucratic-military establishment, as Director-General of the Defense Ministry, 1955–59 and Deputy Minister of Defense, 1959–65; he also laid the foundations for the alliance with France and for Israel's nuclear weapons program in the 1960s; later, since the 1970s, he held every important portfolio in Israel's Cabinets—Foreign Minister, Defense Minister, Finance Minister—and was Prime Minister from 1984 to 1986, and, briefly, in 1995–96; he also made a major contribution to the Oslo Accord with the Palestinians in 1993, for which he shared the Nobel Peace Prize with PLO leader, Yasir Arafat, and Israel's Prime Minister, Yitzhak Rabin. From 2007 to 2014, Peres was President of Israel.

At the beginning of Israel's third decade of independence, 1968, they were all prominent in public life: Allon as Deputy Prime Minister and one of the widely perceived heirs to the first-generation 'old guard' Labor leaders; Dayan as the charismatic Defense Minister and the other perceived heir to the succession; Eban as the eloquent Foreign Minister, widely respected in the chancelleries of the world; and Peres, temporarily in eclipse, as a leader of the Ben-Gurion-inspired splinter party, *Rafi*; he joined the Cabinet at the end of 1969.

There was a striking similarity between Allon and Dayan—in background, experience, and talents. Dayan and Peres were comrades in the national security sphere and in politics for more than 15 years and thought alike on most policy matters; and Allon's outlook was very similar to theirs on core issues of national security. Eban, a Cambridge don before he migrated to Israel, was the most apart of the four and was regarded by all throughout his public life as the least typical of Israeli leaders.

GENERALS AND POLITICIANS: YIGAL ALLON AND MOSHE DAYAN

Yigal ALLON (1918–80) Commander of the *Palmah*, the pre-IDF *Hagana* strike force, 1945–49, and a respected Israeli commander in the 1948–49 Arab/Israel War; Minister of Labor, 1961–65; Defense Adviser to Prime Minister Eshkol, 1965–68; Minister of Absorption and Deputy Prime Minister, 1968–74, and Minister of Education and Culture, 1969–74; Foreign Minister, 1974–77. [Interviews, 1960, 1965–66, 1968, 1973–74, 1977–78]

Moshe DAYAN (1915–81) Military commander in Jerusalem during the 1948–49 Arab/Israel War; a senior IDF commander, 1950–53; IDF Chief of Staff, 1953–58, including the Suez/Sinai War, 1956; Minister of Agriculture, 1959–64; Defense Minister, 1967–74, including the June 1967 Six-Day War and the October Yom Kippur War, 1973–74; Foreign Minister, 1977–79. [Encounter with Dayan May 1969]

Sabra *(Israeli-Born) Roots*

Allon's family ties to the Land of Israel dated to medieval times on his mother's side, to Safed (*Tsfat*), one of the four holy cities of Judaism. His father, Reuven Paicovitch, was brought to Palestine from Russia as a boy in the 1880s. Allon's grandparents were among the founders of

Rosh Pina, the first Jewish settlement in the Galilee. His parents helped to establish *Kfar* (Village) *Tabor* on the slopes of Mount Tabor in the Lower Galilee, where Yigal was born in October 1918. And he himself was a founder of *Kibbutz* Ginossar, a communal settlement on the shores of the *Kinneret* (Lake Tiberias, Sea of Galilee) in 1937. It was his permanent home until his death in 1980.

Dayan, too, had a distinguished *sabra* (literally, prickly pear, native-born) background. His father, Shmuel Dayan, arrived from Russia in 1908, during the Second *Aliya,* and was a prominent figure in the mainstream of Labor Zionism until his death in 1968. His mother was a writer of distinction. Moshe was born in May 1915 in Degania, the first *kibbutz* in Palestine, which his parents helped to found in a desolate swampy area of the Jordan Valley. His family founded the first *moshav* (cooperative agricultural settlement of smallholders), Nahalal; and there Moshe Dayan spent his formative years.

This difference in background—*kibbutz* versus *moshav*—was not without significance in later years. But it was vastly outweighed until the mid-1960s by common experience. Both men were *sabras*, born in Israel, the only ones in Israel's inner circle of decision-makers (until 1974, when Yitzhak Rabin became Prime Minister). Both Allon and Dayan grew up with a plough and a gun. Both received their early education in agriculture, Allon at the Kedourie Agricultural College, Mount Tabor, and Dayan in the high school of Nahalal. Allon went on to the Hebrew University and St. Antony's College, Oxford, in the 1950s and early 1960s, during the period between his two callings, the army and politics. Dayan, too, resumed his studies at an advanced age (42), attending the School of Law and Economics in Tel Aviv and the Hebrew University before entering the Government as Minister of Agriculture in 1959. Allon was to become Labor Minister two years later.

Military Leaders

Their military careers, too, followed a strikingly similar path, beginning with the Arab Revolt, 1936–39. Both men served in the Jewish Settlement Police and then in the *Hagana*, forerunner of the IDF. Both men came under the influence of Orde Wingate, a legendary pro-Zionist British military officer in Palestine who introduced novel tactics with his Special Night Squads. Allon was influenced even more by the equally legendary Yitzhak Sadeh, creator of the Field Platoons and in 1941 of the *Palmah*, (abbreviation for *Plugot Mahatz*), literally, striking platoons or shock troops of the *Hagana*, the main Para-military force of the Jewish community in Palestine until Israel's independence. The *Palmah*, primarily a Left-wing élite commando force, was forcibly dissolved by Ben-Gurion in 1949 and was integrated into the IDF. The two young *sabras* also commanded Jewish units assisting the Australian–British invasion of Lebanon and Syria in 1941.

Allon was the most talented of Sadeh's young men, and he rose rapidly in the *Palmah*: by 1945, he was its commander, at 27. And in the War of Independence, he acquired heroic stature as commander of virtually all the major Israeli campaigns: in Upper Galilee, including Safed; on the Central Front (Lydda-Ramle and the Jerusalem Corridor); and finally, the Southern Front where, in Operation *Ayin* in December–January 1948–49, he expelled the Egyptians from the Negev. Only political pressure from the UK, transmitted by the USA Ambassador to Israel, McDonald, and the order of Ben-Gurion at the end of 1948 prevented Allon's conquest of the entire Sinai Peninsula.

Dayan's record in the first Arab/Israel war was less distinguished; in fact, he served under Allon and Sadeh in the early campaigns (leading to the capture of Lod and Ramle), before taking command of the Jerusalem front at the end of July 1948.

Allon's active military career ended abruptly in 1950, when he left the IDF. He had strenuously opposed Ben-Gurion's enforced integration into the national army, the IDF, of the *Palmah* (and the other Para-military Jewish underground forces, notably the Revisionist-Zionist Right-wing *Etzel* [abbreviation for *Irgun Tzva'i Le'umi*, *IZL*, the National Military Organization, known simply as the *Irgun*], which seceded from *Hagana* in 1938, headed by Menachem Begin, who served as Israel's Prime Minister from 1977 to 1983; and Allon was passed over, by Defense Minister Ben-Gurion, despite what many regarded as his pre-eminent qualifications for the post of IDF Chief of Staff: Allon was a leader of the Left-nationalist *Ahdut Ha'avoda (Unity of Labor)* party; and Ben-Gurion rejected him as not 'one of us', meaning a member of the more moderate *Mapai* (Labor Party). For a decade, Allon was in the political wilderness, though he was a member of parliament, the *Knesset*, from 1954 onwards. He re-emerged as a national figure toward the end of 1961 as Minister of Labor when his party joined a new Ben-Gurion-led coalition. In the May–June 1967 crisis, he was Prime Minister–Defense Minister Eshkol's belated choice for Defense Minister, in a futile effort to keep Dayan, long closely associated with Ben-Gurion, out of this pivotal position; but the mass public, opposition parties, and Dayan triumphed.

Dayan acquired the reputation at home and abroad of Israel's pre-eminent military commander—as Chief of Staff, 1953–58, hero of the Sinai Campaign–Suez War in 1956, and then as Minister of Defense during the crisis preceding the June Six-Day War of 1967, continuing in that position during the 1969 War of Attrition and the 1973–74 October Yom Kippur War. He also became the most compelling Israeli public figure, with a mass following, until the Yom Kippur War, the first Arab/Israel War that was not perceived by Israel as an unqualified IDF victory.

Assets and Qualities

Both men were endowed with impressive assets and qualities. They had deep roots in the society created by Jewish pioneers since the beginning of the 1880s. They were known for personal courage and inspirational leadership—on the battlefield and among their admirers generally. They were more sensitive to the Middle East environment of Israel and understood the Arabs better than most of Israel's first generation of leaders; Sharett was the exception. They had carefully considered views on most aspects of public policy, notably on foreign and security matters. They had many years of experience in political life, including a decade or more in the *Knesset* and the Government. Both were highly intelligent and self-confident about their judgment of men and affairs. Of Dayan, Ben-Gurion reportedly said in 1958: 'You have two diametrically-opposed facets to your character—courage bordering upon the lunatic, offset and balanced by a profound tactical and strategic intelligence.' The same assessment could be applied to Allon. As late as the 1960s, there was a broad consensus that they were the leading contenders for succession to the Second *Aliya* 'old guard', which included the first four prime ministers—Ben-Gurion, Sharett, Eshkol, and Meir. Yet neither became prime minister: Allon, probably because he represented a much smaller wing of the Labor movement; and Dayan, perhaps because he was too mercurial to be acceptable to the mainstream Labor politicians. Both served as Foreign Minister, Allon in the mid-1970s, under Rabin, his No. 2 officer in the *Palmah*.

Differences

Notwithstanding their remarkably parallel roles as the young leaders of the pre-State period, there were differences between these leaders of Israel's *sabra* generation. Dayan was the pragmatist par excellence: his detractors accused him of inconsistency, for he enunciated different policy positions from month to month, sometimes more frequently; this was especially true of pronouncements regarding the occupied West Bank, euphemistically termed by Israelis of almost all political persuasions, 'the territories', or 'administered territories', as late as 2016, almost half a century after they were occupied in the June 1967 Six-Day War. Dayan defended the gyrations in his public policy as a response to changing political circumstances. Allon retained an ideological commitment—to *kibbutz* (collective or communal settlement)-derived agrarian socialism, with a strong nationalist flavor. Both his views and his actions were marked by greater continuity and predictability. Dayan was more flamboyant in speech and manner. Allon gave the impression of greater prudence and caution. Dayan was direct, frank, and easy in manner. Allon was more formal and, to many persons, seemed more the intellectual. Dayan was unconventional in all things. At the same time, he was more restless, obstinate, imperious, contemptuous, and unpredictable—in personality and political behavior.

Dayan was a 'loner', fiercely independent in spirit and an outspoken iconoclast: he aroused passionate devotion and intense hostility among Israelis. There was no one whom he admired, unreservedly—not even Ben-Gurion. 'Let me tell you something about Mr. Ben-Gurion,' he replied to an interviewer. 'He is probably the only person I admire. And finally, no, not even him. I don't admire anyone. But I have a higher opinion of him than anyone else' (MB Interview May 1969).

Allon was much more the member of a team, in the cabinet and his political party. Moreover, he was for years a protégé of *Yitzhak Tabenkin*, the grand old man of the *Ha-Kibbutz Ha-me'uhad* (United Kibbutz) movement, mainly linked to *Ahdut Ha'avoda*, a left-nationalist political party established in 1927, and of *Yitzhak Sadeh*, his military mentor, for both of whom he often expressed admiration.

Sharett was perceived as a Middle Easterner of the peaceful tribe, and Dayan, of the warring tribe. Allon was no less hawkish in policy toward the Arabs than Dayan but he did not acquire his extreme image. Dayan thought aloud and was not averse to hesitation before making decisions. Allon never admitted vacillation and, objectively, was more decisive.

Diplomat: Abba EBAN

Abba EBAN **Israel's Permanent Representative to the UN, 1949–59; Ambassador to the USA, 1950–59; Minister of Education and Culture, 1960–63; Deputy Prime Minister, 1963–65; Foreign Minister, 1966–74. [MB Interviews, 1948, 1965–66, 1968, 1973–74, 1977–78, 1995]**

Eban was the best-known Israeli public figure in the chancelleries of the world and at the UN, where he commanded respect as the consummate advocate of a new state under siege, from 1948 to 1974. To many who heard his masterly flow of words, he was the Churchill of post-WWII diplomacy. Yet Eban's admirers and supporters remained mainly outside Israel, even after decades of continuous exposure to the Israeli public as their high-profile ambassador to the UN and the USA for a decade (1949–59) and holder of senior ministerial posts from 1959 to 1974, including Foreign Minister, 1966–74. To many, he remained 'the outsider', out of tune with Israel's *sabra* generation, its concerns and aspirations, its behavior, its approach to the issues of war and peace, its attitude to the rest of the world.

Zionist Roots and Road to Aliya

Of the four second-generation Israel Labor leaders who held influential positions in Israel's Government and the IDF from 1948 to 1977, Eban was the most distant from the new Israeli society in background and experience. Yet like Peres, though in an entirely different context, his Zionist roots were deep. Born in South Africa in January 1915 of Lithuanian immigrants, he came to England as an infant. His grandfather was a 'fanatical Hebraist', and the young Aubrey was bilingual (English and Hebrew) at the age of five. His mother was the secretary of Zionist leader Nahum Sokolow, Weizmann's chief colleague during WWI in the quest for British support for the Zionist goal of a Jewish homeland in Palestine. Eban himself came to the attention of Chaim Weizmann in 1938, via Sharett and *Katznelson*, as a talented public speaker in the Zionist cause in the then hostile environment of England. By that time, he was a Fellow of Pembroke College, Cambridge, after a brilliant academic record: he graduated from Cambridge in 1938 with First Class Honors in both Classics and Oriental Languages and Literature—Arabic, Hebrew, and Persian.

He worked briefly with Weizmann and Sharett at the London office of the Jewish Agency in 1939—in the preliminary negotiations for the creation of a Jewish Division in the British Army. Major Eban was posted to Jerusalem in 1942, as Liaison Officer at Allied Middle East HQ, with the primary task of training Jewish volunteers for special missions in Palestine and behind the Nazi lines in Europe. Two years later, he became Chief Instructor at the Middle East Arabic Center in Jerusalem, established by the Allied command.

After demobilization in September 1946 and under the influence of the growing struggle of Palestine Jewry, he gave up his academic career and entered the Political Department of the Jewish Agency. He was thus the last of the four second-generation leaders to settle in the Land of Israel, and the oldest (31). In the spring of 1948, he made his first appearance on the UN stage and pleaded the Zionist cause with passion and conviction. Thereafter, for a decade, he was the voice of Israel, from 1949 to 1959 as Permanent Representative to the UN and, simultaneously, from 1950 to 1959, as Ambassador to the USA. He resumed this role after the Sixth *Knesset* Elections, when he succeeded Golda Meir as Foreign Minister in 1966.

Status, Eloquence, Influence

Eban had a unique status among Israel's diplomatic representatives. On more than one occasion during the 1950s, he displayed the courage of his convictions by strongly opposing the Ben-Gurion-Dayan-Peres policy of retaliation. Both Ben-Gurion and Sharett, and later, Meir, had great faith in his capacity to explain Israel's actions, even when they aroused misgivings in Israel and abroad. A notable example was the Lake Kinneret (Sea of Galilee) raid by Israel in December 1955: Ben-Gurion punctured Eban's protest by telling him that, after he had listened to Eban's superb defense of the action at the UN, any doubts he may have had were removed! (MB Interviews in 1960 with officials in Israel's Foreign Ministry and the Prime Minister's Office)

Among his many eloquent speeches, at the UN and elsewhere, perhaps the most memorable was his defense of Israel's invasion of Egypt on 29 October 1956, the launching of the Sinai Campaign: it was delivered before the Emergency Session of the General Assembly on 1 November 1956:

> Surrounded by hostile armies on all its land frontiers, subjected to savage and relentless hostility, exposed to penetration, raids and assaults by day and by night, suffering constant toll of life amongst its citizenry, bombarded by threats of neighboring governments to accomplish its extinction by armed force, overshadowed by a new menace or irresponsible rearmament, embattled, blockaded, besieged, Israel alone amongst the nations faces a battle for its security anew with every approaching nightfall and every rising dawn. In a country of small area and intricate configuration, the proximity of enemy guns is a constant and haunting theme.

As Eban wrote, proudly, soon after: his speech was 'heard and seen by millions, had a tremendous echo, and its impression…was considerable'.

Apart from his admired oratory at the UN, Eban made a major contribution at the height of the Suez/Sinai crisis-war. On 8 November 1956, immediately after Israel's decisive triumph on the battlefield, Prime Minister Ben-Gurion alienated US President Eisenhower and many other Western leaders by his 'victory speech' in Israel's parliament the previous day, including his categorical refusal to withdraw Israeli forces from Sinai: as reported earlier in this book, Ben-Gurion explained the oral blunder by acknowledging, '*You see, Mr. Brecher, I was too drunk with victory*' (Interview 1966). In an attempt to repair the potentially grave diplomatic damage, Eban took the initiative and cabled Ben-Gurion with a recommendation that Israel declare its willingness to withdraw from Sinai when 'satisfactory arrangements' were made with the international force (UNEF) about to enter the Canal Zone, from which British and French troops had withdrawn. Israel's Cabinet, on 7 November, left the decision about an international force in Sinai to Ben-Gurion. He, in turn, in effect, transferred the crucial decision to Eban, asking his ambassador to the USA and the UN whether Israel could afford to accept his formula, saying, in effect, 'if Eban really takes responsibility that it is feasible, then I agree'. Eban did so; and Israel's political crisis with the USA and the West generally on the withdrawal issue at that time was resolved.

Assessment

Eban's behavior in 1956 was a revealing illustration of the important role of a diplomat—sometimes—in the foreign policy–national security decision-making process. Israel's strategic decision to withdraw from Sinai was taken by Ben-Gurion. Eban's recommended formula followed approval by the US Under-Secretary of State—Secretary Dulles was then in the hospital. At the same time, Eban's role was innovative; and the burden of responsibility placed on him on 8 November by his Prime Minister was very heavy. He reacted decisively. Moreover, his formula permitted phased withdrawal and, therefore, ample time to secure concessions from the USA and the UN, the *raison d'être* of the political struggle to follow, until Israel's final withdrawal in March 1957. Eban also exerted influence on other major policy issues, for example, the unsuccessful decision to press for a mutual defense agreement with the USA in 1954 and the decision to decline Communist China's implied offer of diplomatic relations early in 1955 (analyzed in my *Decisions in Israel's Foreign Policy*, 1974). For the most part, however, he was the supreme diplomat, advocate, and implementer of policy arrived at by the Government of Israel.

Eban's speeches in Hebrew sometimes obscured his ideas in the *Knesset*—his Hebrew was too sophisticated for many, more biblical than modern. He was more formal than his peers in bearing, dress, manner, and speech. He was, generally, less quick to make decisions, more inclined to delay while the complex forces at work, both external and internal, and especially the former, unfolded on the stage. As a diplomat, with a donnish air, he had a basic mistrust of 'the generals' and their '*bitzuist*' (activist/technocrat/pragmatist) mentality, with their strong taint of chauvinism, total self-reliance, isolationism, and disdain for the world, an attitude so pronounced with Dayan and Peres until late in their careers, Dayan in the peace process with Egypt, 1977–79, Peres in the (abortive) peace process with the Palestinians, 1993. In this respect, as in others, Allon, although a former general, was closer in spirit to Eban from the time he entered the ranks of Government and the Ministerial Committee on Defense in 1961. Eban's extraordinary appeal abroad, especially with Jewry and the intelligentsia, was not reciprocated among Israelis: the 'alien' image ran deep (Siniver 2015).

Technocrat: Shimon Peres

Shimon PERES Director-General, Defense Ministry, 1953–59; Deputy Minister of Defense, 1960–65; Minister without Portfolio, 1969–70; Minister of Transport and Communications, 1970–74; Defense Minister, 1974–77; Prime Minister, 1984–86; Deputy Prime Minister and Foreign Minister, 1986–88; Finance Minister, 1988–1990; Foreign Minister, 1992–95; Prime Minister, 1995–96; Vice-Premier, 2006–07; President of Israel, 2007–14. [MB Interviews, 1960, 1965–66, 1968, 1973–74, 1977–78]

'Wunderkind'

Like the other three second-generation leaders compared here, Peres achieved influence and success in Israel's national security establishment very early: at 30, in 1953, he became Ben-Gurion's principal aide in the Defense Ministry, as Director-General. Soon after, he was instrumental in forging the (unwritten) Israel alliance with France and achieved secure access to modern weapons of high quality, crucial during the Suez/Sinai War of 1956, including, a decade later, France's support for a nuclear weapons program: both were perceived by all Israeli leaders as vital to Israel's survival in the 1950s and beyond (reported at length by Peres in his *David's Sling* (1970), Chap. 3). (Their view of the security value of Israel's nuclear weapons was challenged with powerful arguments by Israeli scholar *Zeev Maoz* in *Defending the Holy Land: A Critical Analysis of Israel's Security and Foreign Policy*, 2006.) According to Sharett, not one of Peres's admirers, Peres was also responsible for persuading Ben-Gurion to seek early entry into the European Common Market (MB Interview with Sharett, 8 July 1960). Certainly, he played a key role in that initiative. He was, in fact, Israel's Adjunct Foreign Minister to the military establishments of Western Europe, with powerful links as well to friendly new states in Africa and Asia.

Zionist Background and Youth

Peres, too, was not a *sabra*; but, like Eban, his attachment to Zion dated from childhood: he was born in 1923 in the town of Volozin, White Russia, later Belarus. It was a unique environment, for the thousand

Jewish families spoke Hebrew as their mother tongue. Although initially drawn to the left-socialist *Ha-shomer Ha-tza'ir* (the Young Guard), the youth movement of what later became the Marxist-Zionist *Mapam* Party in 1948, he joined *Ha-no'ar Ha-oved* (Working Youth), the youth movement of the *Histadrut*, the trade union bulwark of Ben-Gurion's, Sharett's, Eshkol's, and Meir's social-democratic *Mapai* Party, soon after his arrival in Palestine with his family at the age of ten. He attended high school in Tel Aviv and spent two formative years (15–17) at the Youth *Aliya* children's village of Ben Shemen, with a mixed group of Israeli and Jewish immigrant youngsters. After further training in *Kvutzat* Geva, he settled in *Kibbutz* Alumot until 1947. During that period, he became National Secretary of *Ha-no'ar Ha-oved,* a role which he was to symbolize later in the 'Young Guard' of *Mapai,* along with Dayan.

National Security Roles

Peres was released by his *kibbutz* for work with the *Hagana* HQ in 1947 and remained with the Defense establishment for 18 years. He helped to create Israel's navy in 1949 and then headed the purchasing mission of the Defense Ministry in the USA for two years. He became Deputy Director-General of the Ministry of Defense in 1952 and Director-General the following year. In 1959, he moved into the political arena: he entered the *Knesset,* along with Dayan, as spokesmen of *Mapai* youth, and was elevated to the post of Deputy Defense Minister. Thus, from the mid-1950s to 1965, when he resigned in the Ben-Gurion-generated *Mapai* split, Peres was close to the inner circle of Israel's national security élite.

In 1965, with Ben-Gurion's active support, probably initiative, and Dayan's hesitant approval, Peres created a new political party, *Rafi* (the Israel Workers List), a *Mapai* splinter group, almost single-handed. The years 1965–68 were not quite a political wilderness for him, but the influence and glamour of the previous decade were increasingly removed from his grasp.

Role in Labor Zionist Merger and the 1967 Crisis

Within two years of the split in the Labor movement, Peres played a decisive role, along with Dayan, in bringing *Rafi* back into the Labor Zionist fold: Peres was the first advocate of a complete merger of the then existing four Labor factions—the mainstream social-democratic *Mapai,* the pre-eminent Government Coalition leader from 1948 to 1977, the left-nationalist *Ahdut Ha'avoda*, of which Allon was a second-generation leader, the Marxist-Zionist *Mapam*, and the Peres-created *Rafi*. The merger was consummated in January 1968 as the *Labor Alignment*. Peres became one of its two Deputy Secretaries-General (the other was from *Ahdut Ha'avoda*).

Half a year before the reunion of the four Labor parties, Peres also played an important role in Israel's domestic political crisis during May 1967, triggered by Prime Minister Eshkol's communication fiasco, noted earlier in the discussion of his failed leadership. This crisis led to the Government reshuffle, notably Dayan's appointment as Minister of Defense, despite Eshkol's opposition, in the National Unity Government, formed a few days before the onset of the Six-Day War. Yet Peres remained outside the Cabinet and the then inner circle, for he was, throughout, a devoted aide to Ben-Gurion.

He joined the Cabinet in 1969 and remained a minister for almost four decades, including two brief periods as Prime Minister, once by prearrangement with the *Likud* leader, Yitzhak Shamir, in the mid-1980s and, briefly, as successor to the assassinated Yitzhak Rabin in late 1995, only to be defeated in the 1996 elections by *Likud* leader, Benjamin Netanyahu.

Insight into Peres, Late 1940s-Late 1980s: Prototype of a 'Bitzuist' (Activist)

Notwithstanding the later global image of Peres as Israel's most prominent and influential peace advocate and peacemaker, particularly after his Nobel Peace Prize in 1994 for his role in concluding the Oslo Accords with the PLO the previous year, Peres was, until the mid-1980s, first and foremost, a man of action, a political hawk on the Israel/Palestinian conflict, a '*bitzuist*' (activist), a talented executor of decisions. By temperament and behavior, he was a technocrat, who had abandoned ideology as a guide to policy.

This became apparent at my first interview with him in the summer of 1960, a year after he had been elevated from the post of Director-General of the Defense Ministry to the more visible and influential political positions of Deputy Defense Minister (to Ben-Gurion, who doubled as Prime Minister and Defense Minister) and a *Mapai* member of the *Knesset*. Peres's comments on men and affairs in Israel's formative years, 1948–60, revealed a bright, quick mind, with strong views on a wide range of defense and foreign policy issues, along with candid comments on his second-generation and some first-generation colleagues.

Peres shared with Dayan a pragmatic approach to policy matters and a great respect for science and technology as the keys to solving Israel's social, economic, and security problems. He was ruthless in the pursuit of goals, whether hawkish, in the early years (or dovish in his advanced years). He lacked—and still lacks, at 93—Dayan's and Allon's charisma with Israel's attentive and mass publics; in fact, there has long been a tendency to mistrust Peres's actions—many drawing an analogy with Richard Nixon—long associated with the secrecy of the security network. This was evident in his failure to win an Israeli general election in five attempts as Labor Party leader or the 2000 election by the 120-member *Knesset* to the honorific position of State President. Yet he has a systematic and orderly mind, with a flair for original ideas. His later speeches are lucid, calm, and usually restrained.

THE FOUR YOUNGER LEADERS: A COMPARISON

General

Peres lacked the formal higher education of many of his peers, notably Eban. However, this was partly compensated by a disciple–*guru* relationship with the legendary thinker of Labor Zionism, Berl Katznelson, to whom Peres attributed the greatest influence of his formative years. Over time, he displayed an intellectual flair, no less impressive than that of Dayan and comparable in insight to Allon and Eban, though without the former's originality or the latter's literary and oratorical elegance.

Relationships among these four second-generation Labor leaders of Israel were diverse. As noted, Dayan and Peres were comrades for 15 years in government, party, and the Defense establishment and shared a basic national security outlook. Allon and Dayan acknowledged the mutual respect of outstanding military commanders: neither had ever been defeated in battle, though the latter's role during the 1973–74 War was subjected to critical inquiry soon after. Both were conscious of their role as leaders of Israel's *sabra* generation and as rivals for the political succession to the ageing Second *Aliya* Israeli élite. Both spoke publicly about each other with appreciation and, occasionally, with cordiality—never with a tone of harshness or abuse, or disdain, as Dayan did about Eshkol, Sharett, Eban, and others.

By contrast, Peres did not conceal his profound policy disagreements with Allon, during extensive interviews in 1966. In part, this was a continuation of a political party feud—between Ben-Gurion's (and Peres's) ill-fated *Rafi* splinter within *Mapai* and Allon's *Ahdut Ha'avoda*—and their corresponding clash in basic outlook on policy—Peres's pragmatism versus Allon's commitment to agrarian socialist ideology. In part, it was personal—Peres remembered that Allon's *Ahdut Ha'avoda* had prevented his entry into full membership of the Ministerial Committee on Foreign Affairs and Defense in 1960 because he was then a mere Deputy Minister.

In a similar vein, Eban and Dayan displayed an increasingly hostile attitude toward each other's policies, reaching its peak in the debate over the newly formed Labor Alignment's foreign policy and national security planks in its election platform for 1969. Eban rejected Dayan's 'oral interpretation' of the consensus on this crucial policy issue and virtually called on Dayan to leave the reunited party. The conflict was resolved by two separate formulae in its platform—Dayan's emphasis on 'strategic, security borders' in the security plank, and Eban's advocacy of 'agreed, secure and recognized borders' in the foreign policy plank!

Although Eban and Allon had policy differences, especially toward 'the [West Bank and Gaza] territories', they displayed mutual respect. In 1965, when they served as joint chairmen of the then partial Labor Alignment *(Mapai* and *Ahdut Ha'avoda)* Election Committee, Allon toasted their victory in the Sixth *Knesset* Elections as the only occasion on which Oxford and Cambridge graduates had combined to win an election in Israel! In the 1969 Dayan-Eban clash over the phrasing of the election platform, Eban declared that Allon shared his interpretation—and his assertion was not challenged.

While Dayan and Peres were perceived then, correctly, as hawks on the Palestinians and the West Bank-Gaza, Dayan became disposed to a peaceful solution of the Arab/Israel conflict at the beginning of the 1970s and, especially, during the Egypt-Israel negotiations, 1977–79, as did Peres during the mid-1980s, in his peace 'negotiations' with Jordan's King Hussein and his role in consummating the 1993 Oslo Accord. Eban was correctly viewed as a consistent dove among Israel's first- and second-generation leaders, along with Sharett. In the broadest sense, this was accurate: Dayan and Peres were the proud continuators of the Ben-Gurion activist path in foreign and national security policy, while Eban was the practitioner, as well as the admirer, of Sharett's alternative accommodationist, compromise approach to relations with Israel's Arab neighbors.

Views of World Politics: The USA, the UN, and World Jewry

Allon's worldview revealed the influence of the two main strands in his background. One was the blend of agrarian socialism and militant nationalism which characterized the *Ha-Kibbutz Ha-me'uhad* (Unity of Labor) *kibbutz* movement. The other was his experience as *Palmah* commander during Israel's formative years, pre-State and the first year of independence, 1945–49. The result was an *image* with *greater ideological* content and *flavor* than that of his peers, tempered by a *pragmatic, activist* approach remarkably similar to that of Dayan and Peres, the '*bitzuists*' (activists) in this group. Overall, Allon shared the Dayan-Peres advocacy of self-reliance and the primacy of strategic needs as the sine qua non of Israel's survival as an independent state. He did not dismiss the UN and public opinion; but neither did he attach Eban's importance to external perceptions and pressures.

Allon perceived the global struggle between the USA and the USSR through the lens of the Israeli variant of *non-alignment*. In the early years, he strongly supported the Ben-Gurion-Sharett policy of *non-identification* with either the USA or the USSR, even while the dominant Left-socialist, Marxist-Zionist *Mapam* Party, of which his *Ahdut Ha'avoda* Party was then a partner, was committed to pro-Soviet 'neutralism'. With the reemergence of virulent anti-Semitism and hostility to Israel in Eastern Europe during Stalin's last years, 1948–53, Allon led the move to separate *Ahdut Ha'avoda* from *Mapam's Ha-shomer Ha-tza'ir* youth movement ('Young Guard'), which retained the *Mapam* name and the ideological link to the Soviet Union, 'the bastion of world socialism'. *Ahdut Ha'avoda* returned to its traditional middle-road position on the socialist spectrum of Israeli politics.

In foreign policy, Allon's policy preference for Israel was equidistance from the superpowers or 'genuine' non-alignment. He was no less critical of the *Mapai*-dominated Government swing to the Right from 1951 to 1955, reflected in Israel's attempt to secure a US offer of military alliance, which Eban supported. As Allon remarked in April 1966, '[W]e wasted time and energy in trying to win membership in Western clubs. We failed and wasted our position with the East.' Further, '[M]y belief in the wisdom of Israel's non-involvement [in the Cold War] proved to be correct' (MB Interview, April 1977).

Allon never placed foreign policy on a plane of moral commitment. He once told Ben-Gurion: '[Y]ou were committed to anti-communism; I am not committed to anti-Americanism.' More generally about Ben-Gurion, 'Many dramatic quarrels could have been avoided had we not followed his prophetic zeal' (MB Interview, April 1966). Allon had no illusions about Soviet hostility to Israel. At the same time, he did not adopt a harsh anti-Soviet view in foreign policy and never advocated formal alignment with the USA. This was partly a residue of his ideological antipathy to the excesses of American capitalism, partly to his belief that such a policy would be rejected by Washington, partly because of his supreme confidence that, as he remarked in 1969 (MB Interview), 'thanks to our efforts, the State of Israel today is unconquerable', and mostly because he placed a very high value on achieving mass immigration from the USSR—about which he was optimistic. Stalinism, he claimed, tried to solve the abnormal problem of a nationally conscious Jewry by abnormal means, assimilation, and it failed. Further, Allon perceived precedents of communist states allowing Jews as a national group to emigrate and predicted, correctly, that this would occur under a different Soviet leadership. Like most of his peers and elders in the Israeli leadership, he placed a high value on *aliya* (immigration) from the USSR; thus, accommodation with Moscow was crucial, in his view.

Unlike many in Israel, including Dayan, Allon did not anticipate—or fear—direct Soviet military intervention in the Arab/Israel conflict. In fact, he was among the most ardent opponents of Israel's withdrawal from conquered Egyptian territory, at the height of its triumph in the 1956 Sinai Campaign–Suez War, under Soviet threats of massive bombing of Israel (MB Interviews with Allon and many other Israeli officials and politicians in 1966). And during the 1967 June Six-Day War, he argued strongly against the likelihood of direct Soviet military intervention, whereas Dayan had serious doubts (MB Interviews with many Israeli officials in 1968). The same clash of views was evident during the October Yom Kippur War of 1973, when the Soviet Union once again threatened direct military intervention: Allon thought it was another bluff, and Dayan once again misjudged the threat. Overall, during all of Israel's first three major crisis-wars after the War of Independence in 1948–49 (1956, 1967, and 1973–74), when Moscow threatened military intervention, Allon proved to be correct: he termed the threats a bluff whereas Dayan panicked!

Like Peres, but not Dayan or Eban, Allon exhibited a *strong interest in Asia and Africa*. The center of his attention in the Third World was India; but his attempts to nurture a change in its long-established pro-Arab posture toward the Arab/Israel Conflict proved to be in vain—until

1992, when India established formal diplomatic relations with Israel, long after Allon passed from the scene. Moreover, Allon publicly criticized 'the basic error which we [Israel] made [in 1955] when China was more isolated and deemed important ties even with a small country such as Israel' (MB Interview, 1966). In fact, China invited Israel to establish diplomatic relations (in 1955), but Sharett, Eban, and others rejected this opportunity, fearful of alienating the USA [Brecher, *Israel, the Korean War and China* (1974)]. China's hostility to Israel, thereafter, Allon predicted, accurately, would change only after an accommodation between Beijing and Washington [*Ha'aretz* (Tel Aviv), 12 September 1969].

Dayan's approach to world politics carried the imprint of his primary professional experience, the army. This was evident in his blunt, black-and-white conception of *decisions* and *decision-making*:

> I believe in decisions, not majority opinions.... A decision always implies risks....Moreover, most of the time it's not a question of choosing between alternatives, but inventing a new solution from scratch.
>
> In every situation one must decide. There are two sides to the matter and things are never foreseeable. You can never be sure that things you expect to happen will happen that way. I at any rate am never sure.... If you make a mistake, you make a mistake. But you have no choice. You must say yes or no, agreed or not agreed, do this or do that. (MB Interview, May 1969)

As for Ben-Gurion, the critical test of significance on any foreign policy–national security issue for Dayan was the ability to secure arms. Thus *Euro/America* was always, after 1948–49, central to Israel's struggle against Arab hostility—and, therefore, to Dayan's foreign policy and national security images and decisions.

The main themes of Eban's view of the external world, from 1948 to 1973, even earlier and later, were the Arab/Israel conflict, Israel and the Middle East, internal developments, and Israel's right to security. As for the *global setting*, the three main components were the USA, the UN, and Jewry.

Throughout his years as Israel's pre-eminent diplomat, Eban perceived the *USA* as more important than the *Soviet Union* for Israel's survival, even though the USA denied arms aid to Israel during its War of Independence, as well as in the Suez War–Sinai Campaign, while the Soviets, acting through Czechoslovakia, the first 'Czech. Arms deal', made a notable contribution to Israel's victory in the 1948 war. Until 1955, Eban and other

Israeli decision-makers thought that they could ignore the Soviet Union as a vital factor in the Arab/Israeli conflict. In fact, Eban was predisposed to perceive the superpowers through a pronounced pro-American lens.

Eban's image of the *UN* was in the Sharett tradition. He recognized its limitations and shortcomings in the Arab/Israel conflict but also acknowledged its contribution to Israel's independence. And in the global system, as a whole, he perceived the UN as a stabilizing element of great value. Like his predecessors, Eban always attached significance to Israel's links with Diaspora Jewry.

Both Dayan and Eban recognized the East–West Cold War as a phenomenon with spillover effects on the Arab/Israel conflict. Neither displayed any expectation of Soviet friendship or even non-hostility. Both revealed a greater affinity with the West. The differences in this context were Eban's persistent stress on US aid, with Dayan inclined for a long time primarily to a Franco/German orientation; and second, Eban's greater emphasis on external forces, including the UN, and diplomacy in Israel's foreign and security policy, compared to Dayan's faith in self-reliance and, particularly, in the IDF. Both perceived world Jewry as Israel's most reliable ally. Eban, however, rejected Ben-Gurion's 'two-camp thesis', while Dayan's view was more complex and ambivalent.

'The question is whether we should view the world according to our prejudices or in terms of its objective reality, and try to obtain the maximum benefit from the political constellation that obtains in the world.' Such was the Realist underpinning of Shimon Peres's View of the World, at least until the mid-1980s. The *search for arms* was at the core of his policy orientation and its antecedent global image. In policy terms, this meant, for Peres, *a new look at West Germany* as an ally of France, a major factor in the European community and a source of modern weapons for Israel, as well as a possible entry into Europe via membership in the European Common Market. These ideas he expounded from the late 1950s for decades.

Yet Peres's view of the world and his consequent policy concerns far transcended the search for arms, even in his early years. In a more general analysis of Israel's foreign policy, he perceived *five relevant factors*: (1) its foes attack in word and deed; (2) the Middle East was in flux and was an 'area of inter-power rivalry'; (3) Israel did not belong to any bloc or military alliance; (4) Israel was not just a state but was the only territorial basis of world Jewry; and, finally, (5) '[O]ur political system of permanent coalitions influences policy-making' (MB Interview, 1966). All these, taken together, he declared, play a crucial role in shaping Israel's foreign policy objectives. Notwithstanding his view in the 1960s that Israel practiced real neutralism but did not talk it, he was emphatic on *Israel and the bloc struggle*: 'One cannot be neutral between right and wrong. Israel's place is with the free world' (MB Interview, July 1960). As for the *UN*, he criticized the world body and the then Secretary-General, Dag Hammarskjold, for going beyond its two valuable functions—cooling tempers and providing a bridge between the protagonists—by trying to 'build a house on a bridge', that is, creating a UN-controlled superstate. In the Middle East, he added, the UN role was marginal and negative (*Ibid.*). Like all of his peers, Peres attached cardinal importance to Israel's *links with world Jewry*.

Ironically, in light of his prominent role as Foreign Minister during part of the 1980s and much of the 1990s, Peres showed utter disdain for the ritual and procedure of diplomacy during the early period of his long active public life, 1948–73, and even later. For its substance—negotiations—he perceived a legitimate role within a narrow sphere: 'keep your powder dry and negotiate where possible but do not expect much' was his implied motto concerning *armed force and diplomacy* as instruments of national security and foreign policy. Certainly, he often declared, diplomats should be subordinate to Defense experts in the formulation of high policy (MB Interviews, 1960 and 1966).

Fifty years ago, Peres revealed an imaginative approach to foreign policy by advocating *eight objectives for Israel* in the next decade:

1. 'To build a "second Egypt" in Africa, that is, to help convert Ethiopia's economic and military strength into a counter-force to Egypt (!);
2. To bring Israel into the European Common Market on a political rail, that is, together with Jordan and Lebanon and thus to establish the basis of economic cooperation, the only type of Arab/Israel cooperation that can precede peace;
3. To lay a new basis of France-Israel friendship, by intensifying scientific cooperation;
4. To widen our activities in Latin America and Asia;
5. To build new links between Israel and world Jewry – with a reduced emphasis on money and more on intellect;
6. To bring China into the U.N. and secure recognition of China by all the Powers. This will make its more responsible and therefore reduce its hostility to Israel;
7. To bring about normalization of relations with North Africa; and

8. To reduce our claims on the United States and strengthen our friendship—asking less and appreciating more' (MB Interview, June 1966).

Only one of these goals, item 6, integrating China into the mainstream of world politics, was achieved, with virtually no role for Israel in the process of China's normalization as a prominent member of the interstate community.

EIGHT ISRAELI LEADERS: A COMPARISON OF VIEWS

Ben-Gurion and *Sharett* served effectively to define Israel's foreign policy options for the other inner circle members over *six crucial areas* during Israel's first 25 years.

Sharett assessed the importance of empathetic *global relations* for Israel far higher than did *Ben-Gurion*. Both came to recognize the bipolarity of the international system and the penetration of the Middle East by the superpower struggle. Ben-Gurion's early commitment to 'non-identification' (1948–50), dictated by a 'national interest' logic, quickly gave way to a marked pro-West inclination after the escalation of the Korean War in the autumn of 1950. Sharett's affinity for non-alignment was more ideologically grounded and gave way more slowly: he took care to leave the door open to reconciliation with the Soviet Union.

Meir, Dayan, and *Peres* adhered to Ben-Gurion's view of the *superpower conflict*, relating to the global system principally from the standpoint of Israel's security (access to arms). *Eshkol*, too, tended toward Ben-Gurion's position. *Eban*, like Sharett, counter-posed a pro-American policy to the Europe-oriented posture urged by Peres and, to a lesser extent, by Dayan. And *Allon's* hawkishness on national security issues, that is, his affinity to Peres and Dayan, was somewhat tempered by his ideological commitment to non-alignment.

The *UN*, its role in the creation of an independent State, and its ongoing importance in the Arab/Israel conflict, were subjects of extreme controversy. With rare moments of ambivalence, *Ben-Gurion* dismissed the UN as of no consequence, insisting that Israel's birth and survival owed virtually nothing to any but the people of Israel: 'The State is the result of our daring.' His contempt was best captured in the derogatory phrase, '*oum shmoum*' (oum was the abbreviation for *Oumot Me'uhadot* [the UN]). *Sharett* strongly opposed this view, going so far to assert that 'we owe our State to the United Nations'. In the same vein, Sharett attached significant weight to the UN and to world opinion while Ben-Gurion largely ignored them.

Once again, *Dayan, Peres*, and (to a slightly lesser extent) *Meir* emulated Ben-Gurion's outlook. *Eban* recognized the UN's shortcomings but insisted on its importance as well. *Allon* tended toward the Ben-Gurion pole on the grounds that no words or UN resolutions could supersede in importance the need for strategically defensible borders. *Eshkol's* (for the most part unarticulated) position was closer to dead center between the two alternative approaches.

The area of *relations with the Third World* did not provide a clear division among the eight leaders. *Ben-Gurion* smoothly integrated the notion of Israeli aid to Third World countries into his messianic perspective of Israel as a 'light unto the nations'. *Sharett's* interest in good relations with the emerging states of Asia and Africa derived largely from his ideological preference for a policy of non-identification with either of the superpowers. He played the role of the *architect*, beginning the concrete formulation of policy guidelines for Israel's reach into the Third World. Both were also conscious of the political significance of these links in terms of improving Israel's international standing and achieving the goal of 'leaping over the Arab fence'.

Meir, operating to a large extent on humanitarian grounds, served as the *engineer*, implementing Sharett's and other guidelines. She was successful in establishing the strong links that Israel in 1970 enjoyed with many African states but was unable to accomplish the same in Asia. *Eshkol* demonstrated his awareness of African political leaders' attitudes to the Arab/Israel Conflict concretely with his Africa tour of 1966. *Allon* vainly concentrated his efforts and concerns on wooing India. *Eban* devoted relatively less attention to this area, while *Dayan* was oriented as usual to the priorities of security, notably access to arms. *Peres* on the other hand was close to Golda Meir's concern and worked on military aid policy to Third World states.

All eight Israeli leaders agreed that *relations with world Jewry* were crucial: world Jewry was Israel's principal, some said, only dependable ally; the fate of Israel and world Jewry were profoundly interconnected; and Israel must remain a Jewish state. *Ben-Gurion* claimed responsibility for Jewry—'as we define it'—and split the world into two camps, Jewish and non-Jewish. *Sharett* gave far greater consideration to the needs and interests articulated by world Jewry and rejected Ben-Gurion's 'two-camp thesis'. *Dayan* and *Peres* were closest to Ben-Gurion, and *Eban* to Sharett in this area. *Meir* had a reputation as the supreme ambassador to world Jewry and she performed crucial fundraising functions over the years. *Eshkol* also tended slightly toward Sharett's position but moved significantly toward Ben-Gurion's 'two-camp thesis' after the experience of the June 1967 Six-Day War. *Allon* stood midway between the extremes; he was intensely preoccupied with the fate of Russian Jewry in particular.

CHAPTER 6

Charismatic Leadership: Concepts and Comparisons: Nehru and Ben-Gurion; Other Leaders

During the time of my interim assessments of Nehru as a political leader (1959 and 1964), continuing into the 1970s and 1980s, there was a revival of scholarly interest in the concepts and phenomena of *political leadership* and *charisma*, after a period in which they lay dormant.[1] Most of the relevant literature took as its point of departure Max Weber's classic typology of *traditional, rational-legal,* and *charismatic leadership.* The first rests on 'an established belief in the sanctity of immemorial traditions and the legitimacy of the status of those exercising authority under them'; the second, on a 'belief in the "legality" of patterns of normative rules and the right of those elevated to authority under staunch rules to issue commands'; and the third, on 'a certain quality of an individual personality by virtue of which he is set apart by ordinary men and treated as endowed with supernatural, superhuman, or at least specifically exceptional powers and qualities'. Viewed from the perspective of followers, *charisma* refers to 'devotion to the specific and exceptional sanctity, heroism or exemplary character of an individual person, and of the normative patterns or order revealed or ordained by him'.[2]

The three types of leadership were, for Weber, three bases of 'belief in legitimacy' and that, in turn, is only one of five necessary conditions of a viable leader–follower relationship; the others are custom, affectual relations, material advantage, and idealism. Nonetheless, charisma, only one sub-category of a wider Weberian concept of political leadership, became the major focus of attention in renewed scholarship.

As Rustow noted, 'A half-century of revolution, economic crisis, and war had undermined traditional institutions, challenged accepted ideas and dramatized the role of individual leaders—such as Hitler, Roosevelt, Stalin, Churchill, Nehru, and de Gaulle.' Moreover, '(R)esearch on the new states of Asia and Africa and a more systematic examination of Communist dictatorships led to a revived interest in Weber's notion of charisma'.[3] And as Apter correctly observed, 'the term "charisma" has been applied indiscriminately to most of the "heroic" leaders of nationalist movements who have been instrumental in the founding of new states',[4] a practice elaborated later in this chapter.

Shils, too, following Weber, identified charisma as a valuable basis of transition from traditional to rational-legal authority in the new states, with leaders of national movements exercising personal rule through a populist mass following; charisma is, in this view, a short-lived instrument of domination.[5] [See below for the elaboration of this practice as well.]

Apter challenged this conception by arguing that 'charisma can arise in part when the increase in modernity is not met by a proportioned decline in "traditionalism". Then a charismatic leader is part traditional and part modern, as with Nkrumah in Ghana, and charismatic authority can be more extensive in time.'[6]

In more simple terms, Willner, who cited as indicators of charisma perceptions of a leader as God or Savior, seer or Magician, defined charismatic leadership as a relationship between a leader and a group of followers that has the following properties:

1. The leader is perceived by the followers as somehow superhuman;
2. The followers blindly believe the leader's statements;
3. The followers unconditionally comply with the leader's directives for action;
4. The followers give the leader unqualified emotional commitment.[7]

In the Indian context, this definition clearly applied to Gandhi's leadership—but not to that of Nehru. In fact, Willner ascribed this exceptional quality of leadership only to Gandhi, Roosevelt, Hitler, and Castro. A larger group she termed *probable charismatics*, at least for part of their career: Ataturk, Lenin, Mao, Magsaysay, Nasser, Nkrumah, Peron, Touré, and U Nu, though some of these were more likely *quasi-charismatics*. One type of this last category, *exemplified by Nehru*, is 'the leader with derived or designated charisma..., the heir of the residue of charisma inherited from close association with or linkage to a clearly charismatic leader'.[8]

Historically, legitimate domination often took the form of an admixture of Weber's three pure types. More salient with respect to Gandhi and Nehru is the distinction between leadership and authority, implied by Weber but drawn out explicitly by Bierstedt: 'A leader can only request, an authority can require.... In a leadership relation the person is basic; in an authority relation the person is merely a symbol.'[9] Bendix went further and distinguished 'domination as a result of charismatic leadership...from domination as a result of charismatic authority'.[10] And for Willner this distinction 'rests on the extent of the radius of charismatic support...If and when a charismatic political leader converts the majority of members of a system into his charismatic constituency, his charisma also becomes the basis for authority in that system.'[11] Viewed in terms of this important distinction, both Gandhi and Nehru exercised enormous power over the Indian people through charisma: the Mahatma was endowed with charismatic *authority*, Panditji (Nehru) with charismatic *leadership*.

SOURCES OF NEHRU'S POWER

This discussion of charisma leads to a more substantive question about Nehru's leadership, namely, the *sources of his power and popularity*. As indicated in my 1959 assessment, above, I cited five sources: personal attributes, his relationship with Gandhi, the setting in which his leadership matured, the Indian tradition of hero-worship, and the nature of his ideas. These seem to me no less valid in the perspective of half a century since Nehru's passing.

Perhaps the key to his vast appeal was a combination of personal qualities which was rare among 20th century leaders of global stature and was acknowledged by friend and foe alike: physical courage, integrity, selflessness, sincerity of purpose, generosity, and loyalty to colleagues, honesty, charm, intellectual tolerance, and the abnegation of absolute power. By comparison, the other major political leader from Nehru's generation assessed in this project, Israel's 'founding father', Ben-Gurion, manifested only two, possibly three of these qualities—selflessness, sincerity of purpose, and, perhaps, abnegation of absolute power.

Nehru's special attraction for Indian intellectuals during most of the 20th century after WWI can best be explained by the fact that he was the most complete expression of that social class. Indian by birth but Western by education, modern in outlook but influenced by his traditional heritage, an Indian patriot yet a man with an international vision, he was for them the symbol of a new society—liberal, humanist, and aspiring to egalitarianism. The intelligentsia, like him, was in turmoil, trying to reconcile its goals of modernity with the traditional environment in which it grew to maturity.

Yet Nehru, unlike Ben-Gurion, also appealed to the rural masses, in time acquiring an adulation only slightly less than that of Gandhi. One reason was his constant verbal attacks on the injustice of the land system and his call for fundamental reform. Moreover, he was the Mahatma's designated heir. He possessed, as well, the reputation of an indomitable fighter for freedom, who had sacrificed wealth and leisure in the struggle for India's independence. Along with his personal qualities, Gandhi's blessing, his renunciation, and his articulation of their hopes, Nehru also benefited from the deeply rooted Indian tradition of hero-worship. And, after Gandhi's death, it was natural for India's peasants to transfer their adulation to his chosen successor. In the broadest sense, Nehru's influence derived from his unique role as the strategic link among diverse groups in Indian society. By contrast, Ben-Gurion, during the late pre-State period (1933–48), was the most respected leader of the social-democratic strand of the Jewish working class in Palestine, and during the first 15 years of independence, the most influential political leader of the emergent Israeli nation, especially in the realm of national security, but with unconcealed rivalry and dissent from diverse groups, especially ideologically hostile leaders in Israeli society, from those further to the Left and to the Right.

As for his *weltanschauung*, Nehru was the supreme eclectic, absorbing most of the ideological currents in the first half of the 20th century at various stages of his growth to maturity. First in time was Western liberalism, which expressed itself in his devotion to political democracy and individual rights. At Cambridge, he was attracted to the Fabian Socialism of George Bernard Shaw and the Webbs, as well as to the scientific ethos, both of which were later to provide the stimulus to economic planning and his emphasis on social and economic equality. In the 1920s came the Gandhian emphasis on the purity of means and their inescapable impact on ends, for Nehru, the basic approach to the achievement of that change. And in the late 1920s and 1930s, he was drawn to Marxism, though not its application in the Soviet Union and Communist parties worldwide. The ethical norms of Western humanism, reinforced by the moral precepts of the Buddha, underpinned this myriad of intellectual strands in his worldview. None of these dominated his outlook; all of them influenced his thought and behavior.

The essence of Nehru's humanism, liberalism, and tolerance was poignantly conveyed to this writer in his extemporaneous reflections in the mid-1950s on what constitutes a good society:

> I do believe that ultimately it is the individual that counts. The idea appeals to me, without belief, the old Hindu idea that if there is any divine essence in the world every individual possesses a bit of it. Therefore no individual is trivial. I do believe in certain standards, moral standards. And, if they fade away, I think that all the material advancement you may have will lead to nothing worthwhile.
>
> (As for religion), If a person feels comforted by that, it is not for me to remove that sense of comfort. If it raises him above his normal level it is good for him.[12]

Unlike Nehru's formal education at élite English educational institutions—Harrow and Cambridge, followed by ideological eclecticism, Ben-Gurion was impressively self-educated in the classics of East and West, with a persistent ideological preference for the ideas of national self-determination, as a natural right of the Jewish People, and moderate socialism. Nor did he share with Nehru an attachment to humanism, liberalism, and tolerance. However, both leaders shared and manifested a profound intellectual and emotional commitment to the political goal of independence. For both, the supreme rationale for political leadership, prior to independence, was its attainment, based upon the inherent right of Indians and Jews to self-determination for their nations; and, once achieved, as in 1947 and 1948, its preservation against all perceived external threats to national security throughout their lengthy period at the peak of political power, 1947–64 (Nehru) and 1948–63 (Ben-Gurion).

The concepts discussed earlier—Weber's charisma, Willner's quasi-charismatic, Bendix's charismatic leadership and charismatic authority—relate to the *sources* of power. They say nothing of the ends to which power is directed and the *methods* by which it is exercised. For these concerns, several concepts introduced by Burns are helpful. The most important is the distinction between *transactional* and *transforming* leadership. The first is an exchange relationship, whether economic, political, or psychological in nature. The purposes of leader (initiator) and follower 'are related, at least to the extent that the purposes stand within the bargaining process.... But beyond this the relationship does not go'. By contrast, 'purposes...become fused' in transforming leadership, which 'ultimately becomes *moral* in that it raises the level of human conduct and ethical aspiration of both leader and led, and thus it has a transforming effect on both'.[13] Gandhi is cited as the best modern example of transforming leader. However, for many in India and elsewhere, Nehru, too, fits this type, in the light of his vision, objectives, program, and behavior.

Burns specified two kinds of transforming leadership—*revolutionary* and *reform*. The former he identifies with the pre-eminent leaders of the French, Russian, and Chinese revolutions, namely, Robespierre, Lenin, and Mao. Nehru and Ben-Gurion would appear to fall into the category of transforming reform leadership, given their commitment to democratic means of achieving social and economic change, with a high value on consent. Yet their goals for Indian and Israeli society, especially modernity and egalitarianism, went far beyond Burns's examples of reform leaders elsewhere—Tsar Alexander III, Earl Grey, and the two Roosevelts.

Nehru and Ben-Gurion also fit the concept of *heroic* leader, though not with the same aura as Moses, Joan of Arc, or the Mahdi of Sudan, three examples discussed by Burns. Heroic leadership means 'belief in leaders because of their personage alone, aside from their tested capacities, experience, or stand on issues; faith in the leaders' capacity to overcome obstacles and crises; readiness to grant to leaders the powers to handle crises; mass support for such leaders expressed directly.... Heroic leadership is *a type of relationship* between leader and led.'[14]

Another accurate designation of Nehru's leadership would seem to be *planning* leadership which 'seeks genuine social change for collective purposes, though not necessarily at the same pace, or on so wide a front, as that of revolutionary action. The task of this kind of leadership is political and governmental planning for real social change.... Planning leaders, more than other leaders, must respond... to the fundamental wants and needs, aspirations and expectations, values and goals of their existing and potential followers.'[15]

In that context, Coser's distinction between change *of* system and change *in* system is especially relevant. In the former, 'all major structural relations, its basic institutions, and its prevailing value system have been drastically altered'. While the latter takes place more slowly and is narrower in scope, it may be almost as system-transforming in the long run. This admirably captures Nehru's and Ben-Gurion's intent.[16]

A further contribution to the literature on political leadership is Keren's concept of *visionary realism*, which he regards as more effective in achieving transformational goals than *heroic, messianic*, or *charismatic leadership*: 'The visionary realist is neither a dreamer who ignores constraints posed by reality..., nor a pragmatist overwhelmed by those constraints. In a word, visionary realism is the creative pursuit of daring goals. (V)isionary realism (is) not so much ...a personal quality...as a behavioral trait that can be institutionalized.'[17]

Drawing on the works of Wildavsky and Walzer,[18] he concentrates on the political strategy of Moses who, for Keren, represents the ideal type of visionary realist. In the context of these reflections, at least three of the four principles of the biblical leader's strategy can be said to characterize Nehru's leadership in the pre-Independence nationalist phase, 1929–47, and in independent India, 1947–64, as well as in Ben-Gurion's political leadership in the pre-Independence Jewish community in Palestine, the *yishuv* (1935–48) and in Israel, 1948–63: (1) a contractual relationship—'(n)either the leader nor the followers are conceived as the "sovereign"'; (2) a constructive approach—'the visionary realist advances quite conservatively towards the promised land'; (3) responsibility—he 'uses as much reason as a human being can to ensure responsible politics'; and (4) the principle of ethics—he 'recognizes ethical limits and does not forget that when these are overlooked, the original goals cannot be fulfilled'.[19]

In sum, Nehru's and Ben-Gurion's leadership do not fit any of Weber's three pure types, though they contain elements of charisma, as well as a rational-legal basis of domination of Indian politics from 1947 to 1964, and of Israeli politics from 1948 to 1963. They were transforming leaders of the reform type, even more so, exemplars of the planning leader, and perhaps most accurately, visionary realists.

OTHER POLITICAL LEADERS

How does their record compare with *other leaders* of the 20th century? To this aspect, I now turn, beginning with the third charismatic leader whom I encountered during a lengthy intellectual odyssey.

Pierre Elliott Trudeau

Despite the profound differences—societal, cultural, and historical—among Canada, India, and Israel, Canada too produced a transforming leader of the *reform* type: Trudeau's charisma, during his 15 years as Prime Minister and beyond, reflected the *planning leader*, with an outlook akin to *visionary realism*. Did he merit the accolade of charisma, widely accorded him? Unquestionably, the mass public in Canada accorded him that exalted status from the moment he assumed the role of Canada's political leader in 1968, in the Canadian version of charisma, 'Trudeaumania', throughout his tenure—and beyond.

This status, recognized by admirers and his many critics alike, was exquisitely captured in the opening words of one among several outstanding biographies of the Canadian leader who achieved two transforming acts that were elusive for more than a century: the *patriation of the London-imposed constitution of Canada, the 1867 British North America Act,* and the *enactment of Canada's Charter of Rights and Freedoms, both in 1982*: 'He haunts us still. Six years after he resigned as prime minister, a quarter of a century after he first sought office, Pierre Elliott Trudeau and his ideas remain dominant in the northern attic of the continent, a standard against which other political actors, thinkers, theorists and hopefuls—past and present—measure themselves and are measured' (Clarkson and McCall 1990, 9).

Third World Leaders of Asia and Africa

There were many nationalist leaders in the 20th century anti-colonial era who attained state power in Africa and Asia following independence, notably Senghor and Houphouet-Boigny, Touré and Nkrumah in West Africa, Nyerere and Kenyatta in East Africa, Banda, Kaunda, Neto, and Mugabe in Southern Africa, Bourguiba and Ben Bella in North Africa[20]; and in Asia, Ho Chi Minh, Jinnah, Nehru, and Sukarno. Some ruled briefly and were overthrown (Ben Bella, in Algeria) or died in office soon after independence (Neto, in Angola, Jinnah, in Pakistan). Others held power for a decade (Nkrumah, 1957–66, in Ghana) or much longer (Sukarno, 1949–65, in Indonesia) before being ousted by a coup. Senghor, in Senegal, retired after 30 years. And some remained the dominant figures in their new states decades after independence—Houphouet-Boigny in the Ivory Coast, Mugabe in Zimbabwe, Nyerere in Tanzania, Banda in Malawi, and Kaunda in Zambia. All of them were pre-eminent in the era of nationalist struggle and in the period of national consolidation. There are also some, still active, post-independence Africa *de facto* 'leaders for life', notably dos Santos in Angola, and Mbasogo in Equatorial Guinea, both since 1979, and Kagame in Rwanda since 1994. (Dos Santos announced in

March 2016, unconvincingly and not for the first time, that he would leave office in 2018.) None of these African and Asian leaders matched Nehru's or Ben-Gurion's record of leadership in the post-independence phase.

For African leaders, a Nigerian political scientist summed up the dichotomy with searing candor:

> 'Taking our definition of nation-building as the reference point..., it is difficult to point to a single success story ... (A) clear distinction can be made between the quality and performance of African political leaders under the two phases ...The roll-call of the giant nationalist leaders (demonstrates)... their inability to grapple successfully with the twin problems of national integration and socio-economic development.'[21]

The main reason was the difference between the sharply focused, unambiguous goal of independence, and the vague goal of development.

In Asia, the only commanding figures other than Nehru who linked the phases of nationalist struggle and nation-building were Sukarno and Ho Chi Minh. The former fell from power in an internal upheaval in the mid-1960s, leaving widespread death and economic chaos in Indonesia. The latter was triumphant in war, defeating the French in the first Vietnam War (1946–54) and withstanding the US onslaught in the second Vietnam War, leaving a united successor leadership to complete the expulsion of American forces in 1973 and to unite the two Vietnams by force in 1975. But Ho did not live to achieve the goal of economic development. On the contrary, by the end of the 1980s, Vietnam's failure in the economic domain compelled withdrawal from Kampuchea, conciliation toward the Association of Southeast Asian Nations and the USA, and a reappraisal of traditional policy at home.[22]

Among other African and Asian leaders since WWII, Nasser (along with Ben-Gurion and Cardenas of Mexico) were praised by Migdal as visionary realists who used the state to transform their societies, with varying success. This was partly because of internal factors, but largely due to constraints created by 'world historical circumstances' beyond their control, namely, 'the degree of social dislocation due to external factors, the intensity of the threat of invasion, and the efficacy of possible sanctions by leading powers'.[23]

Nasser's vision embraced a transformation of Egyptian society 'starting with the destruction of "feudal" elements in the thousands of villages along the Nile River'. However, 'the risks of domestic resistance and instability were too high to see his vision through'.[24] Indeed one looks in vain for an enduring Nasser legacy: not in the external arena, for Egypt's prominent role in the non-aligned camp receded after 1970 under Sadat and, even more, under Mubarak; not in terms of political institutions, for the fabric of government remains fragile under Nasser's successors; and not in terms of economic development or social change, for Egypt in 2016 is more dependent on foreign aid than when Nasser ruled (1954–70).[25]

Ben-Gurion's vision was twofold: the transformation of world Jewry into a normal people through 'ingathering of the exiles' into the Land of Israel, and the centrality of democratic socialism in the new society. As noted earlier, he established his primacy through two formidable institutions—the *Mapai* [Labor] Party and the *Histadrut*, a nationwide structure for Jewish workers. At the time of independence and in the early years of statehood, he successfully met three tests to his power: a war imposed by Israel's Arab neighbors; challenges to a unified army from right- and left-wing militias from the pre-state era; and the doubling of Israel's population from 1948 to 1951, through immigration from 60 countries, without undermining the administrative structures or essential unity of the state. In short, Ben-Gurion 'built a state without the need for mediators [between state and society] (unlike Cardenas and Nasser) and effected the social transformation of millions of immigrant Jews'. However, 'his vision, too, was compromised, especially his hopes for a truly socialist society'.[26]

Both Ben-Gurion's and Nehru's were major achievements. However, the Israel case was fundamentally different from India—and from all other new states in Asia and Africa: Ben-Gurion was faced with the task of creating a new state and society from an old, dispersed people; Nehru confronted the task of modernizing a traditional, economically underdeveloped society after two centuries of colonial rule and the schism of partition. Like Nasser and all other Third World leaders, Nehru did not realize his vision in full—a democratic, socialist, egalitarian society in a free India. Nevertheless, none of the post-colonial leaders in Asia and Africa, except Ben-Gurion, approached the Nehru record in nation-building. The basic reason is that effective leadership, as Hirschman observed, requires combination of *charisma* and *skill*. Moreover, 'the most effective leaders are likely to be those who can somehow accommodate both. Charisma can be allowed to predominate in the first period of struggle and mobilization, while the skill requirements are more needed in the next stage, when the leader moves closer to or actually into power.'[27] Stated simply, Nehru possessed both essential components in the two phases. Most other post-colonial leaders did not.

At the time of my interim assessment of Nehru (1959), there were few leaders in the Africa-Asia comparison group—Nkrumah and Nasser in

Africa, Ho Chi Minh and Sukarno in Southeast Asia. Among them, Nehru strode the stage of world politics like a 'gentle colossus'.[28] Thus, it seemed natural to focus on leaders from the first and second worlds—and Mao. In that context, I noted that few political leaders in the 20th century had attained Nehru's stature.

Churchill, Roosevelt, Lenin, Mao

As the pre-eminent figure in India's era of transition, Nehru merited comparison with Churchill and Roosevelt, Lenin and Mao, men who towered above their colleagues and guided their people through a period of national crisis. Only Gandhi inspired greater faith among the Indian masses. Only Stalin and Mao had greater power. Like those notable leaders, Nehru had imposed his personality on a wider canvas. His name conjured up a host of associations, some praiseworthy, some critical. Yet Nehru was universally recognized as a leading actor on the stage of world politics. How accurate is this assessment 57 years later?

Churchill was a war-time leader of heroic stature, widely regarded without peer in the 20th century. Nor is there doubt that, in rallying his people to resist the formidable power of Nazi Germany, if necessary to the bitter end, he saved Great Britain from German occupation, a turning point in WWII. He was also a brilliant Cassandra in the 'thirties who luminously perceived the impending threat from a renascent Germany under a fanatical leader and a destructive ideology. For these contributions he certainly deserves inclusion in the pantheon of great 20th century political leaders. Yet soon after the Allied victory, indeed from that point onward, Churchill reverted to the status of a politician, albeit a distinguished one. His legacy was triumph in a battle for survival; there was no discernible Churchill effect on British society, the traditional polity, or an economy exhausted by war.

Roosevelt, too, was an exceptional war-time leader, though without the genius of rhetoric possessed by his closest ally. In mobilizing America for war, before and after Pearl Harbor, his contribution to the ultimate Allied victory was no less fundamental than that of Churchill. And in the domestic domain, Roosevelt's legacy was of a much higher order, for his New Deal marked a turning point in the history of the USA. It shaped for decades the dominant conception of the role of the state in society and the obligations of government to its citizenry, which reached its zenith in the Fair Deal legislation of Lyndon Johnson two decades later. Despite the demeaning efforts of some successors, the Roosevelt legacy to American society remains fundamentally intact seven decades after his death near the close of WWII.

Lenin's achievements lay elsewhere, though not unrelated to war. Almost single-handed, he forged an élite party which seized power from a faltering social-democratic regime, when the Czarist Empire was crumbling under the impact of WWI. He inspired his colleagues and rank-and-file Bolsheviks to withstand the assaults of Allied forces and white generals in the Civil War from 1918 to 1921. And he laid the foundations of a party-state which also became the beacon light for a worldwide Communist movement. Lenin did not live to see the Soviet Union, under Stalin, become a modern, industrialized, collectivized state, one of the two superpowers in the post-WWII global system. Yet this was undoubtedly Lenin's legacy, for of the 'three who made a revolution'[29] he alone was indispensable: there would not have been a Bolshevik Revolution without him, certainly not in November 1917. Moreover, Stalin's revolutionary transformation was a conscious application of Leninist doctrine to achieve Lenin's vision of an impregnable Communist state to serve as the bastion of the struggle against world capitalism. Lenin may—or may not—have resorted to Stalin's draconian methods of mass killings, slave labor camps, the decimation of the Old Bolsheviks and a vast number of party members, as well as the bulk of the Red Army's leadership. But Lenin shared, in fact, inspired Stalin's goals. And his behavior while in power does not suggest squeamishness about the use of any means to achieve the visionary goal. Whatever Lenin may or may not have done, the Soviet Union, with its formidable influence during most of the 20th century, was his enduring legacy almost a century after his death.

Nehru as a political leader cannot easily be compared with Churchill or Roosevelt—or with Lenin. Theirs were established states of longstanding, great powers, and the beneficiaries of advanced industrial economies. Nehru, by contrast, had to guide a new state emerging from partition and unparalleled mass migration, a small power weakened by an underdeveloped economy, widespread illiteracy, and dangerous forces threatening disunity. He was not a great war leader; in fact, he spent much of WWII in prison, following the Gandhi-inspired 'Quit India' Movement in August 1942. But unlike Churchill and Roosevelt, Nehru was a nation-builder whose legacy, as noted, is evident half a century after his death.

China and India did not face identical challenges in the 1930s and 1940s: Chiang Kai-Shek's Nationalist forces and the Japanese invaders were not the same as the British Raj, civil disobedience, and mass imprisonment. However, the conditions facing Mao and Nehru were much more alike than those of either with Britain and America, or the Soviet Union, during that period of global change.

It is customary to compare Mao and Gandhi, two charismatic figures who adopted qualitatively different means to mobilize large masses of Chinese and Indians to attain power and usher in the millennium, following the dictates of Marxism-Leninism and the Baghavat Gita, respectively. Nehru is generally relegated to the status of Gandhi's principal aide, as Zhou Enlai was to Mao. But this analogy is fundamentally flawed. While Mao was the commanding figure of the Chinese Communist Revolution, as Gandhi was of the struggle for Indian independence, Nehru was not merely an aide to Gandhi. Rather, he was, in his own right, a leader of national—and international—renown from the 1930s onward. And soon after the coming of independence, with Gandhi's assassination in January 1948 and Patel's death in December 1950, Nehru became the undisputed leader of India,[30] as Mao was in China after the Communist Party triumph in China's civil war in 1949. Zhou never achieved a comparable status: rather, he was, always, a talented aide of Mao in foreign and domestic policy, not a nation-builder.

Mao's achievements were herculean, especially before 1949. He survived the onslaught of Chiang's armies and, through the Long March, created a model of courage, persistence, revolutionary élan, and party–peasant integration that was to provide the basis of absolute leadership of China for a quarter of a century. Ruling China as the mid 20th century Emperor of the Middle Kingdom, based upon a peasant-oriented revision of Marxism-Leninism, Mao transformed the China of the Qing dynasty and the war-lords of the 1920s and 1930s into a united, party-led peasant society, the basis for the ultimate communization of a traditional Confucian society. Drastic means of coercion, comparable to Stalin's forced collectivization in the 'thirties, including mass arrests, executions, dispossession of millions of peasants, achieved the goal of Chinese communization, at a price which Nehru the reformer would never have contemplated, even if the objective conditions had been conducive to successful transformation of the Indian countryside to fulfill Nehru's vision. Periodic outbursts of revolutionary zeal, inspired by Mao, notably the 'Cultural Revolution' of the 1960s, sustained Mao's Trotsky-like goal of permanent revolution. Yet the result, at Mao's death, was far from the idyllic society of Mao's dream. Indeed, once in power, the revisionist ideas of Deng Xiao Ping assumed control in 1978. And in the past four decades, China has undergone a profound counter-revolution, seemingly undoing the egalitarian, coercive-driven society of the Maoist millennium.

With the rapid abandonment by Mao's successors of his vision and policies a few years after his death, Nehru's legacy to India half a century after his passing seems more enduring than that of the only other leader in modern Asia and Africa whose record as nation-builder bears comparison with Nehru. At the time of his death in 1976, Mao's place in history stood much higher than Nehru. In 2016, as Mao's revolutionary transformation of China is increasingly rejected by his successors,[31] and Nehru's vision and policies continue to carry forward his much less revolutionary legacy in the political and economic domains, the gap in stature has undergone profound change. At the conference marking Nehru's centenary (1989), I ventured the prediction that the gap might vanish altogether by the end of the 20th century. At this juncture (2016), there can be little doubt that Nehru ranks with Mao as pre-eminent among the 20th century nation-builders of Asia and Africa.

Despite his failure to realize his vision in full, his shortcomings, and the setbacks of his twilight years, Nehru's stature as humanist and leader seems to have grown over time. Nor is there any evidence to alter my appraisal at the height of his power (1959): 'If political greatness be measured by the capacity to direct events, to rise above the crest of the waves, to guide his people, and to serve as a catalyst of progress, then Nehru surely qualifies for greatness. Almost single-handed he has endeavored to lift his people into the 20th century. He is, indeed, India's nation-builder.'[32]

NOTES

1. The most notable publications on political leadership during that period are:

    B.M. Bass, *Leadership and Performance beyond Expectations*, New York, 1985.

    J.M. Burns, *Leadership*, New York, 1978.

    L.J. Edinger (ed.), *Political Leadership in Industrialized Societies*, New York, 1967.

    A. Gouldner (ed.), *Studies in Leadership*, New York, 1965.

    G.D. Paige, *The Scientific Study of Political Leadership*, New York, 1977.

    ———, (ed.), *Political Leadership: Readings for an Emerging Field*, New York, 1972.

D.A. Rustow (ed.), *Philosophers and Kings: Studies in Leadership*, Daedalus, 97, 3, summer 1968.
R.M. Stogdill, *Handbook of Leadership: A Survey of Theory and Research*, New York, 1974.
R.C. Tucker, *Politics as Leadership*, New York, 1981.
———. 'The Theory of Charismatic Leadership'. In Rustow, D.A., *Philosophers and Kings: Studies In Leadership*, Daedalus, 97, 3 Summer 1968, 731–756.
A.R. Willner, *The Spellbinders: Charismatic Political Leadership*, New Haven, CT, 1984.
S.S. Wolin, *Politics and Vision*, Boston, 1960.
2. M. Weber, *The Theory of Social and Economic Organization*, trans. by Talcott Parsons, New York, 1947, pp. 328, 358.
3. Rustow, *op. cit.*, p. 687.
4. D.E. Apter, 'Nkrumah, Charisma and the Coup', in Rustow, *op. cit.*, 762. For a defense of Weber's concept of charismatic leadership, see R.C. Tucker, 'The Theory of Charismatic Leadership', in Rustow, *op. cit.*, pp. 731–756, esp. p. 73a. In a later work, Tucker went as far as equating politics with leadership. *Politics as Leadership*, *op. cit.*
5. E. Shils, 'The Concentration and Dispersion of Charisma', *World Politics*, 11, 1, October 1958.
6. Apter, *op. cit.*, p. 765.
7. Willner, *op. cit.*, p. 8.
8. *Ibid.*, p. 38.
9. R. Bierstedt, 'The Problem of Authority', in M. Berger, T. Abel, and C. Pup (eds.), *Freedom and Control in Modern Society*, New York, 1954, pp. 71–72, as quoted in R. Bendix, *Max Weber: An Intellectual Portrait*, New York, 1962.
10. Bierstedt, *ibid.* See Chaps. X–XIII in Bendix for an elaborate treatment of Weber's three types of domination.
11. Willner, *op. cit.*, p. 16.
12. Brecher, *The New States of Asia*, New York, 1963, 215.
13. Burns, *op. cit.*, 19–20.
14. *Ibid.*, 244.
15. *Ibid.*, 418, 420.
16. L.A. Coser, *Continuities in the Study of Social Conflict*, NewYork, 1967, p. 28, as quoted in Burns, *op. cit.*, p. 418.
17. M. Keren, Introduction to 'Visionary Realism and Political Leadership', *International Political Science Review*, 9, 1, 1988, p. 5.

18. A. Wildavsky, *The Nursing Father: Moses as a Political Leader*, Montgomery, AL, 1984; M. Walzer, *Exodus and Revolution*, New York, 1985; Keren, 'Moses as a Visionary Realist', in *International Political Science Review, op. cit.*, pp. 71–84.
19. Keren, *ibid.*, pp. 80, 81, 82.
20. See R. H. Jackson and C. G. Rosberg, *Personal Rule in Black Africa: Prince, Autocrat, Prophet, Tyrant*, Berkeley, CA, 1982.
21. L. Adamolekun, 'Political Leadership in Sub-Saharan Africa: From Giants to Dwarfs,' in *International Political Science Review*, 9, 2, April 1988, pp. 103–105. See also J. Dunn (ed.), *West African States, Failure and Promise: A Study in Comparative Politics*, Cambridge, 1978; R. Sanbrook, *The Politics of Africa's Economic Stagnation*, Cambridge, 1985.
22. For an assessment of Asian leaders in terms of charisma—Sihanouk and Kim Il-Sung, as well as Nehru and Mao—along with further reflections by Bendix on charismatic leadership, see 'Charismatic Leadership in Asia: A Symposium', in *Asian Survey*, VII, 6, June 1967, pp. 341–388.
23. J. S. Migdal, 'Vision and Practice: The Leader, the State, and the Transformation of Society', *International Political Science Review*, 9, 1988, p. 40.
24. *Ibid.*, p. 36.
25. See R. W. Baker, *Egypt's Uncertain Revolution under Nasser and Sadat*, Cambridge, MA, 1978; and J. Waterbury, *The Egypt of Nasser and Sadat: The Political Economy of Two Regimes*, Princeton, NJ, 1983.
26. Migdal, *op. cit.*, p. 40.
27. A.O. Hirschman, 'Underdevelopment, Obstacles to the Perception of Change, and Leadership', in Rustow, *op. cit.*, 934–935.
28. The title of a book by Indian Communist leader, Hiren Mukerjee, Calcutta, 1964.
29. The title of a book by Bertram Wolfe, Boston, 1948.
30. For perceptive reflections on the Gandhi–Nehru relationship by three Indian scholars, see B.R. Nanda, P.C. Joshi, and Raj Krishna, *Gandhi and Nehru*, Delhi, 1979.
31. A. Doak Barnett, in a wide-ranging assessment of the post-Mao era, refers to his successors' goals as 'a liberalized form of authoritarianism and...a distinctive form of socialism (that, if achieved,) will be the second far-reaching transformation of the country's post-1949 politi-

cal and economic systems'. 'Ten Years After Mao', *Foreign Affairs*, 65, 1, Fall 1986, pp. 64.

A more explicit view of de-Maoization was expressed by one of contemporary China's widely read and respected writers, Liu Binyan, near the end of the 20th century: 'Mao's prestige has been completely discredited only 12 years after his death.' Interview with Fox Butterfield, *New York Times*, Week in Review, 19 February 1989.

32. *Nehru: A Political Biography, op. cit.*, p. 629. A similar view was expressed by Canada's most visible and enterprising diplomat to India since independence, in his 'Reconsiderations' of 1980, more than 20 years after an initial admiring assessment: 'Taking all these criticisms into consideration ... where are we left when we try to assess Nehru's role as Prime Minister? We are left, it seems to me, with a man whose accomplishments greatly outweighed his failures.' E. Reid, *Envoy to Nehru*, Delhi, 1981, p. 272.

Prof. Gopal, too, concluded his three-volume biography of Nehru with a sensitive appraisal in 1984 (Vol. III, Chap. 12) and a moving farewell: 'Rousseau described the maker of a Commonwealth as one who toils in one century so as to reap in another. Nehru was of that category. He is India's once and—we may hope—future king' (p. 302).

Works Consulted

Introduction and Prelude to an Intellectual Odyssey

Allison, Graham T. 1971. *The essence of decision: Explaining the Cuban missile crisis*. Boston: Little, Brown.

Allon, Yigal. 1959. *A curtain of sand*. Tel Aviv: Hakibbutz Hameuchad [Hebrew].

Almond, Gabriel A. 1950. *The American people and foreign policy*. New York: Praeger.

———, and Stephen J. Genco. 1977. Clouds, clocks, and the study of politics. *World Politics* 29(4): 489–522.

Almond, Gabriel A., and G.B. Powell. 1966. *Comparative politics: A developmental approach*. Boston: Little, Brown.

Almond, Gabriel A., and Sidney Verba. 1963. *The civic culture: Political attitudes and democracy in five nations*. Princeton: Princeton University Press.

Anglin, Douglas G. 1994. *Zambian crisis behaviour: Confronting Rhodesia's unilateral declaration of independence*. Montreal and Kingston: McGill-Queen's University Press.

Boulding, Kenneth E. 1956a. General systems theory-the skeleton of science. *Management Science* 2(3): 197–208.

———. 1956b. *The image: Knowledge in life and society*. Ann Arbor: University of Michigan Press.

Brecher, Michael. 1953. *The struggle for Kashmir*. Toronto/New York: Ryerson Press/Oxford University Press.

———. 1959. *Nehru: A political biography*. London: Oxford University Press.

———. 1963a. *The new states of Asia: A political analysis*. London: Oxford University Press.

———. 1963b. International relations and Asian studies: The subordinate state system of Southern Asia. *World Politics* 15(2): 213–235.

———. 1966a. *Nehru's mantle: The politics of succession in India*. London: Oxford University Press; also published as 1966b. *Succession in India: A study in decision-making*. New York: Praeger.

———. 1968. *India and world politics: Krishna Menon's view of the world*. London: Oxford University Press.

———. 1969. The Middle East subordinate system and its impact on Israel's foreign policy. *International Studies Quarterly* 13(2): 117–139.

———. 1972. *The foreign policy system of Israel: Setting, images, process*. London/New Haven: Oxford University Press/Yale University Press.

———. 1974a. *Israel, the Korean war and China: Images, decisions and consequences*. Jerusalem: Jerusalem Academic Press.

———. 1974b. *Decisions in Israel's foreign policy*. London: Oxford University Press; also published as 1975. *Decisions in Israel's foreign policy*. New Haven: Yale University Press.

———. The four questions: A dialogue in Cairo. *The Illustrated Weekly of India*, Bombay, 11 January 1976; *The Asahi Journal*, Tokyo, 5–6 February 1976; *Ha'aretz*, Tel Aviv, 14 November 1975 (Hebrew); *New Outlook*, Tel Aviv, February–March and April 1976; *Queen's Quarterly*, Kingston, ON, Summer 1976; *Das Parlament*, Bonn, December 1976.

———. 1977. Toward a theory of international crisis behavior: A preliminary report. *International Studies Quarterly* 21(1): 39–74.

——— (ed.). 1979a. *Studies in crisis behavior*. New Brunswick: Transaction Books.

———. 1979b. State behavior in international crisis: A model. *Journal of Conflict Resolution* 23(3): 446–480.

———. 1984. International crises and protracted conflicts. *International Interactions* 11(3): 237–297.

———. 1990. India studies in Canada: Origins and assessment of the Shastri Institute. In *India and Canada: Partners for the future*, ed. H. Coward, 1–11. Calgary: Shastri Indo-Canadian Institute, University of Calgary.

———. 1993. *Crises in world politics: Theory and reality*. Oxford: Pergamon Press.

———. 2008. *International political earthquakes*. Ann Arbor: University of Michigan Press.

———, with Benjamin Geist. 1980. *Decisions in crisis: Israel, 1967 and 1973*. Berkeley: University of California Press.

Brecher, Michael, and Patrick James. 1986. *Crisis and change in world politics*. Boulder: Westview Press.

———. 1987. International crises in the Middle East, 1929–1979: Immediate severity and long-term importance. *Jerusalem Journal of International Relations* 9(2): 1–42.

———. 1988a. Patterns of crisis management. *Journal of Conflict Resolution* 32(3): 426–456.

Brecher, Michael, and Jonathan Wilkenfeld. 1988. *Crises in the twentieth century, Handbook of international crises*, vol. 1. Oxford: Pergamon Press.
———. 1989. *Crisis, conflict and instability*. Oxford: Pergamon Press.
———. 1997 [2000]. *A study of crisis*. Ann Arbor: University of Michigan Press.
Brecher, Michael, and Hemda Ben Yehuda. 1985. System and crisis in international politics. *Review of International Studies* 11(1): 17–36.
Brecher, Michael, Blema Steinberg, and Janice Stein. 1969. A framework for research on foreign policy behavior. *The Journal of Conflict Resolution* 13(1): 75–101.
Brecher, Michael, Patrick James, and Jonathan Wilkenfeld. 1990. Polarity and stability: New concepts, indicators and evidence. *International Interactions* 16(1): 49–80.
Brodie, Bernard (ed.). 1946. *The absolute weapon: Atomic power and world order*. New York: Harcourt, Brace.
———. 1973. *War and politics*. New York: Macmillan.
Brzezinski, Zbigniew. 1967. *The Soviet bloc: Unity and conflict*. Cambridge, MA: Harvard University Press.
Bueno de Mesquita, Bruce. 1985a. Toward a scientific understanding of international conflict: A personal view. *International Studies Quarterly* 29(2): 121–136.
———. 1985b. Reply to Stephen Krasner and Robert Jervis. *International Studies Quarterly* 29(2): 151–154.
Bull, Hedley. 1966. International theory: The case for a classical approach. *World Politics* 18(3): 361–377.
Carr, Edward H. 1939. *The twenty years' crisis, 1919–1939: An introduction to the study of international relations*. London: Macmillan.
———. 1942. *Conditions of peace*. New York: Macmillan.
Cohen, Avner. 1999. *Israel and the bomb*. New York: Columbia University Press.
———. Going for the nuclear option. *Ha'aretz* (Tel Aviv), 22 May 2007, B5.
Corbett, Percy E. 1951. *Law and society in the relations of states*. New York: Harcourt, Brace.
Coser, L.A. 1967. *Continuities in the study of social conflict*. New York: Free Press.
Craig, Gordon A., and Felix Gilbert (eds.). 1953. *The diplomats, 1919–1939*. Princeton: Princeton University Press.
Craig, Gordon A., and Francis L. Loewenheim (eds.). 1994. *The diplomats, 1939–1979*. Princeton: Princeton University Press.
Dahl, Robert A. 1961. *Who governs? Democracy and power in an American city*. New Haven: Yale University Press.
———, and Charles E. Lindblom. 1953. *Politics, economics, and welfare: Planning and politico-economic systems resolved into basic social processes*. New York: Harper.
Dawisha, Adeed I. 1980. *Syria and the Lebanese crisis*. London: Macmillan.

Dawisha, Karen. 1984. *The Kremlin and the Prague spring.* Berkeley: University of California Press.
Deutsch, Karl W. 1963. *The nerves of government: Models of political communication and control.* New York: Free Press.
Dowty, Alan. 1984. *Middle East crisis: U.S. decision-making in 1958, 1970 and 1973.* Berkeley: University of California Press.
Easton, David. 1957. An approach to the analysis of political systems. *World Politics* 9(3): 383–400.
Eckstein, Harry. 1975. Case study and theory in political science. In *Handbook of political science*, vol. 7, chap. 3, eds. Fred I. Greenstein and Nelson W. Polsby. Reading, MA: Addison-Wesley.
Fox, William T.R. 1944. *The super-powers: The United States, Britain, and the Soviet Union – their responsibility for peace.* New York: Harcourt, Brace.
George, Alexander L. 1979. Case studies and theory development: The method of structured, focused comparison. In *Diplomacy: New approaches in history, theory and policy*, ed. Paul G. Lauren. New York: Free Press, chap. 6.
———, and Richard Smoke. 1974. *Deterrence and defense in American foreign policy: Theory and practice.* New York: Columbia University Press.
George, Alexander L., D.K. Hall, and William R. Simons. 1971. *The limits of coercive diplomacy: Laos, Cuba, Vietnam.* Boston: Little, Brown.
Hermann, Charles F. 1963. Some consequences of crisis which limit the viability of organizations. *Administrative Science Quarterly* 8: 61–82.
———. 1969. *Crises in foreign policy: A simulation analysis.* Indianapolis: Bobbs-Merrill.
Higgins, Benjamin H. 1958. *Economic development: Problems, principles, and policies.* New York: W.W. Norton.
Hobsbawm, E. J. 1973. *Revolutionaries: Contemporary essays.* New York: Pantheon Books.
Hoffman, Steven A. 1990. *India and the China crisis.* Berkeley: University of California Press.
Hoffmann, Stanley. 1965. *The state of war: Essays on the theory and practice of international politics.* New York: Praeger.
———. 1978. *Primacy or world order: American foreign policy since the Cold War.* New York: McGraw-Hill.
———. 1986. *Janus and Minerva: Essays in the theory and practice of international politics.* Boulder: Westview.
Holborn, Hajo. 1951. *The political collapse of Europe.* New York: Knopf.
Holsti, Ole R. 1965. The 1914 case. *American Political Science Review* 59(1): 365–378.
———. 1972. *Crisis, escalation, war.* Montreal: McGill-Queen's University Press.
———, Robert C. North, and Richard A. Brody. 1968. Perceptions and actions in the 1914 crisis. In *Quantitative international politics*, ed. J. David Singer, 123–158. New York: Free Press.

James, Patrick, and Michael Brecher. 1988. Stability and polarity: New paths for inquiry. *Journal of Peace Research* 25(1): 31–42.

Janis, Irving L. 1972. *Victims of groupthink: A psychological study of foreign policy decisions and fiascos.* Boston: Houghton, Mifflin.

———. 1989. *Crucial decisions: Leadership in policy-making and crisis management.* New York: Free Press.

Janis, Irving L., and Leon Mann. 1977. *Decision-making: A psychological analysis of conflict, choice and commitment.* New York: Free Press.

Johnson, Lyndon Baines. 1971. *The vantage point: Perspectives of the presidency 1963–1969.* New York: Holt, Rinehart and Winston.

Jukes, Geoffrey. 1985. *Hitler's Stalingrad decisions.* Berkeley: University of California Press.

Kaplan, Morton A. 1957. *System and process in international politics.* New York: Wiley.

———. 1966. The new great debate: Traditionalism vs. science in international relations. *World Politics* 19(1): 1–20.

Keohane, Robert O. 1984. *After hegemony: Cooperation and discord in the world political economy.* Princeton: Princeton University Press.

———, and Joseph S. Nye Jr. 1977. *Power and interdependence: World politics in transition.* Boston: Little, Brown.

Kissinger, Henry. 1979. *The white house years.* Boston: Little, Brown.

———. 1982. *Years of upheaval.* Boston: Little, Brown.

Knorr, Klaus. 1956. *The war potential of nations.* Princeton: Princeton University Press.

———. 1975. *The power of nations: The political economy of international relations.* New York: Basic Books.

Krasner, Stephen (ed.). 1983. *International regimes.* Ithaca: Cornell University Press.

———. 1985. Toward understanding in international relations. *International Studies Quarterly* 29(2): 137–144.

Lasswell, Harold D. 1935. *World politics and personal insecurity.* New York: McGraw-Hill.

———. 1936. *Politics: who gets what, when, how.* New York: Whittlesey House.

———, and Abraham Kaplan. 1950. *Power and society: A framework for political inquiry.* New Haven: Yale University Press.

Lebow, Richard N. 1981. *Between peace and war: The nature of international crises.* Baltimore: Johns Hopkins University Press.

Leng, Russell J. 1983. When will they ever learn. *Journal of Conflict Resolution* 27(3): 379–419.

Lindblom, Charles E. 1977. *Politics and markets: The world's political-economic systems.* New York: Basic Books.

———. 1990. *Inquiry and change: The troubled attempt to understand and shape society.* New Haven: Yale University Press.

Maoz, Zeev. 2006. *Defending the Holy Land: A critical analysis of Israel's security & foreign policy.* Ann Arbor: University of Michigan Press.

Mearsheimer, John J. 2001. *The tragedy of great power politics.* New York: Norton.

Morgenthau, Hans J. 1946. *Scientific man vs. power politics.* Chicago: University of Chicago Press.

———. 1948. *Politics among nations: The struggle for power and peace.* New York: Knopf.

———. 1951. *In defense of the national interest.* New York: Knopf.

Neustadt, Richard E., and Ernest R. May. 1986. *Thinking in time: The uses of history for decision-makers.* New York: Free Press.

North, Robert C. 1963. International relations: Putting the pieces together. *Background* 7(3): 119–130.

North, Robert C. 1969. Research pluralism and the international elephant. In *Contending approaches to international politics*, ed. Klaus Knorr and N. Rosenau James, 218–242. Princeton: Princeton University Press.

Palme-Dutt, Rajni. 1940. *India today.* London: Victor Gollancz.

Petrou, Michael. 2008. *Renegades: Canadians in the Spanish Civil War.* Vancouver: UBC Press.

Preston, Paul. 1993. *Franco: A biography.* London: HarperCollins.

Richardson, Lewis F. 1960a. *Arms and insecurity: A mathematical study of the causes and origins of war.* Pittsburgh: Boxwood Press.

———. 1960b. *Statistics of deadly quarrels.* Pittsburgh: Boxwood Press.

Robinson, James A. 1962. *The concept of crisis in decision-making*, Symposia studies series, vol. 11. Washington, DC: National Institute of Social and Behavioral Science.

Schelling, Thomas C. 1960. *The strategy of conflict.* Cambridge, MA: Harvard University Press.

Schuman, Frederick L. 1933. *International politics: The Western state system and the world community.* New York: McGraw-Hill.

Shlaim, Avi. 1983. *The United States and the Berlin Blockade, 1948–1949: A study in crisis decision-making.* Berkeley: University of California Press.

Singer, J. David (ed.). 1979. *The correlates of war*, vol. 1. New York: Free Press.

———. 1980. *The correlates of war*, vol. 2. New York: Free Press.

———, and Melvin Small. 1972. *The wages of war.* New York: Wiley.

Small, Melvin, and J. David Singer. 1982. *Resort to arms: International and civil wars, 1816–1980.* Beverly Hills: Sage.

Snyder, Glenn H., and Paul Diesing. 1977. *Conflict among nations: Bargaining, decision making, and system structure in international crises.* Princeton: Princeton University Press.

Snyder, Richard C., H. W. Bruck, and Burton M. Sapin. 1962. *Foreign policy decision-making: An approach to the study of international politics.* New York: Free Press.

Sorokin, Pitirim A. 1937. *Social and cultural dynamics: Fluctuations of social relationships, war and revolution*, vol. 3. New York: Bedminster.

Sprout, Harold, and Margaret Sprout. 1945. *Foundations of national power: Readings on world politics and American security.* Princeton: Princeton University Press.
———. 1965. *The ecological perspective on human affairs.* Princeton: Princeton University Press.
Spykman, Nicholas J. 1942. *America's strategy in world politics: The United States and the balance of power.* New York: Harcourt, Brace.
———. 1944. *Geography of peace.* New York: Harcourt, Brace.
Thomas, Hugh. 1961. *The Spanish Civil War.* New York: Harper & Brothers.
Toynbee, Arnold, and D. C. Somervell. 1947. *A study of history.* New York: Oxford University Press.
Trilling, Lionel. 1952 [1980]. Introduction to Orwell, George. *Homage to Catalonia.* San Diego: Harcourt Brace.
Turner, Ralph. 1941. *The great cultural traditions: The foundations of civilization.* New York: McGraw-Hill.
Vasquez, John A. 1998. *The power of power politics: From classical realism to neotraditionalism.* Cambridge: Cambridge University Press.
Vertzberger, Yaacov Y. I. 1984. *Misperceptions in foreign policymaking: The Sino-Indian conflict, 1959–1962.* Boulder: Westview Press.
———. 1990. *The world in their minds; information processing, cognition, and perception in foreign policy decision-making.* Stanford: Stanford University Press.
Waltz, Kenneth N. 1959. *Man, the state, and war: A theoretical analysis.* New York: Columbia University Press.
———. 1964. The stability of a bipolar world. *Daedalus* 93(3): 881–909.
———. 1979. *Theory of international politics.* Reading, MA: Addison-Wesley.
Wilkenfeld, Jonathan, and Michael Brecher. 1988. *Crises in the twentieth century*, vol. II. *Handbook of foreign policy crises.* Oxford: Pergamon Press.
Wolfers, Arnold. 1940. *Britain and France between the wars: Conflicting strategies of peace since Versailles.* New York: Harcourt, Brace.
———. 1962. *Discord and collaboration: Essays on international politics.* Baltimore: Johns Hopkins Press.
Wright, Quincy. 1942. *A study of war.* Chicago: University of Chicago Press (2 Vols.).
Young, Oran. 1986. International regimes: Toward a new theory of institutions. *World Politics* 39: 104–122.
Zinnes, Dina A. 1980. Three puzzles in search of a researcher. *International Studies Quarterly* 24(3): 315–342.

Political Leaders: Pierre Elliot Trudeau

Clarkson, Stephen, and Christina McCall. 1990. *Trudeau and our times:* Vol. 1, *The magnificent obsession.* Toronto: McClelland & Stewart.
———. 1994. *Trudeau and our times:* Vol. 2, *The heroic delusion.* Toronto: McClelland & Stewart.

English, John. 2006. *Citizen of the world: The life of Pierre Elliott Trudeau, vol. one: 1919–1968*. Toronto: Alfred A. Knopf Canada.
———. 2009. *Just watch me: The life of Pierre Elliott Trudeau, vol. two: 1968–2000*. Toronto: Alfred A. Knopf Canada.
Nemni, Max, and Monique Nemni. 2006. *Young Trudeau: Son of Quebec, father of Canada, 1919–1944*, vol. 1. Toronto: McClelland & Stewart.
———. 2011. *Trudeau transformed: The shaping of a statesman, 1944–1965*, vol. 2. Toronto: McClelland & Stewart.
Radwanski, George. 1978. *Trudeau*. Toronto: Macmillan of Canada.

POLITICAL LEADERS: INDIA

Select Bibliography

Official Records and Reports

Cmd. 9109, 1918 (Montagu-Chelmsford) *Report on Indian Constitutional Reforms*.
Cmd. 3568–9, 1930 (Simon) *Report of the Indian Statutory Commission*.
Government of India Act, 1935.
Cmd. 6121, 1939. *India and the War*.
Cmd. 6219, 1940. *India and the War*.
Cmd. 6350, 1942. *Lord Privy Seal's* (Cripps) *Mission. Statement and Draft Declaration*.
Correspondence with Mr. Gandhi, August 1942 – April 1944.
Cmd. 6652, 1945. *Statement of the Policy of His Majesty's Government*.
Cmd. 6821, 1946. *Statement by the Cabinet Mission and His Excellency the Viceroy*.
Cmd. 6835, 1946. *Statement by the (Cabinet) Mission dated 25 May*.
Government of India Act, 1947.
———: *White Paper on Indian States* (1950).
———: *Report on the First General Elections in India, 1951–52* (1955).
———: *Report of the States Reorganization Commission* (1955).
———: *Report on the Second General Elections in India, 1957* (1958).
———: Planning Commission: *The First Five-Year Plan* (1953).
———: *The Second Five Year Plan* (1958).

Books and Letters

Birdwood, Lord. 1956. *Two nations and Kashmir*. London: Robert Hale.
Bolitho, Hector. 1954. *Jinnah: Creator of Pakistan*. London: John Murray.
Bose, Subhas Chandra. 1948. *The Indian struggle*. Calcutta: Netaji Publishing Society.
Bowles, Chester. 1954. *Ambassador's report*. New York: Harper & Brothers.

Brailsford, H. N. 1943. *Subject India.* New York: John Day Company.
Brecher, M. 1953. *The struggle for Kashmir.* Toronto: Ryerson Press.
———. 1959. *Nehru: A political biography.* London: Oxford University Press.
——— 1966. *Nehru's mantle: The politics of succession in India.* London: Oxford University Press.
———. 1968. *India and world politics: Krishna Menon's view of the world.* London: Oxford University Press.
———. 1991. Nehru's place in history. In *Nehru and the twentieth century*, ed. Milton Israel, 23–52. Toronto: University of Toronto Centre for South Asian Studies.
Brines, Russell. 1968. *The Indo-Pakistani conflict.* London: Pall Mall Press.
Brown, Judith M. 1985. *Modern India: The origins of an Asian democracy.* Delhi: Oxford University Press.
———. 2003. *Nehru: A political life.* New Haven: Yale University Press.
Brown, W. N. 1972. *The United State and India, Pakistan, Bangladesh.* Cambridge, MA: Harvard University Press.
Campbell-Johnson, Alan. 1941. *Viscount Halifax.* London: Robert Hale.
———. 1951. *Mission with Mountbatten.* London: Robert Hale.
Chanakya [Nehru]. The Rashtrapati. *The Modern Review*, 62, November 1937, pp. 546–547.
Coupland, R. 1942. *The Cripps mission.* London: Oxford University Press.
———. 1943. *Indian politics 1936–1942.* London: Oxford University Press.
———. 1945. *India: A re-statement.* London: Oxford University Press.
Cousins, Norman. 1951. *Talks with Nehru.* New York: John Day Company.
Dwivedi, R. (ed.). 1930. *The life and speeches of Pandit Jawaharlal.* Allahabad: National Publishing House.
Fischer, Louis. 1950. *The life of Mahatma Gandhi.* New York: Random House.
Frankel, F.R. 1977. *India's political economy, 1947–1977: The gradual revolution.* Princeton: Princeton University Press.
Gandhi-Jinnah talks (New Delhi, 1944).
Gledhill, A. 1951. *The republic of India.* London: Stevens and Sons.
Gopal, S. 1976–84. *Jawaharlal Nehru: A biography*, 3 vols. Cambridge, MA: Harvard University Press.
Gupta, Sisir. 1966. *Kashmir: A study in India-Pakistan relations.* Bombay: Asia Publilshing House.
Hanson, A. H. 1966. *The process of planning.* London: Oxford University Press.
Hardgrave Jr., R. L. 1980. *India: Government and politics in a developing nation.* New York: Harcourt Brace College Publishers.
Harrison, S. S. 1960. *India: The most dangerous decades.* Princeton: Princeton University Press.
History of the freedom movement (New Delhi, Collection of Unpublished Papers 1919–1947).
Hutheesingh, Krishna Nehru. 1946. *With no regrets.* London: L. Drummond.

———. Nehru and Madame Pandit. In *Ladies' Home Journal* (Philadelphia, January 1955).
Jennings, Sir W. Ivor. 1953. *Some characteristics of the Indian constitution.* London: Oxford University Press.
Karaka, D. F. 1950. *Betrayal in India.* London: Victor Gollancz.
———. 1953. *Nehru: The lotus eater from Kashmir.* London: Derek Verschoyle.
Khare, N. B. 1957. *Nehru as I know him.* Bombay: Asia Publishing House.
Kochanek, S. A. 1968. *The Congress Party of India: The dynamics of one-party democracy.* Princeton: Princeton University Press.
Korbel, J. 1954. *Danger in Kashmir.* Princeton: Princeton University Press.
Kothari, Rajni. 1976. *Politics in India.* Boston: Little, Brown.
Kripalani, K. R. 1949. *Gandhi Tagore and Nehru,* 2nd ed. Bombay: Hind Kitabs.
Krishnamurti, Y. G. 1942. *Jawaharlal Nehru: The man and his ideas.* Bombay: Popular Book Depot.
Kundra, J. C. 1955. *Indian foreign policy 1947–1954.* Groningen: J. B. Wolters.
Lal, Ram Mohan (ed.). 1929. *Jawaharlal Nehru, statements, speeches and writings, with an appreciation by Mahatma Gandhi.* Allahabad: University and National Book Supplies.
Lamb, A. 1966. *Crisis in Kashmir 1947–1966.* London: Routledge and Kegan Paul.
Lumby, E. W. R. 1954. *The transfer of power in India.* London: George Allen & Unwin.
Mahalanobis, P. C. *Science and national planning.* Anniversary Address to the National Institute of Sciences of India (January 1958).
Malaviyya, K. D. 1919. *Pandit Motilal Nehru: His life and speeches.* Allahabad.
Masani, M. R. 1954. *The Communist Party of India.* London: Derek Verschoyle.
Maxwell, N. 1970. *India's China war.* London: Jonathan Cape.
Mehta, Ashoka. 1952. *The political mind of India.* Bombay: M. Limaye.
Mende, Tibor. 1956. *Nehru: Conversations on India and world affairs.* New York: G. Braziller.
Menon, V. P. 1956. *The story of the integration of the Indian states.* New York: Macmillan.
Moraes, Frank. 1956. *Jawaharlal Nehru.* New York: Macmillan.
Morris-Jones, W. H. 1957. *Parliament in India.* London: Longmans, Green & Co.
———. 1964. *The government and politics of India.* London: Hutchinson University Library.
———. India 40 years on. *South Asia,* X, 2, December, 1987.
Nanda, B. R. (ed.). 1976. *Indian foreign policy: The Nehru years.* New Delhi: Radiant Publishers.
———, P. C. Joshi, and Raj Krishna. 1979. *Gandhi and Nehru.* New Delhi: Oxford University Press.

Narayan, Jaya Prakash. 1940. *China, Spain and the war.* Allahabad: Kitabistan.
———. 1946. *Towards struggle.* Bombay: Padma Publications.
Nayar, Baldev Raj. 1972. *The modernization imperative.* New Delhi: Vikas Publications.
———. 1981. *India's quest for technological independence,* vol. 1. New Delhi: Lancers Publishers.
———. 1989. *India's mixed economy: The role of ideology and interest in its development.* Bombay: Popular Prakashan.
Nehru, Jawaharlal. 1934. *Glimpses of world history.* New York: John Day Company.
———. 1941. *The unity of India (Collected writings 1937–1940).* New York: John Day Company.
———. 1942. *Toward freedom: The autobiography of Jawaharlal Nehru.* Boston: Beacon Press.
———. 1946. *The discovery of India.* Garden City: Anchor Books.
———. 1948. *Nehru on Gandhi.* New York: John Day Company.
———. 1949. *Independence and after.* Delhi: Government of India.
———. 1950. *Visit to America.* New York: John Day Company.
———. *Press conferences, 1950, 1951, 1952, 1953, 1954.* New Delhi: Information Service.
———. 1954. *Jawaharlal Nehru's speeches 1949–1953.* Delhi: The Publications Division, Ministry of Information and Broadcasting, Government of India.
———. 1958. *A bunch of old letters.* Bombay: Asia Publishing House.
Rudolph, L. I., and S. H. Rudolph. 1987. *In pursuit of Lakshmi: The political economy of the Indian state.* Chicago: University of Chicago Press.
Saiyid, M. H. 1945. *Mohammad Ali Jinnah.* Lahore: Sh. M. Ashraf.
Sarkar, S. 1983. *Modern India 1885–1947.* Madras: Macmillan.
Shah, K. T. (ed.). 1949. *Report (of the) National Planning Committee.* Bombay: Vora & Co.
Singh, Anup. 1939. *Nehru: The rising star of India.* New York: John Day Company.
Subrahmanyam, K. 1976. Nehru and the India-China conflict of 1962. In *Indian foreign policy: The Nehru years,* ed. B. R. Nanda, 102–130. New Delhi: Vikas Publishing.
Suntharalingam, R. 1983. *Indian nationalism: An historical analysis.* New Delhi: Vikas Publishing House.
Tendulkar, D. G. 1954. *Mahatma: Life of Mohandas Karamchand Gandhi.* Bombay: Publications Division, Ministry of Information and Broadcasting, Govt. of India.
Thorner, D. 1980. *The shaping of modern India.* New Delhi: Allied Publishers.
Unpublished Nehru Letters (1917–48; 210 to Nehru, 30 from Nehru).
Unpublished Nehru-Mahmud Correspondence (1921–54, 150 letters).
Weiner, M. 1967. *Party-building in a new nation: The Indian National Congress.* Chicago: University of Chicago Press.

Woodruff, Philip. 1953. *The men who ruled India: The founders.* London: Jonathan Cape.
———. 1954. *The men who ruled India: The guardians.* London: Jonathan Cape.
Zinkin, Maurice. 1951. *Asia and the West.* London: Chatto & Windus.
Zinkin, Taya. 1958. *Changing India.* London: Chatto & Windus.
———. The Lonely Man (a review of Brecher, *Nehru: A Political Biography*), *The Economic Weekly.* Bombay: October 24, 1959, p. 1464.
———. 1962. *Reporting India,* pp. 216, 217, 219. London: Chatto & Windus.

Select List of Persons Interviewed by Michael Brecher

In England:

Horace Alexander (prominent member, the Society of Friends).
Earl Attlee (Prime Minister of Great Britain, 1945–51).
Thomas Balogh (Fellow, Balliol College, Oxford).
Alan Campbell-Johnson (Press Attaché to Lord Mountbatten in India, 1947–8).
N. C. Chatterjee (President, Hindu Mahasabha).
Malcolm Darling (prominent writer on Indian agrarian problems).
E. M. Forster (novelist).
P. N. Haksar (Counselor, Indian High Commission in London and later Secretary, Prime Minister Gandhi).
Sir Frederick James (former member of the Viceroy's Executive Council, 1947).
Sir Evan Jenkins (Governor, Punjab, 1946–7).
Philip Mason (author, *The Men Who Ruled India*).
Andrew Mellor (Daily Herald Correspondent in India in 1947).
Sir Walter Monckton (Constitutional Adviser to the Nizam of Hyderabad, 1947–8).
Professor W. H. Morris-Jones (University of Durham).
The Earl Mountbatten of Burma (Governor-General of India and Viceroy, 1947–8).
Mme. Vijaya Lakshmi Pandit (sister of Nehru).
Professor C. H. Phillips (Chairman, Department of History, later Director, School of Oriental and African Studies, University of London).
Sir George Schuster (former Member, Viceroy's Executive Council).
Percival Spear (Bursar, Selwyn College, Cambridge University).
Professor N. Srinivasan (Head, Department of Politics, Andhra University).
Ian Stephens (Honorary Fellow, King's College, Cambridge University, and former editor, The Statesman, Calcutta).
Dr. Solomon Trone (Personal Industrial Adviser to Nehru 1949).
Lieut.-General Sir Francis Tuker (G.O.C., Eastern Command, India, 1945–7).
Guy Wint (leader writer, Manchester Guardian and Fellow, St. Antony's College, Oxford).
Woodrow Wyatt (Private Secretary to Sir Stafford Cripps (Cabinet Mission in 1946).

In India:

Anup Singh (M.P. and author of a biography of Nehru).
Aruna Asaf Ali (prominent Congresswoman, later member, Communist Party Central Committee, Delhi).
B. P. L. Bedi (writer and Kashmir politician).
Freda Bedi (Professor of English, Kashmir University and prominent social worker).
Prem Bhatia (Political Correspondent, The Statesman).
Professor P. C. Chakravarti (Jadavpur University, Calcutta, and sometime acting Director, History of the Freedom Movement project).
Renu Chakravarty (Communist M.P.).
Diwan Chavan Lall (M.P. and former Ambassador to Turkey).
Sachin Choudhury (Editor, Economic Weekly).
Eric da Costa (Editor, Eastern Economist).
Morarji Desai (Chief Minister, Bombay; later member of the Union Cabinet).
U. N. Dhebar (President, Indian National Congress).
Faiz Ahmad Faiz (Chief Editor, Pakistan Times).
Professor D. R. Gadgil (Director, Gokhale Institute of Politics and Economics).
N. V. Gadgil (M.P., prominent Congressman from Bombay and former member, India Union Cabinet).
Feroze Gandhi (M.P., Husband, Indira Gandhi).
S. M. Ghose (M.P.. former President, Bengal Provincial Congress Committee).
A. D. Gorwala (prominent publicist; former member of the I.C.S.).
G. K. Handoo (Deputy-Director, Intelligence Bureau, Ministry of Home. Affairs; sometime officer-in-charge of Nehru's security) .
Shaukat Hayat Khan (Pakistani politician).
Azim Hussain (Ministry of External Affairs).
Raja and Krishna Hutheesingh (brother-in-law and sister of Nehru).
Mian Iftikharuddin (Pakistani politician and owner, Pakistan Times).
H. V. Kamath (M.P.).
R. K. Karanjia (Editor, Blitz).
Khushwant Singh (novelist and journalist).
Dr. Saif-ud-din Kitchlew (prominent nationalist Muslim and President, All-India Peace Council).
J. B. Kripalani (former Congress President and leader, Praja-Socialist Party).
Krishna R. Kripalani (Private Secretary to Maulana Azad and Secretary of the National Academy of Letters).
Mrs. Sucheta Kripalani (M.P. and former prominent member of the Praja-Socialist Party).
V. T. Krishnamachari (Deputy Chairman, Planning Commission).
A. Krishnaswami (prominent Independent M.P.).
Professor Oskar Lange/(economist; adviser to India Planning Commission).
Dr. P. S. Lokanathan (Director-General, National Council of Applied Economic Research; former Executive Secretary, ECAFE).

Professor P. C. Mahalanobis (Honorary Statistical Adviser to the Government of India and Director, Indian Statistical Institute, Calcutta).
Dr Syed Mahmud (former Minister of State for External Affairs).
H. K. Mahtab (Governor of Bombay; later Chief Minister of Orissa).
K. D. Malaviya (Minister of State, Union Cabinet).
D. R. Mankekar (Editor, Times of India).
Minoo Masani (M.P.; former Executive Assistant to J. R. D. Tata; former leader, Congress Socialists).
M. O. Mathai (Special Assistant to Prime Minister Nehru).
Dr. John Matthai (Minister of Finance, 1948–50; later Director, State Bank of India).
Ashoka Mehta (M.P.; a leader of the Praja-Socialist Party).
V. K. Krishna Menon (Minister of Defense).
V. P. Menon (Constitutional Adviser to the Viceroy, 1942–7, Secretary, Ministry of States, 1947–51).
Penderel Moon (Adviser to the Planning Commission).
Professor Hiren Mukherjee (Communist M.P.).
Brijlal Nehru (cousin of Nehru).
Jawaharlal Nehru.
K. M. Panikkar (Ambassador to France; former Ambassador to China and Egypt).
Pandit G. B. Pant (Minister of Home Affairs).
S. K. Patil (President, Bombay Provincial Congress Committee, later member of the Union Cabinet).
N. R. Pillai (Secretary-General, Ministry of External Affairs).
Sri Prakasa (Governor of Madras; former Governor of Bombay).
Dr. S. S. Radhakrishnan (Vice-President of India).
Keshu Ram (Principal Private Secretary to Nehru).
Escott Reid (High Commissioner, Canada to India 1952–57).
Chester Ronning (High Commissioner for Canada to India, 1957-).
Dr. B. C. Roy (Chief Minister, West Bengal).
P. B. Sitaramayya (Governor, Madhya Pradesh and author of History of the Indian National Congress).
C. R. Srinivasan (Private Secretary to Nehru).
K. Srinivasan (Editor, The Hindu).
Y. N. Sukthankar (Secretary of India's Cabinet, and Secretary Planning Commission, later Governor of Orissa).
Saumyendranath Tagore (leader of the Revolutionary Communist Party of India).
Tarlok Singh (Head, Plan Co-ordination Section, Planning Commission).
D. G. Tendulkar (biographer of Gandhi).
S. D. Upadhyaya (former private secretary to Pandit Motilal Nehru and to Jawaharlal Nehru).
Mohammed Yunus (Ministry of External Affairs).

Maurice Zinkin (former member, I.C.S., author of Asia and the West).
Taya Zinkin (correspondent for, Manchester Guardian and the London Economist).

POLITICAL LEADERS: ISRAEL

(a) Primary Sources

(i) Official Records and Reports

Press Bulletin (daily), Jerusalem, State of Israel, Records of the Provisional State Council, Tel Aviv, 1948-9 (in Hebrew).
Statistical Abstract of Israel, Jerusalem (annual).
State of Israel, *Divrei Ha-Knesset* (Official Records of the Knesset, in Hebrew), Government Printer, Jerusalem 1949-68.
State of Israel, Government Year-Book (annually since 1949).
State of Israel, Government Press Office, Newspapers and Periodicals Appearing in Israel 1969-1970, Jerusalem, 1970.
United Nations General Assembly and Security Council Resolutions on Palestine 1947-1961, Jerusalem (n.d.).

(ii) Other Written Sources

Allon, Y. A message to President Nasser. *New Statesman* (London), 31 October 1959.
———. *Masakh Shel Hol* (Curtain of Sand), (Tel Aviv, 1960) (in Hebrew).
———. The Arab-Israel conflict: Some suggested solutions. *International Affairs* (London), 40, April 1964.
———. 1965a. The making of Israel's army: The development of military conceptions of liberation and defence. In *The theory and practice of war: Essays presented to B. H. Liddell Hart on His seventieth birthday*, ed. M. Howard. New York: F. A. Praeger.
———. The campaigns of the *Palmah* (Tel Aviv, 1965b), in Hebrew.
———. December 1965c. Meetings in India, (from the inside). *Ein Harod* 27(4): 355-371.
———. *Interviews in the Israeli Press* 1965-70.
———. Active defence-A guarantee for our existence. *Molad* (Tel Aviv), (24), 2 (212), July-August, 1967 (in Hebrew).
———. The present security situation in a strategic mirror. *Ot* (Tel Aviv), I, 2, Winter 1967 (in Hebrew).
———. The last stage of the war of independence. *Ot* (Tel Aviv), 1 I November 1967 (in Hebrew).
———. 1970a. *The making of Israel's army*. London: Valentine Mitchell.

———. 1970b. *Shield of David*. New York: Random House.
Aridan, Natan and Sheffer Gabriel (eds.). Fall 2015. Moshe Sharett: A retorspective. *Israel Studies* 20(3): 175.
Bar-Siman-Tov, Yaacov. 1988. Ben-Gurion and Sharett: Conflict management and great power constraints in Israeli foreign policy. *Middle Eastern Studies* 24(3): 330–356.
Ben-Gurion, David. 1954. *Rebirth and destiny of Israel*. New York: Philosophical Library.
———. Israel among the nations, *State of Israel, Government Year Book 5713*, 1952–53, Jerusalem.
———. *In the Battle* (Tel Aviv, 1955), in Hebrew.
———. Israel and the diaspora, *State of Israel, Government Year Book* 5718, 1957–58, Jerusalem.
———. Israel's security and her international position before and after the Sinai campaign, *State of Israel, Government Year Book* 5720, 1959/1960, Jerusalem.
———. Towards a new world, *State of Israel, Government Year Book* 5721, 1960–61, Jerusalem.
———. Achievements and tasks of our generation, *State of Israel, Government Year-Book* 5722, 1961–62, Jerusalem.
———. Interviews in Israeli and World Press 1948–68.
———. *Medinat Yisrael Ha-Mehudeshet* (*The State of Israel Reborn*), 2 Vols. (Tel Aviv, 1969).
———. 1970. *Memoirs: David Ben-Gurion*. New York: World Publishing.
———., and Pnina Ben-Gurion. 1971. *Letters to Paula and the children*. Pittsburgh: University of Pittsburgh Press.
Caplan, Neil. 2016. Why was Sharett sacked? Examining the premature end of a political career, 1956. *Middle East Journal* 70(2): 275–297.
Christman, H. M. 1969. *The state papers of Levi Eshkol*. New York: Funk & Wagnalls.
Dayan, Moshe. Israel's border problems. *Foreign Affairs* (New York), 33, 2, January 1955.
———. 1966. *Diary of the Sinai campaign*. New York: Harper & Row.
———. Interviews in Israeli and World Press 1967–70.
———. 1976. *Moshe Dayan: Story of my life*. New York: Morrow.
———. 1981. *Breakthrough: A personal account of the Egypt-Israel peace negotiations*. New York: Knopf.
Eban, Abba. 1957. *Voice of Israel*, 2nd ed. New York: Horizon Press.
———. 1959. *The tide of nationalism*. New York: Horizon Press.
———. Israel in the community of nations. (Address to the 26th World Zionist Congress, Jerusalem, 5 January 1965).
———. Reality and vision in the Middle East, *Foreign Affairs* (New York), 43, 4, July 1965.
———. Moshe Sharett's life was like the national saga itself. *Jerusalem Post*, 8 July 1965.

———. Interviews in Israeli and World Press 1966–70.
———. 1972. *My country: The story of modern Israel.* New York: Random House.
———. 1977. *Abba Eban: An autobiography.* New York: Random House.
———. 1983. *The new diplomacy: International affairs in the modern age.* New York: Random House.
———. 1992. *Personal witness: Israel through my eyes.* New York: G.P. Putnam's Sons.
Eshkol, L. *B'ma'aleh Ha-derech* (On the Way), (Tel Aviv, 1958) – *B'havlei Hitnahlut* (In the Pangs of Settlement), (Tel Aviv, 1966).
———. Eshkol statements on foreign policy. *New Outlook* (Tel Aviv), 7, 6 (64), July–August 1964.
———. Israel and the diaspora. *State of Israel, Government Year-Book* 1964–5, Jerusalem.
———. Points from address by Prime Minister Levi Eshkol at the tenth convention of Mapai, the Israel labour party, Tel Aviv, Feb. 16, 1965. Jerusalem: Government Press Office.
———. Interviews in Israeli and World Press 1963–9.
Eytan, W. 1958. *The first ten years: A diplomatic history of Israel.* New York: Simon and Schuster.
Goldmann, Nahum. 1969. *The autobiography of Nahum Goldmann: Sixty years of Jewish life.* New York: Holt, Rinehart and Winston.
Gorni, Yosef. 2015. Between two mountains: On Moshe Sharett and his relations with David Ben-Gurion and Chaim Weizmann. *Israel Studies* 20(3): 63–76.
Meir, Golda. 1962. *This is our strength; selected papers.* New York: Macmillan.
———. 1975. *My life.* London: Weidenfeld and Nicolson.
Morris, Benny. 1999. *Righteous victims: A history of the Zionist-Arab conflict, 1881–1999.* New York: Knopf.
Oren, Michael B. 2002. *Six days of war: June 1967 and the making of the modern Middle East.* New York: Oxford University Press.
Pappé, Ilan. 1986. Moshe Sharett, David Ben-Gurion and the Palestinian option, 1948–1956. *Studies in Zionism* 7(1): 77–96.
Pearlman, M. 1965. *Ben-Gurion looks back in talks with Moshe Pearlman.* London: Simon and Schuster.
Peres, Shimon, *Ha-Shlav Ha-Ba* (The Next Stage), (Tel Aviv, 1965).
———. Interviews in Israeli and World Press 1967–70.
———. 1971. *David's sling.* New York: Random House.
Prittie, Terence. 1969. *Eshkol of Israel: The man and the nation.* London: Museum Press.
Sharef, Z. 1962. *Three days.* London: W. H. Allen.
———, and Lachower, S. (ed.). 1965. *The writings of Moshe Sharett, a bibliography 1920–65* (Jerusalem), in Hebrew.
Sheffer, Gabriel. 1983. The confrontation between Moshe Sharett and David Ben-Gurion. In *Zionism and the Arabs: Essays,* ed. Shmuel Almog, 95–147. Jerusalem: Historical Society of Israel/Zalman Shazar Center.

———. 1996. *Moshe Sharett: Biography of a political moderate.* Oxford: Clarendon Press.
———. 2015. The Sharett legacy. *Israel Studies* 20(3): 1–17.
Shlaim, Avi. 1983. Conflicting approaches to Israel's relations with the Arabs: Ben-Gurion and Sharett's, 1953–1956. *Middle East Journal* 37(2): 180–201.
———. 2000. *The iron wall: Israel and the Arab world.* New York: W.W. Norton.
Siniver, Asaf. 2015. *Abba Eban: A biography.* New York: Overlook Press.
Syrkin, Marie. 1963. *Golda Meir: Woman with a cause.* New York: Putnam.

Select List of Persons Interviewed by Michael Brecher*

*In the case of Civil Servants, the position noted is that held at the time of the interview. Where more than one interview took place, over a period of time, the position indicated was that held when the last of a series of interviews, some of them extending between 1960 and 1970, occurred.

Benyamin Akzin (Professor of Political Science and Constitutional Law, The Hebrew University).
Yigal Allon (Ahdut Ha'avodah leader; Cabinet Minister 1961– ; Deputy Prime Minister 1968–).
Shmuel Almog (Director-General, Kol Yisrael).
Shimon Amir (Head, Director-General's Bureau, Foreign Ministry).
Yeshayahu Anug (Assistant Head, Western Europe Department, Foreign Ministry).
Meir Argov (Chairman, Knesset Foreign Affairs and Security Committee).
Shlomo Argov (Assistant Head, US Department, Foreign Ministry).
Arye Arokh (Head, Department of International Organizations, Foreign Ministry).
Gershon Avner (Assistant Director-General, Foreign Ministry).
Uri Avneri (Member of Knesset [MK], leader of Ha'olam Hazeh faction).
Ehud Avriel (Assistant Director-General, Foreign Ministry).
Hanan Aynor (Head, Africa Department, Foreign Ministry).
Shaul Bar-Haim (Head, Middle East Department, Foreign Ministry).
Hanan Bar-On (Head, Director-General's Bureau, Foreign Ministry).
Moshe Bartur (Permanent Representative to UN Office, Geneva).
Mrs. Lea Ben-Dor (Deputy Editor, Jerusalem Post).
David Ben-Gurion (Prime Minister and Defence Minister, 1948–53, 1955–63).
Elyashiv Ben-Horin (Head, Asia Department, Foreign Ministry).
Herzl Berger (Chairman, Knesset Foreign Affairs and Security Committee).
Moshe Bitan (Assistant Director-General, Foreign Ministry).
Michael Comay (Permanent Representative to the UN).
Ezra Danin (Adviser to the Foreign Minister).
Avraham Darom (Head, Latin America Department, Foreign Ministry).
Moshe Dayan (Cabinet Minister 1959–64; Defence Minister 1967–).
Simha Dinitz (Head, Foreign Minister Meir's Bureau).
Shmuel Divon (Assistant Head, Middle East Department, Foreign Ministry).

Abba Eban (Cabinet Minister 1959– ; Foreign Minister 1966–).
Eliyahu Elath (Political Adviser to the Foreign Minister).
Elie Eliachar (President, Council of the Sepharadi Community, Jerusalem).
Moshe Erell (Chargé d'Affaires, Nepal).
Levi Eshkol (Cabinet Minister 1951–69; Prime Minister and Minister of Defence 1963–7; Prime Minister 1967–9).
Walter Eytan (Director-General, Foreign Ministry).
Mordekhai Gazit (Assistant Director-General, Foreign Ministry).
David Golan (Head, Department of International Co-operation, Foreign Ministry).
Yitzhak Golan (Department of News and Current Events, Kol Yisrael).
Nahum Goldmann (Former President, World Zionist Organization; President, World Jewish Congress).
Amos Gordon (Director, News and Current Events, Kol Yisrael).
Emanuel Gutmann (Senior Lecturer in Political Science, The Hebrew University).
David Hacohen (Chairman, Knesset Foreign Affairs and Security Committee).
Ishar Harari (MK, Independent Liberal Party).
Yehoshafat Harkabi (Aluf, Director of Strategic Studies, Ministry of Defence).
Ya'acov Hazan (MK, Mapam leader).
Ya'acov Herzog (Director-General, Prime Minister's Office).
David Horowitz (Governor, Bank of Israel).
Mrs. Lou Kaddar (Private Secretary to Foreign Minister Meir).
Nahman Karni (Head, Department of International Co-operation, Ministry of Defence).
R. Mordekhai Kidron (Director of Armistice Affairs).
Teddy Kollek (Director-General, Prime Minister's Office).
Leo Kohn (Adviser to the Foreign Minister).
Haim Landau (MK, Herut).
Moshe Leshem (Head, Africa Department, Foreign Ministry).
Arye Levavi (Director-General, Foreign Ministry).
Ze'ev Levin (Deputy Head, International Department, Histadrut).
Daniel Lewin (Head, Asia Department, Foreign Ministry).
Yisrael Lior (Military Secretary to Prime Minister Eshkol).
Netanel Lorch (Head, Africa Department, Foreign Ministry).
Arthur Lourie (Deputy Director-General, Foreign Ministry).
Ted Lurie (Editor, Jerusalem Post).
Mrs. Golda Meir (Cabinet Minister 1949–66; Foreign Minister 1956–66; Prime Minister 1969–).
Ya'acov Meridor (MK, Herut).
Meron Medzini (Lecturer in Political Science, Tel Aviv University; Director, Government Press Office in Jerusalem).
Michael Michael (Head, Research Department, Foreign Ministry).
Yitzhak Navon (Head, Prime Minister Ben-Gurion's Bureau 1952–63; MK 1963–).

Yosef Nevo (Aluf Mishne [reserve (res.)], Tzahal; military affairs commentator).
Ya'acov Nitzan (Assistant Director-General, Foreign Ministry).
Nissan Oren (Lecturer in International Relations, The Hebrew University).
Don Patinkin (Professor of Economics, The Hebrew University).
Elad Peled (Aluf [res.], Tzahal; Director, National Defence College).
Shimon Peres (Deputy Minister of Defence 1959–65, Cabinet Minister 1969–).
Simha Pratt (Head, British Commonwealth Department, Foreign Ministry).
Haim Radai (Secretary-General, Foreign Ministry).
Gideon Rafael (Director-General, Foreign Ministry).
Moshe Raviv (Political Secretary to Foreign Minister Eban).
Elimeleh Rimalt (MK, General Zionist [Liberal] Party leader).
David Rivlin (Head, Foreign Minister Eban's Bureau).
Pinhas Rosen (Minister of Justice 1948–51, 1952–61).
Shabtai Rosenne (Legal Adviser, Foreign Ministry).
Hanan Rubin (MK, Mapam).
Yoseph Saphir (MK, General Zionist [Liberal] Party Leader).
Ze'ev Schiff (Journalist, Ha'aretz).
A. Schweitzer (Journalist, Ha'aretz).
Ze'ev Sharef (Cabinet Minister 1966–).
Moshe Sharett (Foreign Minister 1948–56; Prime Minister 1953–5).
Haim Moshe Shapira (Cabinet Minister 1948–70).
Ze'ev Shek (Head, West Europe Department, Foreign Ministry).
S. Shereshevsky (Editor of Ner, organ of Ihud).
Emanuel Shimoni (Head, Foreign Minister Eban's Bureau).
Ya'acov Shimoni (Assistant Director-General, Foreign Ministry).
Felix Shinnar (Head, Reparations Mission to West Germany).
Moshe Sneh (MK; Israel Communist Party leader).
Yoseph Tekoah (Adviser to the Foreign Ministry).
Ya'acov Tsur (Acting Director-General, Foreign Ministry; Chairman, Jewish National Fund).
Ya'el Uzay (Secretary to the Government).
Arye Wallenstein (Journalist, Reuters [Israel]).
Aviad Yafeh (Head, Prime Minister Eshkol's Bureau).
Haim Yahil (Director-General, Foreign Ministry).
Moshe Yuval (Head, Department of Information).

CONCEPTS OF CHARISMATIC LEADERSHIP AND POLITICAL LEADERS

Adamolekun, L. 1988. Political leadership in sub-Saharan Africa: From giants to dwarfs. *International Political Science Review* 9(2): 103–105.

Apter, D.E. Nkrumah, Charisma and the Coup. In *Philosophers and kings: Studies in leadership,* ed. D. A. Rustow. *Daedalus* 97(3), Summer 1968.

Axelrod, Robert M. 1976. *Structure of decision: The cognitive maps of political elites.* Princeton: Princeton University Press.

Baker, Raymond W. 1978. *Egypt's uncertain revolution under Nasser and Sadat.* Cambridge, MA: Harvard University Press.

Barnett, A. Doak. 1986. Ten years after Mao. *Foreign Affairs* 65(1).

Bass, Bernard M. 1985. *Leadership and performance beyond expectations.* New York: Free Press.

Bendix, R. 1962. *Max Weber: An intellectual portrait.* New York: Anchor Books.

———. June 1967. Charismatic leadership in Asia: A symposium. *Asian Survey,* 7(6): 341–388.

Ben Simon, Daniel. *Ha'aretz* (Tel Aviv), 23 February 2007, B3.

Bierstedt, R. 1954. The problem of authority. In *Freedom and control in modern society,* ed. M. Berger, T. Abel, and C. Pup. New York: Van Nostrand.

Burns, J. M. 1978. *Leadership.* New York: Harper & Row.

Dunn, J. (ed.). 1978. *West African states, failure and promise: A study in comparative politics.* Cambridge: Cambridge University Press.

Edinger, L. J. (ed.). 1967. *Political leadership in industrialized societies.* New York: R. E. Krieger Publishing.

Gouldner, A. (ed.). 1965. *Studies in leadership.* New York: Russell & Russell.

Hirschman, A. O. Underdevelopment, obstacles to the perception of change, and leadership. In *Philosophers and kings: Studies in leadership,* ed. D. A. Rustow. *Daedalus* 97(3), Summer 1968.

Jackson, R. H., and C. G. Rosberg. 1982. *Personal rule in Black Africa: Prince, autocrat, prophet, tyrant.* Berkeley: University of California Press.

Janis, Irving L., and Leon Mann. 1977. *Decision-making: A psychological analysis of conflict, choice and commitment.* New York: Free Press.

Jukes, Geoffrey. 1985. *Hitler's Stalingrad decisions.* Berkeley: University of California Press.

Keren, M. 1988a. Introduction. Visionary realism and political leadership. *International Political Science Review* 9(1).

———. 1988b. Moses as a Visionary Realist. *International Political Science Review* 9(1): 71–84.

Lane, Robert E. 1959. *Political life: Why people get involved in politics.* Glencoe: Free Press.

Migdal, J. S. 1988. Vision and practice: The leader, the state, and the transformation of society. *International Political Science Review* 9(1): 23–41.

North, Robert C. 1969. Research pluralism and the international elephant. In *Contending approaches to international politics,* ed. Klaus Knorr and N. Rosenau James, 218–242. Princeton: Princeton University Press.

Paige, Glenn D. (ed.). 1972. *Political leadership: Readings for an emerging field.* New York: Free Press.

———. 1977. *The scientific study of political leadership.* New York: Free Press.

Reid, Escott. 1981. *Envoy to Nehru.* New Delhi: Oxford University Press.

Rustow, D. A. (ed.). 1968. *Philosophers and kings: Studies in leadership. Daedalus* 97(3), Summer 1968.

Sanbrook, R. 1985. *The politics of Africa's economic stagnation.* Cambridge: Cambridge University Press.

Shils, E. 1958. The concentration and dispersion of charisma. *World Politics* 11(1): 1–19.

Stogdill, R. M. 1974. *Handbook of leadership: A survey of theory and research.* New York: Free Press.

Tucker, R. C. Summer 1968. The theory of charismatic leadership. In *Philosophers and kings: Studies in leadership*, ed. D.A Rustow. *Daedalus* 97(3): 731–756.

———. 1981. *Politics as leadership.* Columbia: University of Missouri Press.

Walzer, M. 1985. *Exodus and revolution.* New York: Basic Books.

Waterbury, J. 1983. *The Egypt of Nasser and Sadat: The political economy of two regimes.* Princeton: Princeton University Press.

Weber, Max. 1947. *The theory of social and economic organization.* Trans. Talcott Parsons. New York: Free Press.

Wildavsky, A. 1984. *The nursing father: Moses as a political leader.* Montgomery: University of Alabama Press.

Willner, A. R. 1984. *The spellbinders: Charismatic political leadership.* New Haven: Yale University Press.

Wolfe, Bertram. 1948. *Three who made a revolution.* Boston: Beacon Press.

Wolin, S. S. 1960. *Politics and vision.* Boston: Little, Brown.

Index

A
Abdullah, Sheikh, Jammu and Kashmir, 43–4, 105
Afro-Asian Conference. *See* Bandung Conference
Agrarian Reform
  inadequacy of, 88–9
  Nehru interest in, 124
Ahdut Ha'avodah
  on arms deal with Germany, 209
  policies of, 209, 218
A.I.C.C, Indian National Congress, 40, 42, 54, 57, 59, 60, 65, 67, 78, 120, 128, 148
Allahabad, U.P., Nehru family home at, 58
All-India Congress Committee. *See* A.I.C.C, Indian National Congress
Allon, Yigal
  on 'the Arabs', 205–9
  biography and personality, 209
  on China, 213
  on Middle East, 208
  on non-alignment, 219
  policies on security, 218
  policies on the West Bank and Gaza, 218
  publications, 205
  on relations with Dayan, Eban, Peres, 218
  on USSR, 219–20
  view of the world, 219–21
Ambedkar, Dr. B. R., Untouchables' leader
  Chairman, Drafting Committee for India' Constitution, 120
  Constituent Assembly, 120
Amritsar Tragedy, the, 1919, 85
Arabs and Arab States
  Allon, 205–9, 213, 216–21, 224–6
  Ben-Gurion, 170–80
  Dayan, 194, 198, 203–9, 211, 213, 215–22, 224–5
  Eban, 163, 165, 174, 193–4, 196, 203–5, 207, 210–14, 217–23, 225
  Eshkol, 184–96, 199–200

Arabs (*cont.*)
  general Israel views on, 166, 177, 187
  Meir, 184, 195–201, 224–6
  Peres, 165, 170, 203–5, 210–11, 213–20, 222–5
  Sharett, 180–4
  views of Israel's Political Leaders, 118
  views of political leadership, 32–3
Arab/Israel peace agreements, 7, 13
Area of Peace, non-alignment, 138–40, 146
Army, Indian, its role in succession, 78–9
Ashoka, Emperor, 81
Asia (all items), 1–4, 6–7, 23, 28–30, 33, 40–8, 51–4, 60–3, 75, 82, 89, 95, 100, 125, 127, 135, 139, 141, 145–58, 171–2, 175, 184, 199, 214, 220, 223, 225, 228, 234–7, 240
Asian Relations Conferences, 1947, 1949, 89, 118
Ataturk, 1923–38, 82, 228
attitudinal prism of decision-makers in Israel
  preeminent component—security, 182
Attlee, Clement, UK Prime Minister, 1945—51
  announces intended transfer of power to India, 1947, 52

B

Bandung Conference, 1955, 54, 68, 75, 129, 146
Ben-Gurion, David
  approaches to Nasser, 177–8, 235–6
  approach to decision-making, 161, 197–200
  'the Arabs', view of, 169, 176–80, 182, 188–9
  'the Ben-Gurion complex', 174, 222
  biography, 161–2
  on China, 172, 213
  compared with Eshkol, 34, 100, 186–92, 194–5, 199–200, 215–16, 224–6
  on Dayan, 194, 205, 207–9, 211, 215–18, 221–2, 224–5
  on the Diaspora, 162–3, 166, 200
  on goals of Israel's foreign policy, 182–3, 192, 200, 224–6
  indifference to economic problems, 181–2
  Israel's geopolitical position, 172
  Jewish history, 171
  on the Middle East, 162, 166–7, 175–6, 200, 224
  Nazi crimes, 196
  and Nehru's achievements, 236
  on 'the Territories' 209
  personality, 162
  publications, 161
  relations with Meir, 34, 181, 197, 199–200, 208, 215, 224–6
  relations with Sharett, 34, 117–18, 161–7, 169–70, 174, 180–4, 187, 189–91, 196, 200, 211, 215, 219, 224–6
  the road to Statehood, 166–8
  role in foreign affairs, 165
  Soviet Jewry, 191
  statute as statesman, 181
  on Third World, 100, 117, 181, 225, 236
  on the UN, 163, 167, 169, 172–4, 180–2, 200–1, 212–13, 219–22, 224
  on US Jewry, 191–2
  world politics, 170–80

INDEX 269

worldview, 162
Zionist leaders, 165, 186, 221
Bhaghavat Gita, 239
Bhave, Acharya Vinoba, 66
'Bill of Rights,' Canada's, 35
Bombay, 40–2, 59, 96, 102–3, 105, 108
Bose, Subhas Chandra
   Bengal Congress leader, 57
   rival of Nehru, 57
British Commonwealth of Nations. *See* Commonwealth
British India. *See* provinces
British Raj, 52, 57, 122, 124, 238–9
Buddhism, 231

C
Cabinet, the Indian
   Nehru's management of, 110, 121
   under Shastri, 98, 103–4, 121
   working under Nehru, 98, 103–4, 121
Cambridge University, Nehru at, 55, 230–1
capitalism, Nehru's attacks on, 123
caste system, the, persistence, Nehru's campaign against, 78
Caucus (Syndicate) for management of successions to Nehru (1964) and Shastri (1966)
   and Cabinet-making, 104
   composition, 107
   distinctive functions, 116
   and Grand Council, influence, 113
   as managing agent, 103–4
   and Nehru's death, 103
   and second succession, 105
   and succession, 103–4
Central Parliamentary Board, 103
charisma, 227–8
charismatic leadership, 227–43
Charter of Rights and Freedoms, 35

Chaudhuri, General, 105
Chavan, Y. B.
   and battle for succession, 105
   as Defense Minister, 112
   member of Grand Council, 105
   and second succession, 105
Chiang Kai-shek, General, 99, 238–9
China, Nehru's tour of, 1954
   comparison with India, 71
   India's relations with, 71
Churchill, Winston
   hostility to Indian independence, 60
   Nehru compared to, 100, 180, 190, 228, 237–40
Cold War, the, 44, 87, 125, 137, 140, 144, 171, 219, 222
colonialism, Nehru's hostility to, 89, 141–2
commonwealth, Nehru's attitude to continued membership of, 76
communal friction between Hindus and Muslims, 45–6
communalism, Nehru's hostility to, 74, 124
communism, Nehru's attitude to, U.S. and, 86, 88
Communist Party of India, Nehru's attitude to, 239
community development, Nehru's view of its achievements, 70
Congress, Indian National
   dependence on Nehru, 40
   Nehru President of, 1951–54, 40, 54, 57, 60, 65, 78–9, 120, 128
   Nehru's indispensability to, 84
   started National Planning Committee, 1937, 120
consensus
   and Battle for Succession to Nehru, 116
   Grand Council and, 113
   second succession and, 111, 208

D

Coupland, Sir Reginald, historian 253
crisis management, 8
  role of mediation, 11
  'crucial case' approach, 10

D

Dayan, Moshe
  advocacy of retaliation, 211
  on Ben-Gurion, 205–8, 211
  biography and personality, 204, 206
  on German arms, 198
  image of global setting, 221
  on Middle East and 'the Arabs', 208, 209
  on neutrality (non-alignment), 219, 224
  on the Occupied Territories, 209
  publications policies, 218
  relations with Allon, 198, 203–6, 209, 213, 217, 219–21, 224
  relations with Peres, 203–5, 211, 213, 215–20, 224–5
  on 'two camp thesis', 222, 225–6
  on US military aid, 225
  views on defense, 198
decision-making
  comparison in first and second succession, 110, 114–15
  Grand Council and, 113
  Kamaraj's role in, 103
  national and international security, 12, 15
Delhi, 42–3
Desai, Morarji
  anti-Morarji sentiment, 112
  and battles for succession, 102, 112
  blunder of declaring his availability as successor, 106
  defeated in battle, 126
  first and second succession comparisons, 102
  Nehru, relations with, 59, 102–3

Dhebar, U.N., 57, 104
Dixon, Sir Owen, UN Mediator between India and Pakistan in Nehru era, 47
Dulles, John Foster, U.S. Secretary of State, 180

E

Eban, Abba
  analysis of speeches, 200, 211–13
  on 'the Arabs', 174, 222
  on Asia, 220
  on Ben-Gurion, 163, 165, 174, 205, 212–13
  biography and personality, 25, 204, 205, 210
  on the Diaspora, 200, 222
  image of the global setting, 221
  on Israel's presence in Africa, 200, 220, 225
  on the Middle East, 200, 211, 221
  policies, 213, 218–19, 222, 224–5
  and policy planning, 196
  publications, 210
  relations with Allon, 205, 217–18, 220–1
  relations with Eshkol, 193–4, 200, 224–6
  role in decision-making, 203, 213, 221
  on Sharett, 196, 200, 211, 218, 221–2, 224–5
  on the UN, 6, 25, 30, 163, 174, 200, 204, 210–13, 221–3, 225
  on the US, 193, 212–13, 222
  on the USSR, 219
  views on Israel's peril, 6
  on West Germany, 222
economic planning, 120, 123
elections, in India, general, 43, 83, 111, 120

English language, Nehru's mother tongue, 231
Eshkol, Levi
  biography and personality, 184–7
  comparison with Ben-Gurion and Sharett, 189–90
  on the Diaspora, 200
  interest in Africa, 100, 195–6, 200–1, 225
  relations with Eban, 193–4, 200, 217, 225–6
  relations with France, 193
  relations with Meir, 34, 184, 195–200, 208, 215, 224–6
  role in economic matters, 188
  seeks US support, 192–3
  on Soviet Jewry, 191
  style in decision-making, 187–9
  on US Jewry, 191–2
  views on Germany and reparations, 198–9
  views before the Six-Day War, 192, 216, 226
  on West Germany, 192
ethnocentrism, 9
executive council, Viceroy's, Interim Government, 197
external affairs, Nehru Minister for, his office at, 91

F
fascism, Nehru's dislike of, 18, 119
Five-Year Plans, 84, 88, 102, 121, 123

G
Gandhi, Indira, daughter of Jawaharlal and Kamala Nehru
  and battle for succession, 105
  elected leader by ballot, 114
  Nehru's letters from prison to, 53
  official hostess for Nehru, 90
  and second succession, 102
Gandhi, Mohandas Karamchand
  conflicts with Nehru, 60
  his relations with Nehru (*see* Nehru Jawaharlal)
  supports as Nehru as President of Congress, 1946, 57
  supports Nehru, 1929, 86
  supports Nehru as President, 1936, 67
Gandhi, Rajiv, Nehru's grandson, 121, 124
Ghosh, Atulya, and battles for succession
  member of Caucus, and Congress Presidency, 103
  Grand Council member, 103
  influence, 104
  relations with Mrs. Indira Gandhi, 105
  and second succession, 116
  on Shastri, 103
Gorwala, A. D., 59
Graham, Dr. Frank, UN mediator on Kashmir, 44
Grand Council of the Republic, membership
  consensus in, 104
  decision-making, 107
Great Britain, Nehru's attitude to, 79, 237
Gupta, C. B., 108

H
Harrow School, Nehru at, 55
heroic leadership, 232–3
high school (1938–42), 22
Histadrut, 236
The Holocaust (1942–45), 23–25
Hungarian Uprising, 1956, Nehru's attitude to, 83, 137

I

imperialism, Nehru attacks, 137
Indo-China, Nehru attempts to localize conflict in, 44
intellectual Odyssey, phases of author's
  Arab/Israel conflict, 32
  international crises and interstate protracted conflicts, 33
  political leadership, selection of literature, 32
Intelligentsia, in India, support Nehru, 88, 119
Interim Government, Nehru invited to form, 1946, 235
international conflict, 8
International Crisis Behavior (ICB) project, 7, 10
international relations (IR), 1–2
  Almond, Gabriel, 28
  Brodie, Bernard, 27
  Corbett, Percy E., 27–8
  Dahl, Robert A., 29
  Fox, William T.R. (Bill), 27
  Holborn, Hajo, 28
  Knorr, Klaus, 27
  Lindblom, Charles E., 29
  Wolfers, Arnold, 26–7
interstate protracted conflict, 4
Israel
  foreign policy system, 5–6
  formative years (1949–51), 30–2
Italian/Ethiopian War, 19

J

Jallianwalla Bagh. *See* Amritsar Tragedy
Jinnah, Mohammed Ali, unsuccessful talks with Nehru, 54, 60, 234
Junagadh State, 45

K

Kamaraj, Nadar, official author of Kamaraj Plan

and battles for succession to Nehru and Shastri, 103
and consensus technique, 110, 113
Grand Council member, 103–4
member of Caucus, 103
and Nehru, 103
relations with Shastri, 103, 113
role in two successions compared, 113–14
and second succession, 111
Kamaraj Plan, 102–3
Kashmir
  dispute brought before UN, 29, 41, 44–5, 95–6, 125
  Indo/Pakistani conflict over, 46–7, 73–5
  meaning of, 45–7
  Nehru's family origins in, 46
  for Pakistan, 43–4, 45
  struggle for, 1953, 47–8
Keynes, J. M., influence on Nehru, 39
Krishnamachari, T. T.
  Grand Council member, 155
  and Nehru, 155
  and succession, 155

L

leader, unanimous election of Shastri 1964, 106
Mrs. Gandhi elected as successor to Shastri 1966, 102
Left, 108, 115, 121, 141–2, 194, 207, 219
Lenin, 238–9
Library of Congress (1947), 29–30

M

Mahalanobis, Professor P. C., Statistical Adviser to Cabinet
  influence on Nehru, 123
Malaviyya, K. D., 105, 108
Mao, 239–40

Mapai [Labor] Party, 236
Marxism, Nehru influenced by
  his criticism of, 82
  see also communism
Mathai, M. O., Nehru's personal
  assistant, 56
Matthai, Dr. John, 41
McGill, 22–3
McNaughton, General A. G. I., 47
Meir, Golda
  achievement in Africa, 31
  on Africa, 181, 199, 200, 225
  on 'the Arabs', 208
  on Asia, 199, 225
  attitude to West Germany, 196
  biography and personality, 196–200
  compared with Eban, 196, 200, 211, 224–5
  on the Diaspora, 200–1
  as Foreign Minister, 195
  on global politics, 181
  image of the road to peace, 200
  pattern of consultation, 76, 90
  policies on Arab refugees, 181
  relations with Ben-Gurion, 34, 181, 196, 197, 199, 200, 225–6
  relations with Peres, 211, 224–5
  role in decision-making, 197–200
  on security, 181, 224
  on the UN, 200–1
  views on Israel's neutrality, 197
Menon, V. K. Krishna, senior adviser
  to Nehru on foreign policy
  on Britain, 141–2
  on China, 145–9
  on the concept, 'Area of Peace', 138–40
  Grand Council member, 104
  Indian representative at UN, 128
  interviews on non-alignment, 129–32, 134, 135, 139
  on nuclear weapons, 142–3
  äand second succession to Nehru, 127–8
  and succession, 105
  on the Superpowers and the Bloc struggle, 135–8
  on the UN, 140–1
  worldview, 6
messianic leadership, 233
Morris-Jones, W. H., 159
Mountbatten of Burma, 50–5
  achieves reconciliation between
    Nehru and Patel, 50
  Admiral Lord, 50, 51
  last Viceroy, 50, 54
  later Earl Mountbatten, 57
Munich Agreement (1938), 20–1
Muslim League, accepts Mountbatten
  Plan for Partition, 70
Muslims, Nehru's sympathy
  with, 174

N
Nanda, Gulzari
  acting Prime Minister after Nehru's
    death, and succession, 110
  acting Prime Minister on death of
    Shastri, 103, 105, 107
  duumvir during Nehru's
    illness, 54
  Grand Council member, 105
  triumvir, 98
  and second succession, 105
Nasser, 235–6
nationalism, Nehru and, 60–1, 74
Nehru, Jawaharlal
  accepts Dominion status formula, 50, 52
  accepts Partition, 70
  his appeal to the young, 117
  his aptitude for compromise, 126
  his attachment to democratic
    institutions, 76
  attitude to religion, 74
  autocratic tendencies, 65
  at Cambridge, 55, 123, 231

Nehru Jawaharlal (*cont.*)
   his character, his appearance, charm, energy, quick temper, integrity, 65
   combination of revolutionary goals and Gandhian ethics, 83
   The Discovery of India, 79, 81
   disillusioned by Amritsar Tragedy, 85
   early life, 79
   and Gandhi's death, 230
   gestures in favor of Shastri, 104
   Glimpses of World History, 81–2
   at Harrow, 55
   and Hindu Code Bill, 91, 119
   indecisiveness, 78
   and India's Republican status, 99
   indispensability to Congress, 84
   at Inner Temple, 55, 77
   his intellect and opinions, love of reading, 67
   the intelligentsia, 88, 119
   his intentions and preferences, 108
   interest in science, 67
   his political philosophy, 79, 82, 88, 117, 120
   reasons for remaining within Commonwealth, 76
   style of speaking, 66
   succession, 108
   sympathy with the masses, 65
   Toward Freedom, 79, 81
   at Trinity College, Cambridge, 55
   vacillation over States reorganization, 84
   visits China, 71
   Western influences on, 90
   the working class, 71
Nehru, Motilal, relations with his son, 57
Nijalingappa, S.
   and second succession, 103
   and succession, Grand Council member, 103

non-identification
   Israel's policy of, 180
   views of Ben-Gurion, Sharett, Eshkol, Peres, Allon, 181, 219, 225

O
October War or Yom Kippur War, 6

P
Panditji, popular name for Nehru, 62, 66, 80, 135, 231
partition, of India and Pakistan
   Nehru accepts, 33
   his reasons for doing so, 33
Patel, Sardar Vallabhbhai
   comparison with Nehru, 57
   differences with Nehru, 57
Patil, S. K., member of Shastri Cabinet
   Grand Council member, 103
   member of Caucus, 103
   relations with Morarji, 103
   resignation from Cabinet under Kamaraj Plan, 103
   and second succession, 103, 105
   and succession, 41, 105
Patnaik, Biju
   Grand Council member, 105
   resigns under Kamaraj Plan, 103
   and second succession, 105
   and succession 103
Peres, Shimon
   on Africa, 210, 214, 220, 223–5
   'the Arabs', 166, 205, 218, 220, 224–5
   biography and personality, 214–15
   conditions for peace, 213, 216, 218, 223
   on the Diaspora, 222
   on foreign policy goals, 223–4
   on France, 204, 214

on Germany, 222
on the global system, 222, 224
on neutralism, 219, 223
on nuclear weapons, 214
policies, 170, 205, 216–20, 222–3
publications, 214
relations with Africa, 210, 214, 220–1, 223–4
relations with Allon, 204–5, 216–19, 224–6
relations with Dayan, 205, 213, 215–19, 222, 224–5
relations with Meir, 224–5
his request for French arms, 222–3
on security, 215
on Soviet Jewry, 213, 219–23, 225
on the UN, 211, 219–20, 222
Planning Commission, the, 90
polycentrism, 5
probable charismatics, 228
Provinces, Nehru's opposition to, 67

Q
quasi-charismatics, 228, 231–2

R
Radhakrishnan, Dr. S. S., Vice-President, later President, of Indian Republic, 105–6
Ram, Jagjivan
  Grand Council member, 107
  resigns under Kamaraj Plan, 103
  and second succession, 103
  and succession, 105
Reddy, Sanjiva
  Grand Council member, 103
  member of Caucus, 103
  member of Shastri's Cabinet, 105
  and second succession, 105
  and succession, 103
Republican Status, India's, 18

Roosevelt, F.D., U.S.A. president, 1933-45, 237–8

S
Secular State and Secularism, Nehru's insistence on, 76
Sharett, Moshe
  on 'the Arabs', 169, 182, 189, 208
  on Ben-Gurion, 34, 118, 161–7, 169, 180–3, 186, 189–91, 196, 200, 208, 211, 215, 218, 219, 224–6
  biography and personality, 162–5
  Eban on Sharett, 165, 174
  influence as, 117, 163–4, 168, 174
  influence as Foreign Minister, 118, 161, 164, 187, 197
  on Israel's uniqueness, 211
  on Jewish history, 168
  Meir on Sharett, 34, 196
  on the Middle East, 162, 166, 169
  policies and views on non-alignment, 180
  publications and speeches, 163, 180
  relations with Ben-Gurion, 117–18, 161–70, 174, 180–3, 186–7, 189–90, 196–7, 200, 208, 211, 214–15, 219, 224–6
  on retaliation, 169–70, 182
  on security, 218
  on the Third World, 181, 225
  on the UN, 169, 174, 181
  on world politics, 180–4
  Worldview, 165–6
Shastri, Lal Bahadur
  Gandhi, Mrs., relations with, 102
  Grand Council member, 103
  Nehru and, 98, 102, 112, 120, 151
  political style, 100–1
  and succession, 47–8, 111–12
Sinai Campaign 1956, 12
Six-Day War 1967, 6

socialism, Nehru and, 70–1
'Socialist Pattern of Society', 42
South Asia Phase
  Bombay, 40–2
  Delhi, 42–3
  meaning of Kashmir (*see* Kashmir)
Soviet Union, Nehru attitude to, his visits to, 73
Spanish Civil War (1936–39), 17–20
States, the Princely, nationalism fostered by Nehru, 45–6
'structured empiricism', 10
succession, role of chief ministers
  in second succession, chief ministers' statement on Mrs. Gandhi, 107
Suez War, 1956, Nehru condemns, 79, 129, 137, 208, 220

T
Third World Leaders of Asia and Africa, 234–7
Tirupathi meeting, 103
transactional leadership, 231
transforming leadership, 231
Trudeau, Pierre Elliott, 233–4
  early years, 34–6
  goal of political leadership, 38–9
  national politics, 37
  nuclear weapons powers, 38–9
  as Prime Minister, 37
  Quebec intellectual, 36–7
  Roman Catholicism, 36
  'Trudeau-mania', 37

U
The UN (1948), 29–30
United States of America, Nehru's attitude to, visit by Nehru, 172

V
visionary realism, 233–4

W
War of Attrition, 6

Y
Yale Graduate Studies (1946–49), 25–30

Z
Zhou, En-lai, 239

GPSR Compliance

The European Union's (EU) General Product Safety Regulation (GPSR) is a set of rules that requires consumer products to be safe and our obligations to ensure this.

If you have any concerns about our products, you can contact us on

ProductSafety@springernature.com

In case Publisher is established outside the EU, the EU authorized representative is:

Springer Nature Customer Service Center GmbH
Europaplatz 3
69115 Heidelberg, Germany